'In these dashing diaries of his recent years in the movies, Grant shares with candour his wonder at this aberrant universe and its inhabitants'
Sunday Times

'An exceptionally vivid and penetrating insight into Hollywood film-making . . . Qualifies for that exclusive niche reserved for film star memoirs that are worth much more than a casual flick on the bookshop shelf'
Observer

'Lively, hilarious memoirs . . . The lovably nervous, marvellously bitchy Grant is blessed with a fluent style, acid wit and the eternal Hollywood outsider's passion for name-dropping, rubber-necking and raspberry-blowing . . . Grant has produced a classic Withnail himself would be proud of'
Vox

'The honesty and likeability of the man becomes addictive. It's not hard to read two hundred pages in a single sitting . . . this is a fast, scenic and often bizarre tale related by a credible witness . . . it really does stand alone'
Empire

'Proves he can be as witty on paper as he has been on the big screen with this diary of his experiences working with everyone from Paul McGann to Steve Martin . . . an enjoyable read that goes to prove there is at least one true gentleman working in Hollywood'
Maxim

· With Nails ·

Richard E. Grant was born and brought up in Mbabane, Swaziland. He has featured in over sixty films, including *Withnail and I*, *L.A. Story*, *Dracula*, *The Age of Innocence*, *The Player*, *Jack and Sarah*, *Gosford Park*, *Bright Young Things* and *Penelope*, as well as numerous television shows. He is also the author of *By Design: A Hollywood Novel* and *The Wah-Wah Diaries: The Making of a Film*. He lives in London with his family.

Also by Richard E. Grant

The WAH-WAH Diaries

· *With Nails* ·

THE FILM DIARIES OF

Richard E. Grant

With an introduction by
STEVE MARTIN

PICADOR CLASSIC

First published 1996 by Picador

First published in paperback 1997 by Picador

This Picador Classic edition first published 2015 by Picador
an imprint of Pan Macmillan
20 New Wharf Road, London N1 9RR
Associated companies throughout the world
www.panmacmillan.com

ISBN 978-1-4472-8953-1

Visit **www.picador.com/classic** to read more about all our books
and to buy them. You will also find features, author interviews and
news of any author events, and you can sign up for e-newsletters
so that you're always first to hear about our new releases.

Introduction: REG RAW

Between 1995 and 2000, REG (Richard E. Grant) and I communicated by fax—yes, fax—after becoming friends when we worked together on the film *L.A. Story*. REG's faxes to me were composed on a typewriter set with wide margins, jammed up with no spaces between sentences and paragraphs—and very selective capitalization. When viewed from a distance, a single page looked like it had been overtaken by an army of disorderly ants.

I kept these faxes, which grew to a stack over two inches thick, because they entertained me, and because I thought they were valuable esthetic chunks from a screeching mind, a stream of consciousness faucet spewing sentences—sometimes a mile long—without rewriting and bearing just the right amount of acid and alkaline. Here is his description of the director Stephen Poliakoff, transcribed keystroke for keystroke:

He is a miniature clone of Stanley Kubrick in the looks dept.i.e: no chin,pubic beard scrawling everywhere,fat and sloshy lower lip,huge eyes and poodle curly tousled hair,all of which is untidily held together in a cardigan,collapsed tweed jacket and fucked corduroy pants,above his flat-footed scuffed brogues. A walking un-made bed,who slurps coffee,scratches his arse mid conversation with the conviction of someone expecting a tooth to be coming through down below, dribbles, gurgles and re-locates bits of his fast eaten lunch in the lower sections of the beard,is knock-knee'd,a few inches higher than five feet, compulsively says 'ok,alright then,ok?alright then ok?,ok,alright then,'whilst circling round his own thoughts,all the time twiddling a

straw in the left hand,like a miniature helicopter in full flight,and has even called ACTION! before the boom is even dangling or actors fully assembled.YET. He is so passionate about his words,characters , situations,so opinionated about everything, informed and intellectually ferocious,that you CANNOT dislike the little dweezil.

The downside of rereading all of Richard's effervescent faxes to me was rediscovering a computer file that contained all of my letters and faxes to him. I was swept up in his style and tried to emulate it, and consequently my letters lay flat and dead on the page. Plus, in one of them, I was reminded of the headline of a bad movie review I'd received. After a critic had sniped at him, I'd sent it to Richard in order to offer some salve: TIRED MARTIN REHASHES HUMORLESS BORE. You might notice, as I did, that every word of that banner, with the exception of my name, is negative. This is how actors cheer each other up: "I got a review worse than yours."

Richard, I should add, has an ability—which I shall call "charm"—to relax anyone into a state of comfort that might take others three years of regular tea parties and intimate lunches to achieve. Once, after only five minutes of sitting next to a woman at a dinner party, he was asking about the duration and flow of her menstrual cycle. The question seemed reasonable at the time, and no one was bothered or offended. I can assure you this is true because I was there, and the woman was my wife-to-be.

In reading his faxes, most written after his film diaries were published, I noticed many well-known names are mentioned, and some of those well-known names aren't so well known today, yet the observations about them are compelling. I understood that while Richard was writing about individuals, he was also writing about human types, and we no longer needed to know exactly who they were in order to appreciate their foibles (again, keystroke for keystroke):

The penalty for being an aging actress seems especially loaded with cruelties.Currently accruing,with interest,upon the head of [Miss X].Who is now facing a crisis of beauty. For herein has resided the source of all her worldly powers since she stepped onto our screens

FIFTEEN YEARS AGO.Now 36, having coasted through twenty lead roles in films of variable quality,more often than not,notable for how many times she slung off her bra,she now faces the terrors of playing THE MUM.Of a spectacularly gorgeous 20 year old.Upon whose poised young head,our director lavishes all his waking attention. To the point where,having rehearsed [her] in the most intimate one-to-one mode this side of actually licking her all over,announces 'Right,let's go for a take! At which point she yodels up with her plea, 'What about me?'.His eyes momentarily flicker recognition that this other person is actually breathing,looks quizzical,decides "No,you are fine'turns on his heels and moseys to the monitor. Not that she has metamorphosed into an old boiler overnight. BUT.Her powerbase,if you can call it that,was her beauty.The reliable eyelid flutter and dulcet tones that commandeered men,rooms,service,cash, contracts, attention,with the ease and relish that a repulsive,height impaired fatfuck gets from breaking wind violently and daring anyone to sneer…Now this may sound glee-filled and 'serves you right' coming from me,but,for once,I am filling up somewhere with the faintest trickle of pity.Because,this vulnerability is the human stuff that joins us all.

Throughout the pages, with fax headers telling me the exact dates of delivery and typed like archy of *archy and mehitabel* (the early twentieth-century office insect who wrote at night by leaping onto the keys of a typewriter and therefore couldn't use the shift key), are moments of career analysis:

…as the flick I was scheduled to shoot in south africa in may has gone kaput,i may well come to l.a. in june to squat on my agent's horrible little head for a couple of weeks to see whether there is any chance of breathing life into the inert corpse of my american career.

. . . analysis of his profession:

A lawyer in my ski group said, whilst engulfing the chair-lift with her posterior,that 'acting is not that special.Just a job like anything else'.Yeah,thought I,suppressing a supreme urge to tip her out,sure honey : every time you do something,anyone and everyone is a fucking critical expert,in print and in person. You try maintaining some equilibrium in the face of that scrutiny and sure as hell,you will need another lawyer to maneuver your shattered self-esteem back on course.

. . . and self-analysis:

…my self-loathing propensity for vitriol is a warped form of 'intimacy.' This was a form of intimacy between my father and me. so that my most familiar way into a buddy-buddy situation with another human is to establish a slag-fest collusion……..Nothing thrills me more than to sit down at this enclosed, hidden,secret world of my computer,banging out messages.

Along the way, I was re-amused by this observation:

I suspect the number of folk who maintain proper friendships with their ex's,is on a par with,with….Swiss Sea battles?

And this opener from a fax of August of 1996:

Steve—Just got back from a week's break,went to the south of France en famille to our house and had perfect weather,sex and enough garlic to kickstart a dead donkey.

And this one quoting his wife, Joan Washington:

I spoke to Joan (who is in France) and she said 'I think we should just pull up the draw-bridge and not let anyone else in who is full of shit.

And finally this, from one of the earliest communications, received on February 18, 1995

"…I HAVE LANDED MYSELF A LITERARY AGENT AS A RESULT OF MY PRET A PORTER DIARIES PUBLISHED IN THE SUNDAY OBSERVER LAST SUMMER AND SUBSEQUENTLY HAD THE PLEASURES AND TERROR OF A PUBLISHERS' AUCTION. THE HIGHEST BIDDER WAS MACMILLAN-PICADOR WHO HAVE AGREED TO PAY ME TO WRITE UP MY COLLECTED DIARIES AND LETTERS FROM THE MAKING OF WITHNAIL THROUGH TO PRET A READY TO WEAR.ASSUMING MY ARSE IS NOT STRAPPED WITH A LIBEL CASE FROM MESSRS WILLIS,BERN-HARD AND CO.? I CANNOT TELL YOU HOW PLEASURABLE IT WAS TO GO INTO VARIOUS PUBLISHING HOUSES AND HAVE A BOARD ROOM OF ADULTS BLOW SMOKEY PRAISE UP WHERE IT COUNTS,AND FOR ONCE NOT TO BE SOME DIRECTOR'S

OR PRODUCER'S NAME ON A LONG LIST.IT IS THE FIRST TIME IN MY DOZEN YEARS OF DOING THIS SHOWBIZNESS 'THUNG,THAT I HAVE FELT **SOME** RAT'S FART WORTH OF **CONTROL**.THAT THE WRITING IS SOMETHING IN MY HAND THAT I CAN THWATT DOWN ON A DESK AND SAY **TAKE IT OR LEAVE IT FUCKERS**,RATHER THAN THAT MIMSY-MAYBE YO-YO OF THE CASTING CIRCUS...A REVELATION TO THIS TIRED OLD HEAD!!MY DEADLINE IS JUNE FIRST...THE TOME TO BE TITLED **WITH NAILS** AND MAY WELL BE PROPHETIC IN ENDING MY FEW FRIENDSHIPS AND CRUCIFYING WHAT'S LEFT OF MY CAREER.**BUT** ON A GOOD DAY,THE WRITING FLOWS LIKE..........AND ON THE BAD ONES LIKE QUICK DRYING CEMENT.

REG, friend for life unless I do something to upset his moral applecart, is still acting, writing, and directing—the crucifixion did not take place. Restacking all the faxes to put them back into their file, noting that they are as thick as a healthy novel, I realize that all this correspondence makes me feel like I've had a more exciting life than I've had. I, the Zelda B. Toklas to his Gertrude Scott Fitzgerald. Yet, I am happy to write this foreword to Richard's reissue of his film diaries, although in them, I don't come off as perfect as I think I am.

STEVE MARTIN

· *With Nails* ·

FOR MONKEY AND OILLY

Acknowledgements

Thanks to Martin Fletcher for suggesting this idea five years ago, Jane Fergusson at the *Observer* for commissioning the *Pret à Porter* diary, Picador for paying and publishing me, and, most of all, to Georgia Garrett for editing 'my life' so compassionately and saving my arse.

Now for some record-sleeve-like devotions, in alphabetical order: Fred Abrahamse, Brian Astbury, Bunny Barnes and Tom Bayley for inspiration and support beyond measure, Kim Borrell, Chris and Dalene Brand, Annie Christmas, Ray Collins, David and Phillipa Conville, Alan Corduner, Liz Crowther, George and Helen Donaldson, Michelle Fine, Grethe Fox, John Fraser, Chris Galloway, Rod Goodliffe, Henry Goodman, Sam Goodyear, Jimmy and Helen Hayes, Michael J. Jackson, Becky Johnston, Hilary Jones, Penny Lorrimer, Nick and Lisa Love, Neil McCarthy, Steve Martin, who said, 'Write it,' Nick Milne, Roz Monat, Biddy Morrell, Gay Morris, Bryony Mortimer, Terry Norton, Michael O'Brien, Fiona Ramsay, Ian Roberts, Bruce and Sophie Robinson, Barney Simon, Paul Slabolepszy, Clare Stopford, Duarte Sylwain, Mavis Taylor, Sean Taylor, and Leslie Udwin. Heartfelt thanks. Without of course forgetting that chorus of yodelling doubters who belted: 'YOU'LL NEVER MAKE IT!' and have inspired me ever since.

Contents

Withnail and I

WANTED: BOY DANCERS IN DUBAI
— NO PREVIOUS EXPERIENCE NECESSARY

This ad appeared in the *Stage* newspaper in a prominent black box on the vacancies pages and probably still does. After nine months of *resting*, dancing in Dubai begins to seem like a serious option. I get to checking that the ad is still there every week with the vague panic that should they finally fulfil their dancing quota it will be withdrawn, and with it my last chance of keeping the Equity card.

At the close of Orwell's BIG eighty-four, prospects had seemed swimming: a *Plays and Players* Promising Newcomer nomination, and a role in Les Blair's satire about advertising for the BBC, *Honest, Decent and True*. Having emigrated to England from Swaziland in 1982 and done waitering, farting around in profit share, the Fringe and a couple of stints in rep, this television break seemed the ticket. I had a sense that it would open up some possibility somewhere. The transmission date – June 1985 – became a fixed point, with every chip of hope stacked for the big gamble. It was then delayed by six months and I couldn't get out of bed. At least, not the day the news came.

Such is my state of mind that when I chance upon one of those magazine surveys that states your ideal body weight for your height and type, I realize that at six foot two, of medium build, I *ought* to weigh twelve stone rather than eleven. I hatch a plan to find a way to gain the poundage and pump the iron. My wife, Joan, whose patience is bubble-gum stretched by now, tells me about Dreas Reyneke, the body trainer who transformed Christopher Lambert into Tarzan for *Greystoke*. I discover he was from South Africa and grew up two hundred miles from where I did in Swaziland.

I have never drunk milk before, and its nausea-inducing niff mixed with weight-gain powder requires a nose-peg to get it down my gullet. But, gradually, flesh grows where only ribcage has mirrored back before. Dreas teams me up with his most macho body-building client, Richard La Plante, who sees my sand-in-the-face prospects as a challenge to overcome, and has me Tarzaning along the bars in no time. I'm soon flexing and plexing my pecs in a T-shirt. The ritual of pumping and pushing gives some vague purpose to the week, and I spend the rest of the time either staring into space in the middle of a room or clacking out a play about the sexual shenanigans of life in colonial Swaziland, titled *Bongo Bongo*. It sits like an embarrassment in a lowly drawer and hasn't been looked at since.

Marooned, becalmed, beached and increasingly bleached of self-confidence, the magazine rack at my local W. H. Smith's provides some escape. You can stand there for half a day riffling and reading through all their publications. I sometimes make a mental inventory of fellow readers and regulars and assume that they, too, are among the 95 per cent, forty-thousand-odd unemployed members of Equity. Even *Fisherman's Monthly* starts to seem subscribable. Finally I pay for a newspaper, to reassure myself that at least W. H. had earned *something* despite my liberties at the Rack. How can Richmond be so full of people during working hours? On any given day, you'd swear that *no one* works at all. And I'm not talking about the OAP gangs. The *where is everybody going, and what for and why* questions burn away. This existential reverie is interrupted all too infrequently by a call from my agent with news of an audition for something humiliating.

'Know *Frankenstein*?'

'Yes . . . well, I've read it but not recently.'

'Got a pen? The BBC Religious Department are doing a drama-doc in Wales looking at the dialectics, I *think* that's what they said, of

Faith and Medical Advances. Not quite sure, but they're interviewing for monsters. On the fifteenth floor at TV Centre – no, hang on, I think it's the other building next to Shepherd's Bush Theatre where they do *Wogan*. You know. I'll just check on that and call you right back.'

Frankenstein's fucking Monster. Has the woman lost her marble collection? I'm the original eleven stone weakling (though the weight-gain powder is edging things out a bit). What the fuck can she be thinking?

I head for the building next to the *Wogan* theatre, and meet the director in a cramped office occupied by two typists, clacking out bulletins and contracts.

'Would you mind taking off your shirt?'

'What, *here*?'

'Yes, sorry, but the normal interview room is being rewired.'

This is a first. As my buttons obey, the two typers' eyeballs shift briefly upwards without missing a beat. Standing in a room with three strangers, in fluorescent light, shirt off, being appraised for Frank's monster by a stick-insect in a cardigan induces something like self-consciousness.

'Thank you. Could you read a couple of pages for me?'

My relief at buttoning up again is matched by the disappointment in his eyes – my torso had clearly not been up to par. Thoughts of *Why didn't you start the weight-gain powder at fourteen, boy*, scurry round my skull.

'In this scene, the monster argues with, and then attacks, the doctor. Just take your time and then have a go.'

'Will you be reading the doctor?'

'Yes, but I can't act so don't be put off. In your own time.'

Even I am startled by the *Exorcist* gutturals that issue forth from my gizzard. Aside from Linda Blair's 360 degree head-swivels and green projectile vomitings, I *am* monstrous and possessed. The sound of typing stops. Eyes stare and when I drop the script-page and have both hands gripped round the director's neck, I feel primed to hop down to contracts and sign on the dotted.

Just for insurance, I practically rip out my vocal cords with a final MGM roar.

As free therapy, it's worth the train-fare alone.

'Well ... I don't quite know what to say. Nobody has done anything *quite* like that before.' The man's eyes are inspecting the floor, while his left hand massages his reddening neck.

I retrieve the fallen page, and relieve them of my de-roared self. Such is the willingness to delusion, that I seriously imagine my efforts will pay instant dividend. Although I have not physically attacked a director before, a small voice I don't want to acknowledge keeps flashing warning signals.

Going over every detail of the *just happened*, while looking at the suburbs flashing past, all conviction rallies forth to quell the doubt and convince me, despite my lack of pectoral dimension and/or respect for the director's person, that the Monster will, in minutes, be mine. I put in a call to my agent to confirm this.

'How did it go?' she enquires.

'Gave it my best shot, though must admit that *maybe* my torso wasn't quite what they were looking for. But I think the reading made some kind of impression.'

'Well, they're still seeing people, 'cos we have another client going in this afternoon, but I'll let you know if we hear anything. Otherwise, things all right with you?'

Best not to answer that one. Two hours, days, weeks go by and, not having heard a peep, I *have* to take this on board and get me down to the Rack, to oblivion among the faces photographed who are IT or about to be IT.

I sometimes find myself staring accusingly at the phone just sitting there, refusing to rally my talent to work.

Return from wherever and blink disbelief that the answerphone message light is not flashing. Could the little bulb have blown? Or am I truly losing it? Don't ask.

Why endure this humiliation? Get a job. Any job. Go back to Swaziland. *We told you you'd never crack it. Who the hell do you think you are? Marlon Brando? Laurence Olivier? Face it. Even if the BBC* film does finally see the light of day, don't think it's going to change anything. *Grow up.*

Meantime my pitying wife offers as much TLC as she can muster and I detect patronage in her tones when it isn't there, and feel guilty when she offers her unshakeable Faith. Where I have little or none.

One day my dormant laughter cells are temporarily rejuvenated by the Call to Panto that comes down the line. I find myself sitting on the floor and laughing till my ribs ache after the agent declares my eligibility, with encouragement, to audition for Little John in *Robin Hood and the Babes in the Wood*, because I am over six foot tall.

'Lots of money in panto. Everybody does it, specially round Christmas when everything else is shut down and nothing's cast. Oh, and could you take along a song sheet as they want to hear you sing.'

An arctic scout shed somewhere behind King's Cross Station for ten a.m. and a waiting area for the dispossessed. Or so they seem to me. Not much obvious eye-contact, but that hooded surveillance of the competition that charges the room with apprehension. I tot up the height variations to assess how many panto Little Johns are in the vicinity. One is belting out 'MARIAAAAAAA,' in the audition room, and two more are lined up in front of me. A compassionate face with floppy fringe pokes into the waiting room and whispers, 'Won't be long. Name, please?'

The competing Johns shuffle song sheets before going in and I wonder whether my choice of the Swaziland National Anthem is quite appropriate. Different, but maybe deadly.

'SOMEWHEEEEEEEERE!' And out shoots the first Little John.

'DONT CRY FOR ME ARGENTINAAAAAAGH!' The second challenger stamps off, clearly distressed by the off-key note of his finale.

'MEMORY-EEEEEEEEEEEE!' And number three is over and out.

My turn.

A long trestle table at the far end. Three judges, still scribbling opinions, and a pianist, who is the one friendly face. It feels like the first moments in a prison movie, when, standing on the white line, you give name and number, and hand over your worldly goods, only in this instance it's my paltry credits and last vestiges of self-confidence.

'Done panto before?' one spindle-featured face asks.

'No.'

'What are you going to sing for us, then?'

Feeling all of five, I confess to the anthem and detect instant curiosity in the upturned face which, a moment ago, was still scribbling notes on the 'Memory' man. Walk the distance to the piano, offer up the sheet and turn to face the six eyeballs that have the look of vultures awaiting a kill.

Open my mouth after the introductory bars and noiseless air is all that it emits.

'Relax, I'll give you the intro again. And a one two three . . .'

Eyes clamped and face no doubt contorted into constipation expression, I hear a hyena-like caterwaul blast from my mouth. Dizzy with the over-supply of oxygen, I risk opening my eyes and barge through the ruptured anthem, looking into the middle distance, mortified. Blood pounding round my head, I retrieve the song sheet, nod to the pianist and steal towards the judgement table.

'Well, *that's* a first. For all of us. Who is your agent?'

Who fucking *cares*? My legs get me out of there and hurtling towards the underground pronto-presto. Sitting among the mid-morning travellers, I rehash the full horror in slow motion.

I call my agent. 'I don't think you'll be hearing anything about Little John. Sorry about that, but maybe I'll take up singing lessons. No, I'm quite sure.'

David and Phillipa Conville, with whom I had worked at Regent's Park Open Air Theatre the previous year, have mentioned my name to Michael Whitehall, an agent they think might help me.

'*Go smart!*' is their advice.

I get smart and go to smart offices in St James's. Fish tanks and secretaries and phones going. I'm ushered in to see Mr Whitehall, but not before I've had a chance to view the photo board displaying the talent represented in eight-by-ten black and whites.

'Take a seat.'

Michael has a drawly sneery voice that seems to emanate from his sawn-off-shotgun nostrils. He is immaculately dressed in Pringle cardigan, flannels, pinstripe shirt and tie.

Friendly and funny-sarcastic, we size one another up across his desk. He sits in a high-back medieval throne with what look like turrets on each side of the back. My chair is functional and appropriate to my lowly status. Between him and me rests the jagged jaw of a shark.

'We were once attacked by one of those.'

'A shark?' He raises an eyebrow.

'In Africa, Mozambique coast.' What am I *supposed* to talk about?

He is very direct and says that while he is possibly interested, he 'obviously cannot do anything until I have seen your work'. I mention *Honest, Decent and True*, the BBC film to come, and a 'Thank you very much for giving me the time and yes, I will definitely keep in touch.'

'Edward Fox on the line for you, Michael. Can you take it?'

Into the street, which now seems momentarily paved with golden possibility.

This bounding euphoria lasts a couple of days. *Everything* is now fixed on *Honest, Decent and True* which still hasn't been given a new transmission date. Christmas is coming and the staff in W. H. Smith's seem to have become so accustomed to my lurking at the mag stand that I wonder if I've become invisible.

Watching TV induces a head-rant: who *are* all these people, acting and working and getting paid and pointing at weather charts, smiling through snowstorms on the Isle of Skye, and the second episode of *We Are All Famous* will continue after the *News at Ten*.

Lying in the middle of the floor and discerning the intricacies of the plaster rose in the middle of the ceiling has begun to seem a more sane option. *Why not take up further education, boy? Why not read some more Tolstoy? Why not shut-the-fuck-up and die?!*

Six interminable months drag by and then, 'Your picture's in the

Radio Times,' Joan calls out as she arrives home from work one day. Fifty thousand volts up my Khyber would have been sedative to what these six words achieved. '*Where?*'

'It's not big, but your name *is* under it and it's going out on Sunday the thirteenth of January at nine p.m.' I'm not superstitious but at this moment, I am daring fate to thwart me once again by quoting *Macbeth*, walking under ladders, and across the paths of black cats. Sunday the thirteenth, not Friday the thirteenth. Could this be a problem? Could this be the beginning of the end of being invisible?

In the cold porridge reality of Sunday morning, I anxiously scrutinize the *Radio Times* to see what the other TV channels have to offer at nine that evening. *Honest, Decent and True* is on BBC2 so surely that incredibly popular American-something-or-other or last of the red-hot pokers of Yorkshire will be the viewers' first and second choice. And those left over will doubtless be asleep in front of *Gardener's World*. So who *will* watch?

WATCH ME, MAMA. WATCH ME, DADA. OH, JEEZUS.

'Hello, this is Richard E. Grant, I met with Michael Whitehall about six months ago and he asked me to give him a call when my TV film was to be broadcast . . . Put it in writing? Of course I will.'

Hollow-guts watching through the cracks in ten fingers strapped to my phizog. Christ, is *that* what I look like sound like walk like? Nuclear mushrooms cloud up my brain and the bile of embarrassment is coursing fast through my veins. Everyone *else* seems fine, but *oi vey* and a trio of poodles, *what the* . . . WHAT . . . am I doing?

Tears would be too easy an option right now. The temperature in the room seems to have burst the thermometer, or is it just that my head *is* about to implode?

'You're funny.' My wife's reaction is edged with a distinct note of surprise. It dawns on me, too, that I'm supposed to be funny. Maybe not the full ha-ha brand, but certainly satirical and sniggery.

'You're *funny*.'

This note of affirmation is like a benediction. You live with each other all year round, in a kind of close-up, and all of a mosey, tonight, watching, you are seen in *Cinemascope*. And if she is surprised by what is beaming back, then all is clearly Not Lost.

'YOU'RE FUNNY,' she repeats, and I suddenly, blindingly flash upon just *what* it must have been like living with me this past unemployed year, and wonder whether I would be as capable and generous in the reverse circumstance. Tears are streaming down my chops.

'You're all right. Don't be upset.'

'It's not the fucking TV. It's you. Where did they make you?'

'What are you on about?'

Lest I test this poor human's patience any further, I hug and hold and go for a brontosaurus smooch. That all this should originate from with the showing of something on BBC2 on a Sunday night I am sure must strike as ludicrous, but, oooooh, the RELIEF, the brass-bound silver-plated affirmation that, in the eyes of my beholder, I *do* have a chance, crack, shimmy up the old drain-pipe of future and fortune.

When the credits roll the phone starts to ring. Folks I thought had assumed me dead are yodelling and it feels as if I have come back to the land of the living.

Ten a.m. on Monday, it's 'Hello, Michael here. Come and have lunch.'

I am now poncing about the morning with all the bravura of a prima ballerina on pointe. Get dressed, get going, and tube it to Gloucester Road where his new offices are located, punch the buzzer on the brass plate, bound up the three flights with the perfume of future prospects assailing my nostrils, and take a deep, calming breath before footing through the door.

Amanda, priestess of this domain, is *smiling*, as is her assistant, as are all the famous faces pinned to the board, as are the tropical fish in the bubbling tanks. As am I when I'm back in that chair in front of Michael's desk, the shark jaw grinning in between.

'Launceston Place restaurant all right for you? Princess Diana favours the food there.'

My head manages to nod, while my voice merely hides.

'Shall we go?'

Why bloody notsky, comrade?

Everything he is saying *en route* has my head and heart yoyo-ing. 'Very funny ... strange ... why did you play such a weirdo? You're much better-looking than you allowed yourself to look ... My wife liked you, though ...' Fast forward through the pristine white napkins and three courses of cautious praise, topped off with 'I think I could really do something for you, assuming you're willing? And I'd like to represent you.'

DONE.

Circus-skip home, stuffed to the gills and with a promised itinerary to meet the casting directors who decide and guide your thespic fate.

Music is played very loudly this afternoon. It has to be to face the daunt of writing or calling my agent, now my former agent.

I am a Born-Again coward, so the trusty quill will have to do.

I outline my feeble year's worthless auditions for Dr Frankenstein's creature, Little John and the like, and conclude: *I regret to say that I am going to leave your agency and seek representation elsewhere. Thank you very much for everything you have done for me and please know this is no easy thing to write, as I am sure not very pleasant to receive. Yours—*

1st July 1986

'Mary Selway is casting a film for Handmade with a peculiar title, "With-Some-Bloody-Thing" or other. Wants you to read a couple of pages, but I'll send the full script to give you some idea. Says it's a comedy, but no doubt with a different title. Give me a call when you've been in. I'll put you on to Amanda.'

'Gotta pen? You go to a house the producer Paul Heller is renting: Peel Cottage, Peel Street, Camden Hill, Notting Hill Gate. Two thirty.'

The next day a package flops through the letter-box. *Withnail and I* by Bruce Robinson. Light-bulb recognition of the author as actor. I've seen him as Benvolio in Zeffirelli's *Romeo and Juliet* and most recently in *The Story of Adèle H.* Apprehension that this pop-star pretty actor wouldn't be capable of writing anything other than a nursery rhyme to Narcissus. Two pages *in*to the script and an ache has developed in my gonads – I am both laughing out loud and agonized by the fact that the Withnail part is such a corker that not in a billion bank holidays will they ever seriously consider me. This conviction gets stronger as the script gets better and better. Never before or since have I read something that conveys what goes on in my head so accurately.

It's a grey, stormy day and I get the tube wearing a 1940s Oxfam khaki raincoat, carrying a leather-bound copy of *Robinson Crusoe* to read on the way.

Step out of Notting Hill Gate tube into a combination typhoon/monsoon and head through the downpour to the address I've been given. I am met by Mary Selway, who in the way of all casting ladies is instantly reassuring and near-maternal in calming nerves and wobbling egos. 'This way,' and I follow her leggy, toothy self into a dining room and am offered a cup of tea 'as we're running a little behind. Don't touch your hair,' she advises as she leaves the room.

Hear the mumblings of another actor reading in another part of the house and assume he has got the job. This is confirmed when I spy Bill Nighy pass the window on his way out. Cemented when I hear Ms Selway declare in the friendliest of tones, 'Will call your agent. Bye, darling.'

Her head is round the door. 'Come in. Relax. Like the script?'

'*Really* funny.'

'Really?'

Herr Robinson is mid-lager opening, leather jacket, jeans, fag in maw and hair flopped to his shoulders. Like a lost member of the Rolling Stones.

'*Jeezus!*' he exclaims at my appearance.

'Caught in the rain,' I say sideways out of a shit-eating-grin-attempt to *relax.*

'What's that – a Bible?'

'Uhhh . . . oh, this, *no*, a novel. For the tube.' (Oh, fuck.)

'What is it?'

'*Robinson Crusoe* . . . Defoe,' by way of explanation.

'Brilliant book. One of my favourites. D'you read Dickens?'

What is this? Hippie *Mastermind*?

'Yes.'

'Gonna read Withnail for us?'

'Sure.'

My throat is a camel's arsehole and what comes out is scrapy rep Noël Coward. Robinson's mouth twitches and he says to try it again and drop the Noël.

I do, and ask if I can audition standing up as I'm reading the kitchen scene that opens the film and sense that being on my pins might just mobilize whatever talent *might* be lurking *somewhere*.

The 'I' character, read by Mary, identifies 'matter' growing in the kitchen sink, which is crammed with the unwashable. Adrenalin, like a rocket of FEAR, shoots through my system and ignites upon the order to 'FORK IT!'

My script goes flying, my fingers missiling towards Robinson's face. And the morose little fucker *laughs*. He seems even more surprised than I am. Scrabbling around the floor for the dismembered script, whose metal clips had snapped, he asks whether I had attacked any other directors.

'Not yet,' I lie.

'Can you come back tomorrow and read another scene with another actor?'

YOU BETCHA SWEET TWINKLECHOPS, BABY.

'Which scene and when?' is what came out of my mouth.

Mary is now *sotto voce*-ing me towards the front door and whispering that out of all the thesps who have read so far, this is the first time he has *ever* laughed. With this faint *hope* I moon down Peel Street bewildered. What do I say *if* and *when* they ask me whether I chain-smoke and drink a case of vodka per day, as the demands of my character dictate? How many folk are they seeing? Oh, up down and forklifts, this is a kind of dull madness.

Michael Whitehall is on the line when I get home and wants my version of what happened and has already heard from Mary Selway that it went OK.

First ever film audition, first *proper* agent.

A recall is loaded-gun territory: each shot could be your last chance. The last bullet saved to blow yer brains out when they say the *sorry* part.

4th July

Eleven a.m., return to Peel Street. The hovercraft of hope that buoys up my shoes as I walk in is deflated by the torpedo exit of Kenneth Branagh.

I now get to read with another actor, rather than Mary's monotone. Paul McGann's the man, and as blue-eyed and infuriatingly bushy-tailed as you wouldn't want *anyone* else quite to be in such circumstances.

He is apparently casual, confident and chugging down a beer with Bruskie Robinson. Bruce is now up on his feet and giving detailed directions of the kitchen scene, saying, 'If you get this scene right at the start, everything else will just follow.' This has a worrying tinge of *you-just-might-already-have-the-part* familiarity that will be as cold as porridge when regurgitated on the tube home. *What did he mean when he said – Does this mean this –* and round and round the mulberry bush of recall post mortem you thrash.

'Very encouraging . . . indeed. They aren't seeing *that* many more and are short-listing, so hang in there.' I am trying to work out a strategy of how to keep breathing, rather than holding my breath until the second recall, plotted for Monday. Can you *get* forty-eight-hour sleeping pills down at Boots?

7th July

Ten a.m. Turns out I'm now reading with four different thesps and, while hoping above hope, I begin to wonder whether I am being used as some kind of willing stooge to shortlist the 'I' character, while the real contender for 'my' part suns himself in Majorca, doing his deal on a mobile.

There is no mention of a screen test and this too sends missives of doubt to my cranium. Bruce is now asking my opinion about each actor just released from the room. I have heard from Michael Whitehall that the part was originally offered among a pile of others to Daniel Day-Lewis who has just double-whammed America with the simultaneous release of *A Room With a View* and *My Beautiful Laundrette*. He is now doing *The Unbearable Lightness of Being*, which about describes my state of flux; *in* with a chance, thanks to Dan, or, more likely, approaching the *unbearable* of 'Thanks so much. Sorry it's not going to work out this time' and release into oblivion with a kissy 'mwaah' at the door.

Michael Maloney is recalled for Tuesday and they seem to favour him strongly for the 'I' part.

8th July

And it's just *Maloney and me*, two hours' working and gnashing at the script trying to get the funny lines to come out of a real situation and *not* sound like *we* think it's funny. Bruce is cracking open the ales and I wonder whether this is out of brain-busting frustration, or flickers of hope.

9th July

How long can this rack be winched? A very well-known face is just leaving through the front door as I approach Peel Cottage, and my guts have now plunged fifty floors south. He exactly fits the script's description of Withnail, but *surely* – this thought enforced by a facial scrunch and eye-clench designed to transmit it through walls and skulls – *he is too old*!!

I forgot to say that Mary said I'd hear by Thursday evening.

Having now become *intimate* with everyone at Peel Cottage, it seems traitorous that these very smiley faces have their own agendas and are seeing other *Spotlight* subscribers. Over and over we do scenes, I and Michael Maloney, who is wonderfully specific about the 'moment to moment' of every scene, and credits theatre director Peter Gill for this rigour and focus.

Impossible to sleep properly – I am now worried because Robinson has learnt that I don't drink a drop or smoke, and Thursday will be the *last* chance to *get it or goof up.*

Myopic, tunnel-visioned, call it what you will, but I am MANIC!!!!!!

Mr Whitehall is 'hanging in there' with me, making a daily nuisance of himself by hustling Ms Selway.

10th July

'We would like to take you out for lunch and then do an hour or so's work.' Mr Maloney is apparently *not* in a state of the old high wire as I am, and seems able to swallow his three courses *and* talk at the same time. My teeth feel like loose Chiclets, masticating their damnedest, but I suspect the saliva ducts have jammed. Tongue, too, has numbed and nothing tastes of anything other than the approach of bad news. My nerves and napkined nourishment are soulless partners and every sop of sparkly water brings up miniature burps of desperation.

WHY TAKE US OUT TO LUNCH AND NOT TELL? WHAT THE FUCK IS THIS WATER TORTURE?

Bruce is well Barolo-ed by mid-afternoon and by five we're sent packing with a handshake and 'We'll be letting you know today, one way or the other.'

Michael and I schlepp to the tube station. He makes for the public phone box and I hear him tell his agent that even if they do offer him the part he doesn't want to do it.

I am astounded. 'Why not?'

'I just have problems with the script. I'm sure they'll still offer you the Withnail part.'

Going down the rush-hour escalators, my body feels time-suspended, shocked into immobility by this turn of events. Why had he gone through nearly a week of this audition torture? They had been casting for a pair with 'chemistry' so what were my chances now?

Walk home in direst droop of jaw, planning a change of profession.

'*To what?*' retorts Joan with an overflow of impatience. 'It's only a bloody part. *Not* a lunar landing.' I know, but right now I feel like strapping myself to the nearest rocket to Mars.

'Has Michael Whitehall called?'

'No. Call him.'

'I can't.'

More 'bloody actor' mumblings assail the air round her exit. It's nearing six o'clock and my nerves are shredding themselves in a kamikaze pact.

'D'you think I *should* call?' I ask her retreating back.

'I *told* you to call.'

'No need to bloody shout,' I mutter as I dial.

'Can you hold? Michael needs to speak to you. Your phone is out of order. We've been trying to call you for the past hour. Hold on, he's here.'

'Your phone's on the blink. Where are you?'

'Home. It must be just incoming calls.'

'Well, sit down I've got some news for you.'

At this juncture, agent am-dram is *almost* suicidally inappropriate. My mind has derailed and is scudding towards Dubai.

'You've got the part . . . if you want it?'

GOT THE PART GOT THE PART GOT THE PART signals the SOS standby through my charged circulation. Some kind of scream must have hurtled from my mouth because Joan's face is two inches away and registers STARTLE.

Share the phone earhole for: 'Mary Selway says you *must* have known it was yours. Anyway they're offering [more money than I had earned doing theatre for four years] for a seven-week shoot, Shepperton Studios, and the Lake District, with a couple of weeks' rehearsal. *Congratulations!*'

Sphincters are winking, neck hair is rising, tears are welling and Joan is tut-tutting about mood swings and extremes.

'Oh, and by the way, Mary asked if you could go in tomorrow because they want you to read with one of the McGann chaps. Maloney pulled out.'

'Does that mean they could still change their minds about me?'

'The part is YOURS. *Congratulations!!*'

Grab my wife, squeeze, jump, hug, blub and make for the sofas to jump up and down. Braying donkey noises are emanating from my bowels.

YAAAAAAAAHOOOOOOOOOOOWOWEEEEEEEEEEEEE!!!!!!!!!!!!

Right now, I could happily convert to Catholicism, the Ayatollah, Dalai Lama, Jehovah Witnoids, you choose the denomination – I am obeisant.

I have a bone deep conviction that *this* is *the* BREAK. I suspect this sure, centred sense of *something* happens rarely and some part of me is grateful that I am conscious of it *now*, and not in the mists of nostalgia and disappointment years down the line.

11th July

A week after my first drenched meeting with Them and, to everyone I pass in the street, *all* is as per, but in my head and heart a Dixie jazz band is stompin' ma joints.

Bruce greets me with 'Well, Granty, we're gonna make a fucking *masterpiece.*'

Paul arrives and we read, and today it's his turn to be nervous and needy. His hair is similar in length to Bruce's and sitting together they have a likeness that aptly fits his character, which is Bruce twenty years ago.

Mary Selway is hugging and kissing and 'I told you so-ing' by lunchtime and Paul is confirmed and contracted. We now go to the same restaurant, and it feels like the end of school! Bottles *are imbibed* and food forked south. Bruce claps a paw across my shoulder on the way out and says, 'I'd like you to lose about a stone to look really wasted.'

Skipping, levitating, long-jumping, I am airborne back to the underground and on my way to Boots for weight-*off* powder. Sorry, Dreas. Apologies, Richard La Plante. I contact Gary Oldman, who is currently porking-up to play Joe Orton, for weight-loss advice. He says that for *Sid and Nancy* he ate nothing but a small piece of steamed fish every day and lots of melon. But warns that he got so obsessed that he was briefly hospitalized and had to gain weight. He points me in the direction of a 'diet-agent' who assures me that, following her regime, within two weeks a stone will shed itself from my beefed-up frame, and armed with food-supplement tins and a few nutrient bars I am ready to De Niro it in East Twickenham for Art.

A lead role in a first film that *isn't* written by Rumpelstiltskin about topples my equilibrium. It is ridiculous that an offer of work could be so instrumental in restoring a sense of self-worth. But it does. This pre-rehearsal weekend *is* sunny, beautiful, calm and loved to the hilt of its hours, pulsed through with this part. Every mollusc that squelched doubt and 'You haven't a flea's chance' BE BOILED. And SLOWLY.

Love is made, shops are shopped, vases are flowered and talk is peppered with possibility.

Our baby is 'baking' and we are nearing seven months safe, after three previous miscarriages at three months. She is kicking inside as am I on the out.

14th July

Everything feels like a Virgin First, from the chauffeur-driven Benz that motors me down to the studios, to the meeting with George Harrison, who is Handmade Films' chief honcho, aside from being one of the Fab Four.

We rehearse in a wood-panelled drawing room in the Old House which was once the Manor of someone Born. Valerie Craig is the production Girl Friday, and is clearly feared by *everyone*, except David Wimbury, the other producer whom Bruce refers to as The Pot (in reference to his gut).

Bruce and Paul arrive and Bruce is giving a monologue on the state of the British Motorway at this historical juncture.

Away from Peel Cottage, reading the lines aloud in this new location is deadly. Sentences putter out without any life and 'I'm sorry we have made a dreadful mistake, Edward Tudor Pole is on his way down' is bleeping through my solar plexus. All notion of *how* to play this part has deserted me and I just hope to whoever that Bruce does not detect this. Having been an actor, however, he is acutely aware of the anxiety and his 'Well, boys, how are we going to get this fucker off the floor?' eases us up. Everything comes and goes and just when you *think* you have *something*, the next scene squirrels off to Slough. He is incredibly patient, but knows exactly how he wants the lines delivered; nothing is improvised; and the luxury of the writer being the director short-circuits *any* doubt as to what the author might mean.

A couple of weeks have passed since Peel Cottage and costumes have been fitted, the sixties revisited, our own backgrounds mined for 'experiences', hair and makeup tests completed and the script known by heart. Bruce tells us the background for the film, and where, why and how it came into being.

He wrote the script in 1970, basing it on his drama-school days in the mid-sixties, but it wasn't until his Oscar nomination for writing *The Killing Fields* that he could get the venture financed and build in the proviso that he would direct it. Paul Heller has raised money through Handmade and a philanthropic American billionaire called Larry Kirstein. The 'I' character is based upon Bruce himself and Mickey Feast, Withnail modelled upon Vivian MacKerrell, who never really worked as an actor, contracted throat cancer some years later, and has now fetched up in a hospice in Gloucestershire.

Bruce declares without a hair of humility that he 'was as gorgeous-looking as a fucking Renaissance prince' when he left drama school and various gents 'wanted my arse'. 'Uncle Monty' is the rotund apotheosis of this 'harassment'. Bruce decides to cast Richard Griffiths in the role 'because he is so sweet and *simpatico*, like Billy Bunter', which ensures that Monty will not be perceived as some saturnine predator.

'This film is bittersweet, sweet and sour, like King Curtis's definitive sax version of "A Whiter Shade of Pale",' is Bruce's oft-quoted mantra. 'The comedy comes from character and situation. There are no *jokes. No poncing.*'

While Paul and I understand the theory of this, the practice is still eluding us and cruellest yet is the day Bruce has the camera team and script supervisor in for a rehearsed read-through. Instinctively, Paul and I are seduced into trying to *perform* as they are the first *audience* we have experienced. Working to explicate our characters comes across as commenting on them – or third-eyeing – and it's disastrous. We sense that the room is now as solemn and silent as Tutankhamun's tomb and we both start rushing, which only compounds the problem.

Bruce is chalk-white-grey. No sooner has our audience all filed silently out, than he turns and lays it on with, 'Well, what the fuck do you think I feel like? Apart from a TOTAL CUNT.' Head pounding with the shame, eyes snailing the carpet for clues and he despairs of us and calls it quits for the day. Says the next morning that he had to put The Fear up our arses so that we *never* make the mistake again.

His oven-scouring honesty and wit make his damnation all the worse because you can't retort with the usual *who the fuck do you think you are?*. The tension is leavened somewhat by a casting session for the drug dealer, Danny. He is based on a record-shop bloke near the Central Drama School, who did a side trade in drugs. Bruce is moronic and funny when he imitates him and warns the three actors he is auditioning for the role that whoever plays it is going to have to put up with him demanding a near replica of the weak 'R'd' dude voice. Ralph Brown turns up, bare-footed with painted black finger-nails, long wig, shades, eye-shadow, attitude and a pair of those bell-bottom pants with criss-crossed string where a zip might be. He is IT and as good as gets an offer from Bruce there and then. I only realize later when he actually comes to film that he is nearly bald and does not look *anything* like what came down to Shepperton that day.

21st July

While all this can-we-or-can't-we-get-this-comic-stuff-right was occupying time and space, *nothing* prepared for the horror that happened this morning. Joan, who for some reason apparently common to the offspring of doctors *never* admits to needing to see one, is ashen and asking, 'CAN YOU TAKE ME TO THE HOSPITAL. NOW. I THINK MY WATERS HAVE BROKEN.'

She is only seven months pregnant.

Bewildered and panic-stricken and ignorant, we get into the car and, trapped in early-morning rush-hour traffic, she tells me she has been *spotting* for a week. I am nearly yelling my disbelief: *Why the fuck didn't you tell me?* We could have gone to the hospital and got advice, help, whatever.'

'STOP SHOUTING. STOP IT!'

The car has now mounted the pavement and lights flashing, horn honking, we career along to the Hogarth roundabout and, blindly, hobble and bump to Queen Charlotte's Maternity Hospital.

Joan is now holding the roof of the car, stretched and in agony. Crying. 'HELP ME. GET A STRETCHER.' Someone does. White coats and aprons crowd round and we are moving towards the lift like an instant rugby scrum. Shoes and wheels squeak and slide along the polished corridors and there's that disinfected smell of institution. OH, JESUS. OHHH, JEEZUS. NOT NOW. NOT THIS. PLEASE NO!

Labour Ward. Still doesn't register with me. Wheeled along and sharp turned into a ward, green curtains drawn and I know by the look and sound and whispered stuff that we are in *trouble.* A tiny West Indian sister takes me to one side and says, 'Your wife is in labour.'

My head is shaking NO and she softly tells me that 'The waters have broken and we will try and do everything we can.'

And still it does not enter rational thought that *this* is *it.*

I hold Joan's hand, tight, and her face is contorted with the onset of pains and the disbelief that *this is happening.*

I haven't exactly read the books or done the breathing classes, but I do know that *all* this is happening too early. But at least we are now in the hospital and everyone seems to know exactly what to do and how to be, which we do not. Over the next four hours, the sister and doctors gradually give me information, clearly knowing that to have told me in one dose would have been unwise. It is coming at us criss-crossed with *percentages* and *chance* and *probability.*

I do not dare ask why a Caesarean is not an option, as everyone seems to be acting as though *this way* is *best*.

I am stationed at the head of the bed holding Joan's hand, shielded from the medical team by a green cloth which divides us and the lower body like a windbreak on a British beach.

Undiluted *fear* is all that courses through every vein and the *what if* and *if only* variations collide.

The room temperature is getting higher by the minute and this is explained as being necessary to help the baby.

And *still* the imminent reality of what is presaging *does* not get through. Everything is out of joint. What should be a journey of unimaginable pain towards the safe birth of a baby, is now an upside-down event at the wrong time with the wrong noises and the wrong expressions on every face. IF ONLY, IF ONLY . . . Joan's face is just tortured and streaming tears.

'Your baby will be very small, because it is so early and will have to go into an intensive-care incubator. It can be very distressing, but we have a great success rate.'

Whatever. Wherever.

We have a name already, Tiffany, as we know she is a girl but when she is born there is no sound. No cry. No sight of her. But just the terrible *rush* of hands and doctors and nurses doing something in a huddle. For half an hour. Like half of eternity. A doctor comes away and has tears in his eyes, as does the tiny sister and they say words that are unbearable to hear. Unbearable to say. 'Her lungs were too small. We tried everything we could to save her. We are so sorry.' *Were* and *could* ricochet through me. How *can* this be the past tense? We are here *now*. Joan is just *shaking*. As am I. This intense activity, commotion, tubes, bleepers, scanners, pumps, hyper-this and dermic-that, is now all abated. Falling away. And then the words that you hate the speaker for saying. 'Would you like to hold your baby? . . . We find this helps . . . not to just take the baby away . . .'

She is handed to my stricken wife first, and had I all the powers of Mars and miracles I would give this child life. After I don't know *how* long, my baby is put in my arms. Hand. For she is the size of a little bird. She is warm but dead. And PERFECT. Ten toes, ten fingers. Eyes, mouth, *all*. Broken. No breath.

Our hearts are broken and will we *ever* cease weeping.

To have and to hold, through sickness and in health ... and we are blind with this grieving.

Her little body is lifted and put in a blanketed tray and, most bizarre of all, a Polaroid picture taken, once then twice. The baby blanket arranged as though preparing for sleep. The sister says, 'Odd as it may seem, having a picture will be very important and precious for you both in the coming weeks. We are going to leave you here with her for as long as you like' – with which the last of the team leaves us to the room that is silent.

Later, I go to the sister's office. 'What do we do now?'

'Your wife will have to stay overnight and we have given her some sedatives.'

'I mean, about our baby?'

'Well, we could perform an autopsy, but it's up to you. Her lungs were just too under-developed to survive, but if you want further investigation . . .'

'Please! No autopsy.' (The thought is beyond this nightmare.)

'We have a garden of remembrance here if you choose to have the body cremated or you can have a burial, but we find that most parents opt for the former.'

HOW DO YOU BURY YOUR CHILD?

The question is not a question I want to be asking, but it *is* when I speak to an undertaker who is saying, 'We do a very simple, classic white casket, if you choose burial.'

Hammersmith Municipal Offices are the next port of call while Joan sleeps and a human blimp shuffles forth a form on which I am legally required to write down our daughter's name, date of birth, date of death. One little half-hour. Same day. Same hour.

This confuses the counter cretin who whines that I will have to do the form again ''cos it's not possible to 'ave the same date of burf 'n' def on the same line'. Behind me are folk waiting to register. I lower my voice and say, 'Excuse me, I don't want to argue with you, but my baby daughter was born and died within half an hour of birth on the same day, within the same hour, and is therefore registered on this form on the same line in the same section.' A couple of sullen eyes meet mine with the distant blink of a light-bulb going on in a place which has been switched off for a couple of aeons and I wonder if she is *ever* going to stamp the fucking paper—

'Get a move on, love,' comes from someone behind and her hand is galvanized and grips the stamp, inks up and blots down on the words that I never thought would relate to me.

'Here are some pills to help you stop lactating. They will reduce the build-up of breast milk. Every hormone and heartbeat is programmed for the coming child.' COME AND GONE.

'I'm so sorry. I'm so sorry.' This keens from my wife and, no matter how I try to absolve her, she relentlessly repeats this, rendering what sounded like apology as an elegy, lullaby for a lost babe.

Joan accepts a job in Sicily coaching Christopher Lambert for *The Sicilian*. She is not keen to go but it seems better to be abroad while I am filming on location in the Lake District than to be alone at home with a baby's room that has no infant.

Flowers have come from the Handmade team as well as others from all over and the house is full of pollen.

I drive to the cemetery alone. I am handed the tiny white coffin by a lone man in black and, having no religious conviction or ritual of prayer, close my eyes tight and just *bust*. Find my way to the open grave where three coffins are stacked one atop the other, unmourned, unclaimed, and I give the coffin to the grave-digger, who is actually in the enlarged hole. He places it on top of the unknown adults. 'I'm sorry, mate.'

This will be an unmarked grave, but I know where it is. And I am relieved Joan is not here. The unbearable has to be borne.

I must have called the studios during the labour hours to say what was going on, because everyone knew what had happened when I went back to rehearsals. Because a premature birth is perceived as a miscarriage, people find it hard to credit such a death with as much gravitas as they would a full-term child and I was bleached by the 'Never mind, you're sure to have better luck next time round ... Nature's way ... for the best ...' palliatives.

Bruce's wife Sophie is nearing her full term and all joke and joust about these two *Withnail* babies is abandoned.

29th July

'I want you and Paul to get absolutely legless tonight, stay up all night, come in first thing tomorrow and we'll stagger through the whole screenplay. I want you to have a *chemical memory* of what it's like to be arse-holed beyond Withinsnape.' Wasted. Fucked. Horizontal.

Since trying every alcohol variation in teenagerdom and never succeeding in keeping any down me for more than half an hour, I know this planned *Walpurgisnacht* is going to be some trial. Joan thinks the idea completely insane and in the light of what has just happened to us, no doubt it *is*.

Get a couple of bottles of champagne from the off-licence, don't eat, and start off at around nine. Any publican's fart would be capable of rendering me askew so it is no surprise that by nine thirty I have already lurched to the loo for the first of what will be many hurling-up visits thither.

By about two a.m., my innards have obviously acquiesced and alcohol *does* stay down and there is now a serious focus on measuring out my intake so that I maintain this state until dawn. My bereaved and bewildered spouse has retreated to bed with mutterings of 'Wanker, why don't you just try *acting*?'

30th July

Nine a.m. and I am dragged out into the car and driven to Shepperton where there is a generous wet bar laid out in the corner. Fearing that I am not quite far enough gone for Bruce, I fill a large tumbler to the three-quarter mark with neat vodka. What to top it off with to get it to go down? Ah – I spy with my totally bleary eye, a row of Pepsi cans beckoning. Grab the ringpull, *whish*, spill some and frotz the last quarter of the glass with liquid black. I put the can down and lift the tumbler to my chops, hold my breath, which is Vulcan's stithy by now, and gloop the bubbling Pepsi bomb down in one. Burp, eyes squirt tears of shock and in a nano-second the whole fucking room is turning in on itself. Bruce and Paul arrive and start laughing. We start rehearsing, and I suppose because we know this script to Bognor and back, the words are firmly enough lodged *not* to get displaced by the alcoholic onslaught.

I must have fallen as my trousers are gaping at the knee. Both knees. Lurching and crying and laughing and flailing and the more it goes on, the more hysterical are Bruce and Paul. Who seem to me *totally* sober. Right now I don't care a fuck about anything or anyone and this limbless lunacy gets us almost all the way through the script. Or so it seems. French windows line the far wall with a narrow side glass door into the garden. An *ocean* of nausea bolts through my system and brain cells convene upon one single thought: GET THROUGH THAT DOOR. NOW! Only it seems very far away and movably mobile. Fall on the way, grab the doorknob and get outside. Blazing sunlight and fluorescent green grass come up at me fast as a flying Persian carpet of champagne vodka cocktail comes spewing from my gullet and I still feel duty-bound to carry on the dialogue. On my knees, vomiting, crying and berating the wide world and its invisible masters.

31st July

That was Friday morning. Today is *Saturday* and I am at home, in my own bed, and my stomach is on fire. Tongue stapled to the roof of my mouth, throat scorched and head housing an orchestra of pneumatic drills playing Beethoven's Ninth. All for Art? Terrible stink coming from somewhere close. Not a fart, but, uh-oh, I have dribbled some nasties onto my shoulder when comatose. Still, the exercise seems to have paid off as when I grope my way downstairs Bruce has left this message on the answerphone: 'Granty? You did it. Break-through. Gonna make a fucking *masterpiece*, boy.'

1st August

Joan flies to Sicily. I meet Paul at Liverpool Street Station at midday, and we board for the Lake District. I feel slightly uneasy that he witnessed my utter arseholedom on Friday but he says it is the funniest thing he has ever seen. Regales with tales about shooting *The Monocled Mutineer* up this way last year, and my brain is clocking my endless months of unemployment and how changed *everything* is just now.

On the outskirts of Penrith near the motorway is our hotel. It is brand new, American ranch-style, and is full of tourists and badge-and-briefcase conference types.

No turning back, boyo, is boing-ing through my brain as I ginger towards the bar to meet the assembling crew, *all* of whom smoke and drink and, oh, fuck, will they suss that I do neither, playing this part?

Everyone knows this film is being made for a flea's pittance, but loyalty, friendship and a sense of what this script *might* be, if pulled off, pervades us all.

I speak to Joan in Sicily and she says she is helped by the change from everything familiar. *No* one asking 'How's the baby?' Says she is enjoying the work and has met a great young actor called John Turturro. Go to bed listening to Otis Redding on earphones singing 'Tenderness'.

And the grief is uncontainable.

I suffer nightmares of what has happened to her little body.

2nd August

Mini-bus together out to the location in Wet Sleddale, supposedly the wettest corner of the United Kingdom, through numerous gates, up a mountainside to an abandoned cottage on the water board estate. Perfect. Exactly like the script suggests. A hammering Art Department is getting it ready for the first day's shoot. Black drapes have been erected round the kitchen area, as we start with a day-for-night scene – when the two characters first arrive in the middle of the night. Everything now is practical and hands-on and how to get from A to B and where to put the camera and lights and which props and where do you want this and how do you like that and suddenly it is all *very real* and very close and *very* adrenalin-friendly!

Bruce is poncing around with his hands fixed in I-am-a-camera mode, *and* sending himself up for doing so.

He has a very simple but strict dictum for the camera crew: everything has to be seen from the I character's point of view. *Nothing* can be shown that strays from this discipline. He also declares his loathing for over-the-shoulder shots and challenges the team to come up with alternatives. All of this is new to me, but his sureness alongside his total honesty about knowing *nothing* technical has the desired effect of giving *them* the responsibility, rather than arsing about with a lot of 'I think we should go for an 85 mil. lens on this one chaps, followed up with a quick pan, zoom or what you will up my collective.' This ant-hive activity is fuelled by lack of time and an overload of nerves. All round.

3rd August

The dialogue for the first day is very short but, even so, it lops around my head like a pea in a tin. I am deluded, despite having had the experience of the TV film a year and a half ago, into thinking that the shooting will go quickly. Hurry Up and Wait is what it turns out to be. Much fixing and flagging the black drapes round the door, rain-machine for the window and seemingly endless tweaking of lights to effect the I character's beat-up Jaguar headlamps outside. When all is dingy and complete I am doused down with tepid water and I reprise the drowning rodent-look with which I first presented myself to Robinson.

Paul is to light a match and then get a paraffin lamp going. As it's from *his* viewpoint, we follow his hand to the lamp, and then up to the walls and around the derelict room to discover Withnail slumped in a chair. Only Wesley – the American-football-sized props boy – is busting his balls to get the taper to ignite, with everything now poised and waiting. Fingers fumble and 'haven't we got another lamp?' unwelcomes its way out of someone's mouth. I hold my breath.

An aeon later it catches and we do the short scene, which has me answering I's question about what's going on with 'I'm sitting down to enjoy my holiday.' Uttered with as much contempt and despair as I can muster.

By which time it's lunch-time and we are *off.*

The catering is set up in an old barn, and, half-way through a mouthful, rumblings are to be heard from nearby.

Bruce is arguing with Denis O'Brien, the incredibly tall, incredibly bald Big Noise from Handmade Films who is a Bilko identikit on a giant scale.

O'Brien says something about the film being behind schedule and suggests cutting the Bull scene.

'How can we be behind schedule? It's only lunch-time on the first day?' Bruce retorts and, to my horror, spits out his resignation.

David 'The Pot' Wimbury seems unperturbed and says it's par for the course. 'Intimidation, dearie. Not to worry.'

NOT TO WORRY? Food is now paralysed in my ocsophagus. Paul doesn't seem bothered and his nonchalance is rewarded by the news some time later that Bruce has been reinstated and that 'over my dead carcass will we cut the Bull'.

I reflect into the sponge pudding at the bunjee-jump-and-drop that my nervous system has endured these past four weeks. Is life always like this – or is it just me?

Back at base, I chart the drunk progression through the story to keep my head in order as the scenes are being shot out of sequence.

Richard Griffiths arrives in the evening, roasted and in agony from too much sun in Tuscany, which doesn't stop him enjoying five courses, cigs and plento vino and tales of Thespia. His larger-than-life avuncularity comes as a great relief, for we have been so wound up rehearsing that it was beginning to feel as if we were the *only* characters in this lark.

Paul and I are in the hotel jacuzzi when Paul Heller comes in and in reverent tones tells us that 'The dailies are *great*! Don't tell Bruce I told you because he doesn't want you to know, but, take my word, we are *very* happy.'

At which I manoeuvre my arse towards one of the subterranean water-jets for a comforting blast of the hots.

Slept on this slim compliment.

What we hear from Bruce is Bile High: 'O'Brien says it's a fucking disaster. He thinks it's all too dark, funny as cancer and that you, Grant, should be like Kenneth Williams, throwing your arms in every direction. I told him you were playing a manic alcoholic in desperate circumstances and that the comedy was *cumulative* not Benny Hill joke-a-minute, SO!'

Battle lines are drawn. FUCK YOU! FUCK THEM! FUCK 'EM ALL, SOLDIERS! There is nothing like establishing the enemy to galvanize and glue us together, and bonded are we! (This bravado is tempered by the terror of being fired and/or the film closing down on us.)

Peter Frampton, Makeup, is a second-generation panstick-pedlar, his father having been a famous makeup man through Peter Sellers' career and many others, so there are endless anecdotes and stories and catchphrases that get repeated all over the shop. The current favourite this week, it being Uncle Monty's mounting Mr McGann scenes, is BRING ME MY BRASS-BOUND BUGGERY BOX! THIS BOY'S BURST! delivered in fulsome Donald Wolfit basso profundo with a vibrato undertow. Bruce describes how, as a young beauty, he was 'targeted' by rovers of the same sex who spun sexual innuendo into the most ordinary conversation with the result that he was often tongue-tied and trapped and says he understood *exactly* what a woman must feel like when hit on by a lounge lizard. He tells of going to a disco and responding to one such predator with 'The music is so loud it goes right through you,' to which came the reply, 'I would like to go through *you*, baby.' I would have thought this would translate into an unsympathetic portrait in Uncle Monty. Yet his loneliness and humour are what Bruce has expressed and this avoids any hostile homophobic portrayal.

'The sky is beginning to bruise, and soon we'll be forced to camp.' This Mont-Montyism is catching as lines from the script are picked up by crew members and become part of the daily yak. It is a particular pleasure to hear a molto-macho electrician come out with Uncle Monty's 'As a youth I used to weep in butcher's shops.'

The scene of Withnailian complaint about the lack of proper nourishment climaxes with my grabbing a fencing rapier, standing bolt upright like an erection and braying, 'I WANT SOMETHING'S FLESH!' This gets a laugh from the crew and is the first time I experience that *thing* you always seek: the Click. When you innately *know* something has worked. Robinson is on to it like a laugh-seeking missile. To *kill*. He instantly wants another take, saying that 'If it's funny *now* it'll be funereal in the cinema' and blathers on about 'what is funny at the time *never* is, out of context'. I know in my gonads that this has worked. And bet it will be the take that's used.

12th August

The Bull scene, which was threatened with being *cut* on the first day by the powers that be, is now being set up on a steep hillside with a veritable tapestry of classic English countryside all around. I don't know whether you know this already, but bulls aren't really trainable for film roles. As I am playing a total coward, I do not have to face the snorter's ring close up, and Paul is its somewhat trepidatious victim. Cameras are loaded and the scene staged with the bull 'safe' behind a wall and gate, which leads into a walled road down the hill, myself safely ensconced on one side of this central road, the crew on the other. A couple of farmhands are crouched down at the back end of the beast, ready to prod and push it towards the gate through which it is supposed to go to meet Mr McGann.

After what seems like five years of preparation, upon hearing 'Action!' the poor animal starts with fear and instead of going forward through the gate to scare Paul, reverses and tries to scramble over the wall that the crew are crouched behind, assuming themselves to be safe.

From my vantage point on the opposite side, I have a clear view of the bull careering off in one direction, while hitherto leisurely-moving riggers and electricians are Linford Christie-ing in *any* direction. Having established that the bull is far more frightened than us, they brave tethering it into the 'corridor' with Paul and some fruit-filled shopping bags nearby. In one take, the rope is released, Paul goes *mental*, screaming, gnashing his teeth, and the bull shits itself, swerves round, gets momentarily jammed in the gate, makes it through and *cut!* Farmhands appear from their hiding places and run after the departed four-legged one.

'Told you we'd get it,' says Bruce, cracking open an ale.

15th August

'If you draw a line with chalk in front of a chicken, it will be mesmerized and stay put.' Such is the wisdom of someone, and none of us being too familiar with the ways of the Hen, we acquiesce to the possibility. The clucker is duly placed on the kitchen table, head 'guided' to watch the chalk trick and it stands its ground, blinking, without *once* checking its mark. The props department have a stuffed hen at the ready, but the live one stands obediently behind the chalk line until we've finished shooting. What I haven't counted on is that *this* fowl will be the *actual* one to be sacrificed and baked on a brick.

Somehow, knowing the hen as we do after a morning's shooting, it seems fair to let it go back to its life of peck and lay. I assume that the plucked carcass necessary for the subsequent scene will be *done* by a butcher. Discover otherwise when going for a pee down the mountainside and spy to my left, while buttoning-up, the freshly severed head lying on its own. It gives me a terrible *turn* and gut lurch. Get back indoors and see Wesley plucking off the last feathers, ready for Paul to try stuffing it into the kettle. It won't fit and he heads for the oven and props the carcass upright on a brick. I am now feeling distinctly queasy while Robinson is convulsed by this grotesque/funny sight.

16th August

'You were lucky you got in to see me, Granty,' says Bruce, inhaling like it was his last request on Death Row. 'Selway had shown me your fat mug in *Spotlight* three fucking times and each time I refused to see your unknown boat and she says, "Well, you'll have to, he's in the next room waiting." What the fuck – ready to give you the heave-ho and next fucking thing you're flying at me with the script and bellowing "*Fork it*". Got the part. Two words. Thought, if he can do that, *maybe* I can work the little rat up into something. But you had to lose the weight. Right *porker* you were when you came in.'

During this harangue I detected the begrudging tones of friendship, 'in the beaten way', as young Hamlet was to say. As well as a colon-twisting cramp of *what if* Mary Selway *hadn't* been so sure that I, the Unknown Soldier, might fit the bill, Bruce having turned away the well-known mortals . . .

In this loquacious state of mind, Robinson says he has *another* film for me, some time in the future, if this one *goes*, which it will, ''Cos it's gonna be a *masterpiece*.' The project is called *How To Get Ahead In Advertising* and is the story of a man who grows a talking boil on his neck. Comedy. 'You're my man.'

Getting a compliment such as this, however coded in cut-and-thrust, is something to make me levitate inside for a good long couple of days.

18th August

'How d'you like yer lamb cooked then, guv'nor?' the props boys ask, though why they are called this when they are clearly *men*. There seems no end to what they are required to do, and I am shown the kilo of roast potatoes at the ready, two legs of lamb and 'We got Ribena for ya, to make like it's wine. Can't dilute it too much, else it looks namby, all right?' This in readiness for a day of *eating* chez Monty. Honeyrose herbal cigarettes, which are tobacco-free and chain-smoked by myself, cause these grown men to WHAT THE FUCK? and cough at the stench.

This is a scene where Uncle Monty, nearly having mounted

McGann in the kitchen while preparing the luncheon, is now salivating at the prospect of 'burglary' come nightfall, as Withnail has let slip that his friend is a 'toilet trader' in order to secure the cottage for the holiday.

As I am not supposed to have had a square meal for a couple of moons, Bruce requires that the eating be a veritable *stuffing*. 'Get the *lot* down.' Which I duly oblige on the first take, *not* anticipating that this has to be shot from various angles, will take most of the day, and at this rate will require a Monty-Python-sized gut to cope. I now see *why* those folk in *Dynasty* always pick at their food. I stupidly thought it was to preserve the lip gloss. Beg for a pee at one point and establish an impromptu vomitorium in a bucket out the back of the house, made all the more surreal by the sounds of sheep bleating on the grassy slopes.

Roast lamb and Ribena are *not* a happy combo and I swear there and then *never* to let either pass my lips again. Richard Griffiths so enjoys his lunch and lines and has developed a sort of exclamatory 'AH'-sound that has us all corpsing, which surprises him into laughter. Which means the scene takes that much longer to complete, and the *more food* I have to eat. 'Bucket o' spuds down ya, guv. Both legs-a-lamb. Bloody marv'lous.' A strange thing to be complimented on. Sore from vomiting, sore from laughing. Sore with the sheer pleasure of doing a scene that ping-pongs along so sweetly. I just hope this transmits.

19th August

I have a couple of days free to roam Penrith while they shoot Uncle Monty in makeup and dressing gown, making lusty advances on Paul, and spend my time endlessly mouthing the *Hamlet* soliloquy that ends the film. I console myself that if it's badly acted, I can argue that Withnail is a lousy actor; though I know this won't wash with Bruce as it's his favourite play.

Many mutterings of 'I have of late ... I *have* of late ... I have of *late* ...' Drives me mad.

Paul assures me over dinner that 'There are *no* tall movie stars. All shortarses like me – Hoffman, Pacino, Newman, Brando, Bogart, De Niro . . .'

My brain put on momentary hold before retorting with 'What about Eastwood, Stewart, Caine, Connery, Wayne and – uh . . .?'

'Nah, I'm talking 'bout the *greats*. Look at Chaplin.'

My ego is not quite up to this competition just now. Acquiesce with 'You're right.'

Returning to London after being all together on location dissipates the sense of camaraderie somewhat, as wrap-time looms and 'normal' life beckons.

3rd September

Come the day of doing the *Hamlet* scene in Regent's Park, it's too sunny, and rain-machines and filters simulate the drear and depression. False railing is erected in front of the wolves so that I don't have to get in there with them.

'Will you be wanting the old menthol, governor?' asks Peter Frampton.

I sense this is something I am *supposed* to be *au fait* with, and take a gamble, saying, 'No thanks. They contain tobacco and the Honeyrose fags don't.'

Frampton is the Chris Tarrant of the makeup world and for him to take a beat sets off alarm bells.

'Not fags, you blithering idiot! Tears – for the goodbye. Thought you might want some help?'

Suppressing a faint blush, I blathered on about being a good blubber.

'Well, I've got this on standby if you run out on the fifty-seventh take.'

Rain-machines, saying goodbye, don't require a Lee Strasbourg Lifetime Achievement Award to get me teary. For some reason I have an overwhelming wish for my father still to be alive to see that things have worked out and that I am not tearing tickets at Waterloo Station as he predicted one dark night. Although we still have more filming to do after this end sequence, principally the opening scenes set in

hen, the premature rush of _Is that it?_ comes up fast and
_s_ me.

he Hamlet has to compete with the stampede of rain on to the
brella and Clive Winter, the sound chief, is shaking his head and
mouthing, 'Have to post-synch.'

'Fuck that,' says Bruce. 'Never be the same.'

Which may be true. For once Herr Robinson seems happy not to
do too many takes and I wonder whether it's because, not having
written the lines himself, he's giving Shakespeare and me the benefit
of his doubt.

10th September

We are filming the interior night journey scene to the cottage and sit
around waiting for the Jaguar to be rigged. I am supposed to be
arseholed, starved and suffering a headache '_like a pig shat in my
head_', and this scene seems to have given the director the cue to get
himself into the mood. Once all is lit, the camera clamped to the side
of the car, we motor out of Shepperton studios and spend most of
the night cruising up and down the road adjacent to the reservoir.

Bruce is squashed up with camera operator, sound guy and
continuity gal, quaffing back a Molotov of ale and vodka, and is not
convinced by my performance: 'Not enough _pain_ in there, Grant.'

It is the only time during the whole shoot that I formulate plans to
murder the fucker. It seems to me as though, ensconced in the
comfort of the back seat, he could happily stay there for a couple of
weeks, so long as SUPPLIES do not run dry _or_ his heart give out.

'It's gotta have _more_ pain.'

The only pain I can envisage is a Light Brigade of Red Hot Pokers
going up his charger, preferably in fourth gear.

Some voice, somewhere, tentatively suggests we might 'Have it?'

'BOLLOCKS,' is the encouraging reply.

After a while, saying the lines _over and over_, all meaning escapes
and it becomes Kafka-esque.

'Gotta wrap, Brucie.' Peter Kohn, the American first assistant
director, adopts the full beside manner to our _auteur_ in the back seat

and, with a cancerous tone, Bruce moans on about 'Not got it yet. Probably have to reshoot.'

Needless to say, come the rushes, no reshoot is required.

Because he is so well liked and respected by this crew and company, this minor *lapse* is accommodated, amid often-voiced declarations that 'This is one of the happiest films we have ever worked on.' A veteran lighting man, who I nicknamed Nipper on account of his permanent tan, Tintin kiss-curl and pint-size frame, says to me, 'Worked on over seventy features and none of 'em 'as been as good as this. You don't know, right, 'cos it's yer first but, you mark my words, in years to come, you'll look back on this one as really special, 'cos it is. You ask Reg.'

Reg, known as the Phantom Farter on account of his Petomaine skills, leans in. 'Wot's that?'

'Talkin 'bout the guv'nor, Number One.'

'BINGO! On the money, 'e is.'

Bruce projects about the 'Boil' film and claims *if* and *when* it happens he will use the same crew if possible. 'Truffaut taught me that. Did *Adèle H* and reckoned if I couldn't enjoy acting with the Master, it was best I got out of it for good. He used the same crew through most of his films. Had a real shorthand going. Can't put a price on that.'

14th September

The Art Department have located a pub in Westbourne Grove, off the Westway, that is suitably nicotine-stained and has the external advantage of a council tower block, lone toothing in the distance, for when the two thesps escape the violent advance of the Irish Frankenstein within.

Extras are selected on the basis of their facial decrepitude and propensity to chain-smoke relentlessly. Which they do.

The props boys are offering variations of non-alcoholic beer to try, as I am supposed to down a pint in one. Frampton has lined my lower lid with magenta crayon. Moving my head first and letting the eyeballs catch up a second after mimics the effect of alcohol well enough for a crew member to ask whether I am a reformed drunk, which I interpret as a great compliment.

Here at the bar Paul and I hatch the plot to hit on Uncle Monty for cash and a weekend at the cottage in the country. We are interrupted by a vast Irish punter who denounces us as PERFUMED PONCES. I am directed to swivel on my barstool with some bravado intact and refute with 'WHAT FUCKER SAID THAT?' By happenstance, I have just bitten off a mouthful of bread to help swill down the pint o' 'lager', with the result that when faced with the mountain of Irish Threat, I smile a tepid 'It's not me, sir!' kind of smirk, with a bread-lump that resembles an additional tooth in my face. Bruce laughs hard and long, and the more I try to fathom why, the more he yelps. He keeps imitating the smirky-smile back at me, and to have raised a laugh out of the old reprobate is pleasure indeed. Some key has been found and I understand, for the first time in practice rather than just theory, that playing someone *funny*, you have wilfully to imagine that *nothing* is funny. Almost as if you have *no* sense of humour. All Withnail's outrage at the world he wants to put to rights, plus a Yorkshire pit's-worth of self-hatred, make for a dented soul in search of some panel beating. Bruce has been banging on about Comedy being a Very Serious Business and while thinking I have grasped this, it is only now that it has all clicked and cogged.

It's a strange process because, knowing the script so well and finding the lines and scene descriptions very funny, you have to put all that aside and inhabit the mental furnishings of failed rage. '*How dare you?!*' seeps into my head like a mantra for this character. It silently goes through my mind before every new scene and keys me in.

17th September

The opening scenes, set in Withnail and I's Camden Town squat, are filmed in a condemned house in Notting Hill Gate. This allows the Art Department to wreck relentlessly although they need do very little to the kitchen, which already had a sink that *stinks*. Someone says that *matter* has been growing for a month, but I don't bother to verify this. Everything accords with the script description and the minute Paul and I are in our squat we feel as though we have always lived there. Michael Pickwoad has detailed everything and the whole place has the perfect sense of history and near collapse. Bruce is now demonstrating with his fists how he wants the acting to WELD itself to the celluloid. That, somehow, *everything* has to be cranked up a notch and intensified until you *earn the right* to commit the thing to film. All the while he's punching his fist into his other paw. STAMP IT ON TO THE SCREEN is about the measure of it.

In other words, commit everything to the max ... and then some. As the two characters have not eaten anything for thirty-six hours, and are out of booze supplies, the whole situation is *desperate*. Normality is left behind as the eating of soup becomes a near-nuclear bowl of contention, which culminates with Withnail threatening to DO THE WASHING UP with as much misplaced zeal as Thatcher declaring, 'WE'RE GOING INTO THE FALKLANDS!'

This is the source of the comedy and Bruce is like a bloodhound in relentless pursuit of attaining this extreme. Even though it is the scene rehearsed forever during the auditions, now that we have completed most of the film coming to it again throws a completely new slant on it. 'It's the reason I *had* to get you arseholed and carrying *a chemical memory*, because you can't be drunk when we shoot these scenes.' My line, I FEEL UNUSUAL, is instantly catch-phrased through the crew and applied to every variant and situation, from overtime hours to the pleasure and surprise of meeting Ringo Starr, who turned up to watch the filming one day. I *did* feel unusual – for here was one of the four icons of the sixties. He delighted in the whole look of the place and said it was *exactly* how things looked in the Cavern days.

I wondered whether to mention that I first kissed Patricia Brook underneath a twelve-year-old's birthday party spread in Swaziland, 1969, to the sounds of 'Hey Jude', or that 'Ob-La-Di, Ob-La-Da' was what got us out from under the table and jumping about, me wearing my first pair of hipsters with a wide belt and a green paisley shirt.

Caught my reflection in the set mirror and what beamed back was a gaunt greasy junkie, so I spared Ringo my reminiscences and, anyway, Paul as a fellow Scouser had more immediate chat in hand.

A dastardly trick is pulled upon my unsuspecting tonsils during the Drinking of Lighter Fluid scene. During the camera rehearsal, water is the fake fluid, no doubt matched by the faked gaspings of my actings. Come the take, and 'ACTION' has me upending the little yellow tin down my gullet, and undiluted vinegar hits my pipes. I gag, gasp and hope I haven't swallowed Swarfega, demand, 'GOT ANY MORE?' with demented relish, and then collapse out of sight and vomit.

'That's the one. Print it,' announces a satisfied Robinson, full of delight at having duped me.

The props boys are very proud of the switch and feel it necessary to show me *just* how they did it, and what brand of *mega-brute* vinegar they had found. I do *not* tell them that my oesophagus was presently ON FIRE but nod sagely at the smilers.

'Got you that time, Granty,' Bruce growls with pleasure. Conclude that he probably *is* the Marquis de Sade. For a moment, anyway.

Certainly hope this little section gets stuck to the celluloid as directed.

Full-Frontal Method Acting is required for stripping down to baggy Ys and I'm basting myself with Deep Heat, while berating the world for the temperature being 'Like Greenland in here', in a menthol-perfumed vapour, fingering a rubber glove for warmth, and bemoaning the lack of work, 'Why doesn't Gielgud retire?'. The *manics* have set-in. Feel completely crazed and possessed, combusting with desperation and disgust.

Painting myself with the cream and wearing the scratchy wool coat sends my system into *irritability overdrive*, which speeds up and motors the *mania* required. Working on Bruce's theory of Comedy Reality in direct proportion to *actual pain* cues me in, 'And,' he assures me, 'the deeper the rage and sense of injustice, the greater will be the comic result. It's what I tried to explain to those fuckers. This script has no jokes. It's cumulative and *has* to be real. Otherwise it's just a load of old wobbly bollocks.' *Quite*. Mine, right now, feel the first of menthol approaching. Please God!

All that separates my scrotum and the unstoppable menthol fumes is a rib of cotton Y-front, so I turn tail, grab a towel and rub a neutralizing line of Nivea as a fire-break to prevent Ball Ache. Or, perhaps, FLAMING GONADS?

AAAAAAH. *All this for Art!*

Robinson says that he *needs* to be in his cups to be able to write as it is such a pain-filled process. Getting it to sound right is like dragging out his guts every time – it explains just *why* he is so meticulous about *nothing* being improvised and all the focus on getting the rhythms right, so that it sounds 'like it does in my head'. It's then the actor's job to make it seem like their *only* way of speaking.

Seven shooting weeks and a couple of weeks' rehearsal, plus the week of audition and recall, make a total of ten between my first 'FORK IT!' and actually FORKING IT. With a crew of seasoned professionals, home-cooking-style producers and three 'virgins' to feature films, in Paul, myself and Bruce (though he had acted and written for film) and all the incredible highs, and the unbearable sorrow of Joan's and my personal loss, coming to the *end* doesn't seem possible, the whole process being so intense and *funny!* For me, anyway. But the promise of a partnership, of sorts, with Bruce that would last beyond the final wrap is of some comfort.

The last scene to be shot is the arrival outside Uncle Monty's London home, which requires Paul to park the crocked Jag.

It being the last shot, without dialogue, other than a murmur from me, 'That's Monty's car,' Paul and Bruce have downed some beers. With the result that when Paul comes to manoeuvre the old Jag into position, he scrapes the side against a skip. A few dodgy reverse-gear jobs later, having got the motor vaguely in the right position, we get out, meander to the door past the camera, *wrap* is called and it's *over*. I just stand in the dark and quell a terrible lurch of blub. I hand out my presents – vodka bottles for the camera crew and Bruce, beer for the boys, and homemade amateur cartoons of each crew member – to say thanks. Corks pop, plastic cups are filled and a mixed chorus of GOOD ON YERS, BOYS accompanies the packing up of equipment, cables, generator, ladders and lamps and all the industrials of filming two blokes arriving in a car and getting out.

Drive home in shocked silence, flushed and wondering whether to let it all heave out in bucketloads or just go for solo tear-down-the-cheek option. Turn out a bit of both.

8th December

Wardour Street screening room. Seven p.m, rough cut, not fully colour-graded, some sound-effects still to fill in, without credit titles. Bruce stands up and gulps out some excuses about this *not* being the finished thing, but more a LOOK-SEE.

I sit in the back row. I can hear my heart pounding its ribcage prison to *get out* and begin to feel slightly damp all over. It's not the central heating, but a hideous internal combustion.

Hold Joan's small Scottish hand *tight*. She leans near and kisses my neck. HANDMADE FILMS logo starts as a dot centre-screen and then comes at you like a fast train, accompanied by the unique whine of King Curtis giving it 'A Whiter Shade of Pale'. Credits *do* come up, and when I see my name I am gently tipped over the other side and want to weep that my father is not alive to see this.

To say that things are getting a little on the emotional side, is an understatement. Seeing myself up there for the first time, from all the angles impossible in real life, short of a four-way mirror scheme, is *so* horrifying that I'm now trembling and wondering *if* there is *any* plastic surgery on earth that can fix what is so obviously lacking. Oh, sweet Jeeezus! Vanity aside, it's the H'ACTING that's now capsizing my senses. So *that's* what registers. *That's* what comes across. The next ninety minutes are a gradual slide down the seat, IN SHOCK.

My left hand is welded to my face, allowing one eyeball to see the thing out, my right hand has drawn blood, such is the crab-clamp on to Joan's hand.

NUMB. NUMBED. NUKED.

'You were great,' whispers Joan. My eyeballs swivel at her, as if she is Judas revisited. 'Let's go and have a drink.'

Into the pub and Paul, who is as chipper as can be, put his arm round my shoulder and says, 'We've done it. Fucking GREAT.'

'*You* were great, Paul.'

I feel like I'm at my own funeral.

'What d'you think, Grant?' asks Bruce.

My eyes have blurred up, head is shaking side to side and I know all the blood has mutinied down to my toes and is fighting to get out.

'Fucking good flick we've made. Always a killer to see yourself for the first time. It's why I never let you see any of the rushes.'

I stand with a glass of ginger ale like a stunned warthog.

'I can't stand this any longer. Let's go,' pleadingly to Joan.

Watching myself in *Withnail and I* taught me that the self-obsession of a first viewing obliterates all judgement. However, the dubbing process, in which actors re-record lines, allows you to see the film in bite-sized morsels and affords some objectivity.

By the time I watched it with a packed BAFTA preview audience, I could see the film that I'd originally found so funny *as a whole*, rather than as a catalogue of my own shortcomings. And people laughed a lot. At Paul and me, speaking Bruce's words.

I had no notion that, almost without exception, *every* film offered since then would be the result of having played an alcoholic out-of-work actor. *Withnail and I* led to working with *Altman, Coppola and Scorsese*. To name but three ... And the title *wasn't* changed. And *all hail* to the advent of video and cable, for it has ensured longevity beyond six weeks in the Odeon and assorted one-night-stands in London repertory cinemas.

Warlock

'It's Michael. Got an audition for you at the Four Seasons Hotel off Park Lane. Six p.m. tomorrow for an American picture. Producer won an Oscar last year for *Platoon*. Sean Connery role – he turned it down. Tough adventure-thriller type thing. Sending the script. See what you think. They've asked to see you. Apparently saw *Withnail* in Los Angeles.'

Script arrives with a biker and I speed through this tale of a warlock, hounded through the seventeenth century, then catapulted to the twentieth. The warlock-hunter role requires ... well, Sean Connery, twenty years ago.

Resolve to look as tough as possible, which seems ludicrous but get up in cowboy boots, jeans, and leather jacket with slicked-back hair, and get off to the hotel, all the while intoning a silent mantra ... MY NAME IS BOND ... JAMES BOND ... MY ... This hotel is soundproofed by carpeting and my boots sound like ballet slippers. Arnold Kopelson, the newly Oscared producer, greets me at the door of the suite and beams me in. He cannot contain his excitement about anything and is telling a tale of how he was a carpet salesman, then film distributor and now producer of *Platoon*. Steve Miner, the director, is pencil slim, top to toe in cowboy gear, including string tie, but minus the Stetson. Claims he is a WASP from Connecticut.

'SIT DOWN. WHADDYA WANNA DRINK? WHADDYA THINK OF THE SCRIPT? LIKE THE ROLE? MIND DOING A BIT OF READING?'

'Sure.' I attempt to lower my voice to what it might have been had I been blessed with demolition-sized bollocks, and *growl*.

They let me gruff through a page and then interrupt with, 'Can you do a SKUTTISH accent for us?'

Suppress all signature 'shh' sounds of Sean and Highland fling it. Probably doing a dialect tour of Inverness via Aberystwyth.

'That is so neat. You English guys! How d'you do this stuff?'

Read further, and their seeming so pleased is totally disarming and I realize during the chat that follows that, were these gents English and the same age, *everything* would be different. Americans seem to have this direct, almost childlike enthusiasm that seems unfettered by class or formality. Leave half an hour later on first-name terms, 'Thanks, Arnold, thanks, Steve.'

'We'll be calling your people.'

True to their word, I get a call next day and an offer. Is this the *call from the coast* that actor-autobiogs are signposted by?

I have never been to America. Grew up on Hollywood movies. None of this seems *real*. *Withnail* opened over there to wonderful reviews and a small release, but seemed as distant and inaccessible as Mars.

My memory is banked with movie memorabilia, F. Maurice Speed's annual *Film Review*s, teenage subscription to *Photoplay* and *Films Illustrated*, and every birthday and Christmas present a book about the cinema. Scrapbooks. Stolen lobby stills, posters, biogs, autobiogs. *Films and Filming, Sight and Sound.* ANYTHING. OBSESSED!

20th January

I'm bolt upright in bed and it's two a.m. *How could they have cast a skinny Englishman to play this macho warlock-hunter?* They never saw me without my leather jacket ... Eyes are stalked like Malcolm McDowell in *Clockwork Orange* as I'm now running around trying to pack in the middle of winter for Californian sunshine. Convinced I've forgotten something important. Answer the phone, my brain doing U-turns and backflips off the top board, Adam's apple jogging 'mmmmMMMMmmmm's' of agreement with whoever. Passport, visa, cash, diary check. Eye-fondle my way round the contents of the house, as if it might be the last time I ever see it. *Daft.* Charged farewells at the door and into a cab driven by a greaseball to Heathrow, FAST.

Everything slow-motions for a while. I'm ushered into the first-class lounge with *would you care for a drink, sir,* caressing the cushioned airwaves.

Use the courtesy phone to call the agent.

'All going *raaather* well,' drawls Michael. I am quietly, calmly *combusting* with excitement *and* the upheaval at the prospect of it all.

The Khoi Kalahari Bushmen have a philosophy that THIS IS ALL A DREAM THAT IS DREAMING YOU and, right now, my head and my heart are dislocated and scudding about in search of new signposts. The existentials become concrete by the *real* thought that were this happening to my best friend it would somehow be more thrilling and comprehensible, I suppose partly because the *imagined* 'journey' or composite of every Rags-to-Riches route is finite. Whereas the *actuality* is flying into the Unknown, which translates as The Fear. Which must explain why my hands are shaking.

After a ten-hour flight in the nose of a 747, LA stretches to the left and right, and through my porthole, like a railway miniature mountainscape, stands the HOLLYWOOD sign. My guts have figured eight. All the palm trees, freeways, cars and the domed airport building seen in a hundred movies. And I am *here* to be *in* one. Through Immigration and when asked what I'm doing here, drop volume in case they yell, 'FAKE!' when I declare my intent. Through, and meet my name-on-a-card and 'Hi, my name's Chuck. I'll be your driver for today. Lemme take your luggage cart.'

While he twanged and nasaled his way through his *life plans*, I gazed off. EVERYTHING IS SO FLAT. Nothing seems higher than two storeys and everywhere there are scaffolded wooden 'flats' that look like the back of film sets. Shall I say something to Chuck?

'Are these film sets?'

'Are you *kidding*? They're just buildings-in-progress. Sets, huh? That's kinda cute! This yer first time?'

As it *is* Los Angeles, I had dumbly assumed films were being made on most streets.

'HOLLYWOOD IS A SLUM!' claims Chuck, and twiddles up the volume of Kiss FM.

Drive for ever through the Flatlands. Seems to be one vast sprawling suburb. More of the same. FLAT FLAT FLAT. I never thought it would be so *flat*! Glide sideways and park outside a stucco adobe. WIG SPECIALTIES.

'First port o' call,' hails Chuck, opening the door. Is he kidding me? I've just flown in and it's two a.m. bodyclock time. A walking ice-cream tub called Del swings in and declares, 'HI! I'M DEL AND I'M GONNA FIT YOU WITH SOME HAIR EXTENSIONS, RIGHT?' With which he attacks my frail scalp with elastics and clips, and in no time he has attached the wig and I have shoulder-length hair.

'FIT OK?' He *does* speak in capitals.

I now resemble an oblong-faced, minor rock'n'roll band member.

Julian Sands, playing the warlock, saunters in for his fitting and is incredibly laid back and oh-so-ca-su-al, compared to my oh-so-strung-up state.

'See you at the read-through tomorrow.'

'ADIOS, RICH.' Del, all swell and familiar.

Chuck outlines his detailed plans to avoid the rush-hour and we finally ascend from the flats up to West Hollywood. Fancier houses and sub-tropical plants.

The Sunset Marquis Hotel and Villas, on steep Alta Loma, just south of Sunset Boulevard. Dusk, and the trees and foyer all twinkling fairy-lights.

'All the rockers and music people stay here,' Chuck assures me. Orange-ochre, low-lit and plant-filled. Live one at the piano playing Broadway, and it's like stepping into an evening Hockney. 'Hi and welcome and how are ya? Suite 333 and we have a package and some phone messages for you, Mr Grant.'

Luggage trolleys and bellmen, waiters and whoever else swarm about and I walk across the poolside terrace to the elevator.

Irv the agent, the Californian counter-partner of Mr Whitehall, cues his call perfectly. 'You got in OK? We are so excited. Gonna be great workeen tugether. Good hotel. I'll see you get *per diem* right off and let's do lunch at your earliest. Or maybe even a breakfast. See how your skedule pans out. OK. Bye.'

Is it just the jet-lag or *does* everyone have this habit of saying the most mundane thing as though it was SOS important and pressing? Like a NASA launch when all that's being said is *Your room is on the third floor*? I ponder the idea of '*per diem*' – the glorious cash-in-hand expenses which actors get when shooting – and pass out.

22nd January
Read-through at Lion's Gate Studio, a couple of freeways yonder.

Julian says the movie is basically a kind of cartoon. Chase movie. Action. Special effects, horror and clearly *commercial*.

Steve, the director, is easy-going and laid-back. He and the writer David Twohy forthrightly discuss what will play for the audience ... who they will like and identify with ... how each scene will do this to achieve that. This is rather like overhearing a couple discussing the ingredients of a successful washing-powder formulation. So much of *this* will get *so* much of *that*. Lori Singer, best known to me as the cellist who never talked much in the TV series *Fame*, is the third person in the triangle.

While Lori wades in with the psycho-*Angst* of her character, Julian counters with his conclusion that it's a straight narrative drive-through and shouldn't be side-tracked by psychology. Fierced my eyes round the dialogue to convert to Connery-cadence.

Lori's concern that her character does not garner sufficient sympathy and has *too many negatives* culminates in her making calls to her agent and lawyer. Strange irony here as her character is the *funky-chick-who-doesn't-give-a-shit* type, and her brass-balls dealings with writer and director seem *perfect* for the role. Yet it is this very aspect she wants changed or at least soft-pedalled. She asks me for dinner, then cancels, then calls to say, 'I have decided to be friends with you right away, rather than let things develop gradually and grudgingly as in the script.'

Is this what they mean when they talk about the METHOD?

Makes sense as we're shooting the thing out of sequence and back to front.

I meet Bo, the wrangler/stunt co-ordinator who's going to teach me how to use the whip my character brandishes. Bo is a *Real Man*.

'Let's git down to the car park. Find some space.' We cowboy-boot-click-heels to the tarmac. 'Now you gotta get in the right gear 'n'all, Dick.'

'Sorry, my name's Richard. Never been called Dick – to my face, that is.'

This flies off into the blue stratosphere without *any* response other than 'OK, Rich.'

Bo is too busy shunting me into a black alpaca jacket, gloves and racing helmet to concern himself with my neurotics. 'For your protection. Believe me, I seen some nasty stuff go down with folk who ain't prepared. Now you just holler any time you feel uncomfortable with anything.' He sounds like he's talking on TV, and the swaying palms and cobalt sky look like a backdrop. Bo outlines the technique required to handle the whips and I quickly work up a sweat inside the alpaca.

'Dammit, man. You done this kinda of stuff b'fore? You're a nat'ral. Feelin' good?'

I'm ten feet above myself, looking down at Swazi Boy doing Indiana Jones cracks and swirls with a twelve-foot coil of cowboy whip, and Bo enthusiastically offering instruction and encouragement.

Two ARSE-BUSTING hours later, drenched from the gruel of swing, curve, shuffle, withdraw and THAAAA-WACK! my right arm feels as if it has been wired up to an artificial wanking machine. Numbed. But felt High.

Bo entrusts me with the whip 'So's you can practise any time you have to spare.'

Yeah, like round the pool patio, you mean?

Julian suggests a trendy hamburger station for lunch, where the portions are apocalyptic and the waiter-verbals bullet-speed.

I manage to catch 'rye' in the torrential choice of breads being offered. But she loses me, or I her, when it comes to what dressing I can choose. She eyeballs me with an important stare as if to say, 'GET YOUR ACT TOGETHER, WHITE BOY.' I end up just pointing and nodding. She swishes off and is back in seconds with iced tea in glasses the size of jugs. Julian canters through the protocol of life out here and asks, 'Do you know anyone?'

'Not a soul.'

'You will. Pretty curious about newcomers.'

Ominous Boarding School. Bells a-ringing.

Tyrannosaurus rex-sized platter arrives and I do my best to demolish a corner.

The afternoon is spent with Bo and whip work.

I have a week before going to Boston to start filming so apart from some rehearsals I am free in the evenings. Paul Heller, the independent producer of *Withnail and I*, asks me to dinner and regales with talk of LIPOSUCTION. Says they insert straws into your flab, vacuum it out and you minge around for six weeks with Very Sore Sides. All this while eating. Heartily! Extremely welcome to meet a known face *and* eat in a house in Beverly Hills.

25th January

The Art and Costume Departments are peopled by Brits so a guaranteed laugh at least. Off into Beverly Hills to have my seventeenth-century boots fitted by an ancient miniature Italian elf who has touched the feet of 'all de grate stars, Ricardo!'

Then to South Central LA, the antithesis of all the Bev Hills hoopla. Dead eyes on every street corner and the colour is all drained to grey and dust. Pull up at a warehouse that looks like it's in a movie starring itself as the ideal location for stranglings. Get kitted out in a knee-length coat of coyote skins, with hidden Shoulder Enhancement to beef me out.

Bewigged, bewhipped, bestubbled and becoated, I am *very* grateful that the assembled seamstresses and passers-by are not openly laughing at this attempted transformation from stick insect to Steve Reeves.

They have made me look and feel *bigger*. And I realize that *everything* here *does*. They don't refer to the Pacific as 'the sea', it's THE OCEAN. The *streeetch* limo, the triple-decker sandwiches that could feed a family of six, the freeway of multiple lanes, the menus of multiple choice, the tooth-capped whites of waiters' gleaming dentals, the apples like footballs and Michelin humans trolley-shuffling and doing the 'big' Diet Coke straw-suck on a gallon carton. The billboards on Sunset Boulevard with faces blown up four storeys high . . .

Julian Sands takes me to lunch at the Farmer's Market which is an urban version of what I imagine to be your neighbourhood down home fruit and veg co-op with Ma's home-made lemonade and brownies on cooling racks. Except it's mainly stalls, waffle shops, fruit, and old Yiddisher Ladies on their constitutionals, alongside sharp-suited execs from the NBC TV studios next door. Jodie Foster half-jogs by in a grey tracksuit and comes over as she's a friend of Julian's. Takes a seat, is bright, direct and no-shit-Sherlock. Lasers me with the compliment that she has taken four sets of people to see *Withnail and I*. Oh, sweet waffle syrup, yes, please, thank you, Jodie. My brain is bleating to try and act casual, like this happened a hundred times before, but body parts have curled up their toes.

Jodie eats a hen's leg that she has stored in a small Tupperware box, while expounding on her passion for all things English. Having seen her in movies since she was a tot, her strenuous normalness is strange and exotic.

26th January

'Takin' you to a premiere, OK?!' Irv the Agent.

He drops by and picks me up in a shiny convertible plus fellow travellers. Hits a button and the hood is humming back over our heads and concertinaing into neat folds. His friend does publicity for something and he and Irv are giggling away, all Anglophilic Burberry reserve dropped. We turn into Hollywood Boulevard and before my eyes is an eighties replay of *Day of the Locust*. Crowds of people mill about outside the Egyptian Movie House. Plus sky-sweeping searchlights, stretch limos, screaming fans and a red tongue of carpet, just across from Syd Grauman's Chinese Theater where *Locust* fictitiously exploded. I AM IN A MOVIE. We join the ticketed throng moving down the roped-off entrance and there is no disguising the brutality of *stare* as you are sized: WHO YOU? WHY YOU? FUCK YOU!

It seems as though everyone is head-swivelling to find *someone* they recognize. The movie finally starts and the stench of hair-spray and popcorn is stifling. During the titles and credits, applause erupts from the various fraternities with the odd strangled cheer. There then follows an awesomely terrible teenage tract about dating.

Irv has a client in the movie which is titled *You Can't Hurry Love*. Well, come the credits you couldn't have hurried the crowd out any faster if you tried. And by the time the house-lights were up, the place was deserted. We cross the road and see the hand- and footprints outside Grauman's. So *this* is HOLLYWOOD? It was never so sleazy in my dreamings . . .

We convertible down to the Hard Rock Café where Irv wedges me between big bellies and bozooms and the rhetoric of 'YOU'RE AN ACTOR? DO YOU DIRECT? WHO'S YOUR AGENT? PUBLICIST? MANAGER? GURU? SAW YOU IN *WITHNAAAALE AND AY*. SO WHADDYA THINK OF THE MOVIE, HUH?'

Double-glazed eyes – either drunk, disappointed or dumb. Can there really be as many *stupid* people here as I think there are?

'Gotta remember this is not an A-list event, but kinda gives you a taster. Fun, huh?' Young women with piles of peroxided hair switch on like mega-watt bulbs when an agent or director is radared. I meet an English agent who is trying to itemize it all with irony, but before I can mutter Davey Crockett, Irv is at my side and reacting like the Brit has lured me away.

'*Beware of the people poachers*,' he whispers in my ear.

I gasp for some fresh air outside, pocketing the traitorous card clipped me by the English agent, and am delivered back to the hotel by Irv. Get a room service sandwich that must have taken four grown men to prepare. I haven't yet asked *how* you're s'posed to get your jaw wide enough for a bite without double jointing.

It's impossible to imagine what this place does to your psyche and soul if you aren't working. The divide is *ruthless*. Every waiter seems to be an actor and they deliver the menu like an audition speech.

'HI, MY NAME'S WARREN AND I'LL BE YOUR WAITER FOR THE NIGHT. NOW THE SPECIALS GO LIKE THIS: TONIGHT WE HAVE CLAMS ON THE HALF SHELL, SHARK STEAK WITH A PIQUANT LIME AND DILL SAUCE, OR SAUTÉ OF LAMB'S BRAIN WITH A GUACAMOLE ACCOMPANIMENT AND I KNOW I SHOULDN'T BE SAYING THIS BUT THANKS FOR YOUR PERFORMANCE IN THAT MOVIE.'

28th January
Few days free before heading to the Boston location, in NEW YORK, NEW YORK!

Afternoon flight across this continent and it's like the whole world is below: from desert to snow, Rockies to oceans, all reduced at this altitude to Jasper Johns-scapes and Jackson Pollock patterns. Glee at the request to fasten our seat-belts ... Indigo evening sky, the plane banks sideways and I see this Oz from a God's eye view. *Dazzling*. I can clearly see the Empire State, Chrysler, Liberty and the dark oblong of Central Park.

Later, crossing Queensborough Bridge in my chauffeur-driven limo, I swear I have a mini-hovercraft levitating under my bum. My head is jammed with Gershwin going GAGA. Yes, I have seen this skyline of 'scrapers all my movie-going life, but *Jeeezus*, this is that Coke slogan come true. *It's the real thing.*

Pedestrian crossings read WALK/DON'T WALK. Nothing in between, like these sparkling monoliths fingering the sky. Shimmering. Lacquered. *Confident.* Glossy glass-scapes. Art deco wedding cakes, Towers of Sheer. Where do they make people with the *confidence* ... call it what you will ... to have dreamt and constructed this ... NEW YORK. With its Twin Trade Towers. And double-barrelled title. Big Apple is the last thing that comes to mind. No Cinemascope, Technicolor, 3D, Cinerama, Mega-scope can convey what you *get* through the retinas. Maybe *this* is what they meant when they said you haven't lived till you've dropped acid. This will *more* than do!

Into, onto and within Manhattan and push-button down the window, despite the arctic air out. *Swazi Boy!* Fix your lugs on that sound. Steam jets like breath from the road and it's *Taxi Driver.* Horns honking and *maybe* Gene Kelly's gonna skedaddle by. Sirens wailing somewhere close and it's *Shaft* and 'Papa was a Rollin' Stone'. Boom boom BOOM. Yellow cabs and neon and cops on horseback, and drugstores with light-bulbs and glossy oranges and brown paper bags and it's *Annie Hall*, 'cept I can't quite see Woody or Diane. But as near as dammit. And Frankenstein's full voltage has plugged into my bolt.

A gloved hand opens the door and is getting my holdall and me into the lobby of the Algonquin Hotel pronto! Inside, it's a wood-panelled Edwardian gentleman's club. The loose sexy style, you'd never encounter anywhere else. Punters are cocktailing and clinking glasses and fur-coating up for the short walk to the theatres.

Up in the old elevator with the bell-boy and holdall and into some cosy chintz, which feels like staying in someone's house, *without* the hassles. Tip here, tip there, tip every-bloody-where. The dollar sleight-of-hand is a magician's manoeuvre, known to one and all. Unspoken. Into hands. Unavoidable. Warm radiator-hum in here, knowing that at least ten million people and double that many light-bulbs are *out there* beyond the door. Put on the thermals and bound down the stairwell and into 44th Street and *run* to Times Square on Broadway. GUYS AND DOLLS FOR REAL. Bright, brash, busting with people and I feel about as *alive* as I think I ever *will* be!

A third voice is coming up from way back in my head saying, 'sssssSSSSSSSSEEEEEEXY!' And *yes* it is. *Sexy*. Get a grip, boy, you're talking about a *city* for Chrissakes! All the *characters* are here. That's what gets me. Hookers, tramps, tourists, oldies, Occidentals, sharpsters, hucksters, cops, cabbies, gawpers, Brothers, 'Ricans, sleazeters, mothers, fathers, kids, families. *Danger?* Must be but it's too cold and too bright and too BRAIN-BUSTINGLY BRILLIANT to worry. Strong smell of smoke, gasoline, hot-dogs, cheap scent and something else ... *sweet and sour*. Sound and sight like the electric fizz and *shhplicks* you get above dodgem cars. And *time* to try to get it all without someone editing anything or cross-cutting or cross-fading. Every corner and angle is mine.

Added to which is the sweet jelly-roll of having a great friend, Alan Corduner, previewing in Caryl Churchill's play *Serious Money*, which has just transferred from the Royal Court Theatre in London to the Royal Theatre *on Broadway*. He is the only English actor to transfer and I stare at his name on the billboard outside. Leave a note at the stage door for him.

Someone with whom to share this first sight of NYC.

The vast electronic billboard in Times Square fixes the temp at minus 15 degree C. With wind. Understand the meaning of wind-chill factor for the first time and duck into a bookstore to try to restore circulation to my numbed ears.

Flick some pages, but all the print I can see says, HERE YOU ARE, SONNY! DREAMIN' THE DREAM THAT'S DREAMIN' YA!

No cold or wind can bolt this feeling *down*. Come signs of circulation and I am *out there*! This *time*, these *moments* have been YEARS in the making. Selznick! Cecil B. de Mille. KING STOMPIN' KONG.

Gulp some ice-air and meet Alan backstage.

'Want to tread a Broadway Board?' he asks. It's like the movies said it would be: naked light-bulb, air still strained with perfumed human, and the last stragglers struggling into their furs. You never saw so many dead furry animals walking the streets.

My euphorics are put on hold as Alan is nervous and twitching about the show's prospects on Broadway. This is about as far from the Royal Court as you can get. And it's WALK/DON'T WALK out here. Or more like WORK/DON'T WORK.

Alan has planned the sightseeing tour: Rockefeller Plaza to see the open-air skaters, Radio City Music Hall, up Fifth Avenue to the Plaza Hotel – just as F. Scott Fitzgerald said it would be. Into Central Park and on cue it starts snowing, topping up the night fall. Almost black and white and as near as dammit to the credits of *Manhattan*.

Downtown and up the Empire State to breathe the rarefied air and ever endless view of – below, beside and beyond – NEW YORK.

Movie matinée to warm up and the aisles are patrolled by a policewoman with baton and gun. This is a *first* for me. Maybe it's just because it's on Times Square?

Then to the preview of *Serious Money* – which is how you could describe the bejewelled punters. It's a fast, foul-mouthed City of London comedy and meets with deadly silence. Like the gagged fox heads swathed round wrinkly necks. The interval applause is more a retarded hand-clap and the man to my right growls, 'I don' come to the the-ay-tah tuh hear people say "cunt". Fuckin' disgustin'. C'mon, Hazel, we're outta here.'

Crush to the bar for a drink, and as I reverse out of the scrum I find myself parked next to a diminutive Paul Newman and Joanne Woodward, who are in the clear minority of praising the play, while all around people are fighting their coats on to get *out*. You don't *have* to eavesdrop here. *Everyone* has the volume turned up full – even when whispering, 'CAN YOU BELIEVE HOW SHORT HE IS?'

This is cut across by another matron yelling, 'SYDNEY! THIS SHOW AIN'T NO SHOW AND IT SURE AIN'T NO COMEDY. WE GOTTA GO!' I swear she hoped that by yowling, the audience would respond to the herding instinct and follow her lead.

Friends of Alan's invite us to dinner at an Italian restaurant called La Primavera, which they are trying out for the first time. More like La Prima Donnas. Hair in here is a real 'do', faces taut, diamonds sharp, toupees fixed and ties sapphire-pinned. New money, old flesh. Child-sized pasta portions clock in at thirty dollars. Talk is all deals and dollars and dumping money here to dough it up there. The artistic endeavour of making movies is relegated to a corner of minor irritation and inconvenience. *Yet* it seems *everyone* wants to know the stars. Meanwhile Alan is getting *major* attention from everyone in the place – maître d', waiters, other guests, and we cannot work out *why*. Until the owner 'compliments' him with 'You have lost so much weight, Mr Kissinger'. We were taken aback long enough *not* to dispel the mistake and settled back for the five-star service, laughing all the way through complimentary dessert and liqueurs. *Must be these new glasses.*

Our hostess is renting her Hollywood house to Alan Rickman, who is shooting *Die Hard*, and the house could be mine to rent once he leaves. Money is discussed up front and agreement is fixed, between the various verbal meteors slinging through the air about so and so. Corduner and I repair to the Algonquin lounge to unravel it all. You have to *plan* when to get some sleep in this city.

1st February

I take a shuttle flight to Boston to resume Warlock work. First day of shooting and we're in a mock seventeenth century village, shooting the opening sequence with extras, camera cranes, geese, children and sub-zero temperature in this cocaine-snowed landscape. Big test: will the crew laugh when they see me for the first time? Neurotic, I grant you, but a genuine anxiety. Makeup and wig and coyote-coated and bewhipped, I manfully stride out and silently survey the small crowd of crew whom I will get to know over the next two months. Introduce myself. Everyone in lookalike lumberjack gear and called Hank, Crank or Brick.

Leading lady and director are loggerheading. Makeup man and hair lady are sniping. She tells me, between stories of having her saddle-bag thighs unsuccessfully fat-suctioned, that my makeup man has *gotta go*. Meanwhile I am gearing myself up to say with a straight face and Scots accent, 'Damned be these hell besmeared and black Satanic fartin' holes.'

What *is* welcome is the work format being so clear and adhered to. Get to set. Straight rehearse through for crew and camera. Breakfast and costume and makeup. Everyone knows what is going on. Obvious, but not always the way.

9th February

I cannot believe I am not in London for the première of *Withnail and I*. Spend the day *raging* around, like my limbs were amputated. After all this time and here I am ice cold in Boston. BUGGER!

Spiky as a Sea Urchin.

My mood is dispelled with a day off in New York and dinner with Alan. His show is ailing, with mixed reviews and tiny audiences. We mope into Orso's for dinner with yet another group of his acquaintances, one of whom is a well-known Republican senator. Coincidentally Julian is dining with John Malkovitch who, it turns out, has seen *Withnail* twice, as has Kate Nelligan who leans over from an adjacent table, lifting my mood and worsening the doldrums of poor Corduner.

Unavoidable awareness that *everyone* in here is checking *everyone* out. There's a hierarchy of *fame*: the not-so, half-famous, were famous and maybe will bes. Someone interrupts our senator with, 'You're doin' a great job and makin' for a better country.' The senator then declares his extreme satisfaction at this, prompting a bushel of name-dropping from Ronnie to Nancy and down.

Appointment to meet Photographer Supremo Richard Avedon in his studio. Sixty-five going on twenty-five with extraordinary eyes, and charm by the carat load. I'm photographed and then video-taped improvising stuff for a Calvin Klein commercial. Love-talk. Just for the experience. I kid myself.

Alan is crabbed and crazed with the demise of his play: having played it in London where it was a great success, to have it dribble and die here on the Great White Way. I took him to see a comedy flick of no consequence to try to cheer him up.

Up ... Down ... Up ...

Spare the strings, but it *is* this push-me-pull-you elastic that undoes you. It's so close a call most of the time, and trying to maintain *some* equilibrium is hard.

Everyone knows when you have *bombed*. And, as much as you console yourself that what's printed today will wrap fish and chips tomorrow, I have yet to meet an actor unable to quote VERBATIM their worst reviews. The ones you believe *somewhere* might be true. Actors compare bad reviews in the same way old soldiers compare combat notes. Both deal in Death. One absolute, the former Living. Both laugh. In the dark.

15th February

Get back to LA and the makeup man is fired; they reckon the cheek-shading on my face looks like mud. Claims he will sue. More *Withnail* cuttings are coming through and it is strange to read so many reviews that fixate on my physiognomy: Tombstone-featured. Sepulchral. Lantern-jawed. Pop-eyed. Acres of Forehead. Sloe of Eye. Slab-faced. Sort of like an undertaker's catalogue.

We travel out to the Mojave Desert and put up in a motel on the highway that is pure *Paris, Texas*, down to the flies and sullen staff. Country and western twanging the hot airwaves and, despite my prejudice, I have begun to succumb to its charms.

The pool is bordered by a fake grass carpet, incongruous against the desert surround. Trucks megalith by at all hours. We are shooting at a Victorian farmhouse and I'm required to do part of a stunt with my whip, trapping Julian round the ankles and then falling. They set up a mound of cardboard boxes on to which I fall back, accompanied by applause at 'CUT'. We are three floors up on the turret of the house. The stuntman then does the full fall and I cannot believe that this human being is going to go through with the three-storey drop. Insane. But he does – and has to be carted off on a stretcher as he has cracked his shoulder. After which, trying to control the flighty Warlock with my whip, I am dragged forwards, holding the whip attached to a crane, through a field of fake cabbages. Like water-skiing on the ground. Then ker-thumping into a barn door. My supreme bravery earns me *huge* respect from the moustachioed macho crew.

'You're not a Method actor, are ya?' and *this* clearly a compliment.

As the stuntman is incapacitated, I end up doing a lot more than planned and, come nightfall, I am bruised and bashed all over. Monika, the German masseuse, is sent over and pummels me like so much dead veal.

Back in LA for the weekend and I'm convinced that every Brit out here buys a regulation crumpled cream suit before going through Customs.

The crew have nicknamed the English 'Teabags' and we have

retorted with 'Hot-Dogs'. I strongly suspect that *obesity* is what will bring about the Big Bang here. Not drugs or crime or cable television. Herds of folk as round as the Albert Hall perambulate about as if it is *normal* to be this size. There is a preponderance of 'pookie-cute' personages around shopping malls; ladies of a certain age in Bo-peep pink tracksuits, zipped, nipped, tucked and sucked in – not a brain cell out of place.

22nd February

Back in the Mojave Desert. Lori is *kvetching* about the heat and discomfort of her old-age prosthetic makeup. She decides to add a club-foot effect for good measure. It seems no one, even when faking it, is prepared to face old age with a wrinkle in California.

In the midst of all this cartoonery in the desert I am 'quaked by the following news. It seems that, due to a failure by Bruce Robinson's producer and my agent to inform and/or negotiate with one another, my filming schedule for *Warlock* makes me unavailable to do *How To Get Ahead In Advertising*, Bruce's 'Boil'. The mix-up is due to the ever-changing start dates for shooting *Advertising*, which finally got the go-ahead once *Withnail* had opened so well in London, by which time I was already shooting *Warlock* in Boston. 'Betrayal of trust', 'Selling out to Hollywood': these, and any other insult that fits, are bandied across the Atlantic by the parties involved, while I sit on my bed in the hotel room shaking my head in disbelief that this role and my friendship with its creator has gone belly-up. It would be more honest and accurate to report that my legs feel paralysed, my tongue is tied and heart on the rack. All this for a role? you might well ask. Yes, but a role wrapped in friendship and trust, the like of which comes along only a very few times in life. I can't bear to accept that Bruce has written me off and offered the part to somebody else and, worse still, that our friendship has been jettisoned in the process. What to do? What *did* I do? Begged. And after more to-ing and fro-ing, and attack and counter-attack, and who said what to whom and not to A. N. Other, a rapprochement is brought about by the producer, who acts as intermediary and calms both sides. Before my warlock-hunting is over, the deal is done for me to play the lead, Bagley, an adman who grows a talking carbuncle on his neck. Knowing that this situation has been saved makes the rest of my hunting days easier to handle, be it flying machines, smoking weather-vanes, or a monumental graveyard finale shot at Raleigh Studios opposite Paramount Pictures in which I vomit up ectoplasm in an intercosmic battle across time. However, I never want another week like that; never want to be strapped to the bedhead and the foot-rail and pulled in opposite directions, unable to speak for the sheer anxiety and frustration of it. Suffice to say that this was the beginning of the end of my relationship with Michael Whitehall.

17th March

Betwixt oozings and schmoozings with various agents from rival agencies, another fandango gets under way, over and above the daily schedule of my warlockery.

25th March

Milos Forman, the Czech director Oscared for *Amadeus*, is casting *Valmont*, the rival to *Dangerous Liaisons*, to be directed by Stephen Frears.

I get word that, despite having turned down Richard Avedon's commercial (after a plethora of conflicting agent advice), Mr Avedon has had the generosity to recommend me to his friend Milos, who is staying round the corner at the Sunset Marquis. Arranges a look-see the following day.

'Come back on Friday, Reechard.' I do. It's Good Friday, 1st April. 'Don't act. Just be. Say the lines. Think through. Like this.' He then demonstrates the very thing I have understood he does not want me to do: act. But Forman is charismatic, funny, disarming, and he knows that I know 'Valmont' is a great role.

It has been in the industry papers that he is seeing every actor in town, so all of this is an apparently breezy diversion. I kid myself.

Alan Corduner turns up from New York, where *Serious Money* has indeed folded due to lack of any at the box office.

5th April

Another summons to a meeting with Milos, at the end of which he declares, 'I want you to come back tomorrow to read with Kim Basinger.'

6th April

Four to seven p.m. with Kim and Milos. Intimidated at first. Absurdist by dinner.

7th April

Take Joan to Disneyland as we are free! A day of the longest queues on Earth, for two-minute rides. Idiotic.

9th April

Shooting more graveyard antics and Julian says congratulations for bagging 'Valmont'. It's news to me. Apprise him of the truth and worry all weekend about the rumour. Someone else calls and says I am on the shortlist.

The *Warlock* special effects are taking for ever and I wonder how anyone can stand the python pace of making action films, judging by how long everything takes to set up.

15th April

Further recall for Milos. Getting to feel mightily avuncular and chummy round here.

19th April

Milos tells me he is 'seriously interested' and states that we will do a final screen test when he is in London in a couple of weeks' time, and I am finished on *Warlock* duty.

25th May!

I get the promised call to screen test. This appointment is sandwiched between rehearsals with Richard Wilson for *How To Get Ahead In Advertising* and its multitudinous prosthetic head-mould fittings. Get to Commercial Studios at the far end of Ladbroke Grove for ten a.m. Told by an abrupt assistant to find from a rail a frock coat that fits, don a white periwig and 'wait'. As warm as the Sunset Marquis was, this environment would feel cold to an Eskimo.

Bleepers in my head are going, 'Get out! Get out! Get out!' Especially when I see like-kitted-out contenders lurking in the corridor muttering their lines and stubbing out their fags. No sign of Kim round here! Twelve thirty a.m. and it's 'Mr Forman will see you now.' I trot into the studio and am directed to the chair at one end opposite a video camera on a tripod at the other. In between is Milos. But not the version I had begun to think I knew somewhat. This is a no eye-contact, gruff-voiced, non-greeting grump who prods me towards the centre of the space, mumbles an order to speak the prepared text and get on with it.

Standing there, marooned in acute embarrassment, in a dank, ill-fitting frock coat, powdered wig and no one to act with, I feel simultaneously surreal and horribly duped. I think someone says 'Thanks' at the end, by which time I am out of wig, coat and W10 before I can spit out 'Prague.'

1st June

Lord Snowdon eases me through a funny morning sit for a *Vogue* portrait, followed by the less-than-earth-shattering news from White-hall that 'indeed you were right. Not going to work out with Forman. Sorry.'

10th June

Joan is pregnant!!!!!!! Amniocentesis result: it's a girl. We bow our heads, hold tight and hope.

4th January 1989

After three months in hospital with complications Joan gives birth to our daughter Olivia, one month premature. A little bird. Alive. 'Oh, God. Oh, God, Oh, God.' To register this takes more than writing.

5th May

Thirty-two today. *Warlock* and *How To Get Ahead In Advertising* were supposed to open simultaneously in the USA. However, New World Pictures are bought out by another company; *Warlock*'s release date is altered and delayed, and I am in Los Angeles doing the chat-show rounds and press for *How To Get Ahead In Advertising* alone.

Finally leave Michael Whitehall, having been told it 'highly unlikely you will ever work in the States', and join ICM under the guidance of another Michael – this one a Foster, to be known affectionately hereafter as the Dwarf. His American counterpart, who takes over from Irv, is Steve Dontonville, he tells me. Sincerely hope this is it and that I never have to go through another changeover.

Henry and June

I am summoned to the Portobello Hotel to meet director PHILIP KAUFMAN, he of *The Right Stuff* and *Unbearable Lightness of Being* repute. He is now casting a film about Henry Miller and as this *meeting* is a euphemism for an *audition* the question is what to wear. How to be. This daft consideration takes up some brain space along with the colliding images of astronauts and Czech liaisons recalled from the two movies of his that I've recently seen.

I was twelve and living in Swaziland when I heard the Apollo Moon landing on the wireless and resolved to dedicate my life to Space and becoming an Astronaut. This idea was as ridiculous to my father as my notion of becoming an actor. My conviction was reinforced when samples of Moon rock were exhibited in the American Embassy to queues of local Moonies.

'Unlikely to be the real thing,' quipped my pater.

'*What do you mean?* Of course it must be,' squeaked I.

'Don't be so daft. Think about it. Do you really think they brought back enough lunar rocks to populate every Yank embassy on the planet?'

This possibility wobbled my axis for a moment – maybe I could ask Mr Kaufman if *he* had any idea. Might provide a conversational segue into talking about Henry Miller and Co. My dad, dead and buried eight years ago, and me a sort of grown-up standing like a lost Girl Guide, wondering what to wear.

*

The venue for these meetings with American directors is invariably a suite in some discreet, quintessentially English hotel. A homely kinda atmosphere, with lots of thick carpet and well-stuffed chintz. Going in midday when the hoovers are out and discretion lingers in the slow-swivelling eyeballs of the concierge who checks out your face for signs of Fame.

Philip Kaufman's handshake is the firm don'-fuck-with-me-fellas kinda shake. All American and direct eyes. Deep voice, black beard and Chicago slow-drawl accent. Like a Talmud professor. Reassuring and almost academic.

'So excited you could come and meet with us. We loved, that is, my wife Rose and I loved, your work in *Withnail and I*. So funny.'

'Thank you. I loved *The Right Stuff.*'

We love each other up a bit before he gets down to discussing the character he has in mind for me.

'We're looking for a James Stewart kindova guy. Sweet, uncynical, pure, faithful and straight as an arrow.' All of which you will appreciate I have *become* as each adjective has spooled forth. 'In fact, the exact opposite of your *Withnail* character. Now the thing is, this character Hugo Guiller, the husband of Anaïs Nin, must be played by a strong actor, although, to be honest, he is the "weak" character and cuckold of the piece. Have you read any of Miller or Nin?'

This is the moment when you *really* have to ACT. And try to lie convincingly that of course you are *au fait* with much of the collected canon when *Tropic of Cancer* is as far as you got in your late teens. I recall seeing a picture of Ms Nin and thinking she looked a bit of a poseur and finding much fartaceous humour in the mispronunciation of her first name. *Read any Anus lately?* ghosts up from school. But this is not the moment for that. Mercifully Phil – please-call-me-Phil – does not interrogate or cross-question my literary knowledge. Though if he had asked whether I could ride a dolphin free-style I would no doubt have said aye. He tells me with a totally straight face that *Hugo* had a famously huge penis. I suppress a chortle and only manage to half-listen to his analysis of *why* Anaïs might have strayed into a relationship with Henry and June.

By the end of the conversation, I swear my Member has grown to such a length that a small barrow might be in order to wheel it out. I swear too that the very spirit and soul of every Jimmy Stewart movie has by auto-suggestion invaded my being. Righteous grace is pulsating from every pore and, as we shake hands, I am already planning my three months in Paris and speaking to the Props Department about Penile Enhancement.

Of course, by the time I reach the underground station, doubt has settled in like rising damp. *Who d'you think you're kidding? They'll never cast an Englishman to play an American.* But as each station clatters by, hope re-emerges through the replay of the remembered conversation. Part of you says, 'FUCK IT, who cares?' The rest yells, 'We do.'

No sooner said than the Dwarf is on the phone. The billing will read Alec Baldwin as Henry, Uma Thurman as June, Maria de Medeiros as Anaïs, and Richard E. Grant as Hugo. Universal Pictures are producing and they hope to 'go' in early August. Money is ... Yippee time.

I am now speed-reading EVERYTHING ever written by Miller and Nin. Which is a LOT.

The opportunity to re-create their lives and milieu galvanizes every minute, and even though I am not playing Miller, reading his and Nin's correspondence has become somehow personal. It also helps to clarify *why* Hugo Guiller was so attracted to this world and why he tolerated his wife's infidelity.

The wonderful illusion that good writing induces is the belief that, were you around with them then, you would have been one of them and definitely best friends. This is the honeymoon, when your head runs rioting through another time and place, at the end of which you feel you KNOW these people and are perfectly equipped to breathe your breath into their reputations.

I scour the photographs, knowing I am playing a real person, for clues. Get the magnifier out and scrutinize Hugo's pants for signs of endowment. No visible trace. Philip and Rose Kaufman have co-written the screenplay and it is unreasonable to expect a hundred pages of scenes to re-create what happened over years. Inevitably whole chunks are missing, and the best you can hope for is some kind of spirit suggested by Miller and Nin's fiction and documented doings. I can feel the Miller and Nin aficionados preparing their condemnations.

17th August

Major wobble: Alec Baldwin has withdrawn two weeks prior to shooting. Panic stations. Rumours fly in every direction about the whys and wherefores. The delay will mean problems for the location scouts, who have secured the use of certain buildings and streets on the condition that filming is completed in the holiday month of August. The budget spirals and there is overall pandemonium. Who will play Miller? Suggestions and possibilities are flung around like so much confetti and Fred Ward, one of the astronauts in *The Right Stuff*, is tracked down and cast. He is in his mid-forties, Uma just twenty, Alec in his early thirties. Concern is voiced about the suddenly widened age gap. And how can anyone get their head around playing Miller with so little notice?

22nd August

Leaving London. Olivia is seven months old and this will be my first time away. Joan is having to work and cope *sans* 'usband. What should be love-crammed prior to departure is rather nerve-ridden and tetchy. Suspect you subconsciously irritate the shit out of each other so that the parting is welcome when it comes. Unlike the sweet sorrow stuff of which movies are made. I am not exactly footing it off to the Crimean War and Paris is a mere forty-minute flight and phone call away, but there is still the unspoken neurotic fancy that *this* could be the last time we clap eyes upon one another, and Glenn-Miller-in-the-fog scenarios loom up.

Pack in the dark, out of sight. Hard to sleep. Wide-eyed *before* the alarm does the damage. Big hugs. No words. Car picks me up and I indulge myself in a quiet blub all the way to Heathrow. Leave *terra firma* nursing a throbbing mouth ulcer that has grown carbuncle-like overnight and which precludes eating the pre-packed breakfast. Everyone is in suits with briefcases and expressions to match. No signs of ADVENTURE AHEAD here.

At Charles de Gaulle Airport I am met by a driver, fag in mouth, with my name scrawled on a card, and how different this all is from when I first hitched into France as a student. We stop-start our verbal way into Paris; he speaks pidgin Anglais, while mine is more ferret-Franglais and we splut and barter our way in Nursery Talk.

Got to learn the language.

The Wardrobe Department is in the midst of a pre-shoot nervous meltdown. All pins and needles and tight jaws sucking the life out of Les Gauloises. I am set upon by four strangers who demand I strip down. Which I do, relieved for once as it's so hot. Then I'm pinned, prodded and patched up with pieces of fabric, which are then drawn over with chalk to indicate where sleeves and pockets and knees *will* be. Exactly like my own 'unstitched' mental state. *How the fuck are these clothes ever going to be ready in time?* The question Le Mans around my skull awhile and by the look on these faces in here, *they* feel the same way!

Next stop the Production Office which is a warren of offices and typing and people on the move and photoboards of various locations and actors' photos on a noticeboard and lurking actors waiting to meet the casting director for the smaller parts, phones and bike messengers and shouting.

'Hi, I'm, Peter, Phil's son and your producer. Welcome. Welcome. Phil and Rose are out scouting new locations right now and sorry they can't be here to meet you, but we'll be meeting up later, and now if it's OK with you we could go check out possible accommodation for you and your family.'

Peter is an uncanny clone of his father, down to the beard, accent and expressions. We head across the Champs-Elysées to Place de l'Alma on the Seine opposite the Eiffel Tower and park in front of a vast wedding-cake of a building. An ancient old crock with a moustache greets us; she guides us up a curving staircase and into a miniature palace.

'Would this be all right for you and your family?'

They must be under the misapprehension that I am a big breeder and have ten kids. My brain is whirring at speed at what it must be costing old Universal Pictures for this embarrassment of rooms.

My baggage is brought up and Peter and Jean-Claude announce that they must be off and that I have the rest of the day free. And it's only lunch-time, yet it feels as if London is a lifetime ago. Is this what amnesia feels like? Here five hours, and my other life seems to have no connection with this new one whatsoever. Julie Andrews has popped into my head and is standing outside the convent gates humming, 'What will this day be like, I wonder?' before running over the mountain-tops to sing, 'The Hills are Alive with the Sound of Music'.

GET A GRIP!!

What *will* this film be like? A story *so* intimate, sexual and exposing and all the actors as yet total strangers.

23rd August

Rehearsal Day One. Maria de Medeiros and I take part in a sexual chemistry test, presided over by Phil Kaufman, who adjudicates our every mutual reaction. Maria is an identikit of the real Nin, and we tell one another how like the Real People we look.

'WHEN DO WE DO OUR BED SCENES?' she asks, wide-eyed and beguiling and ironic and teasing, and peels off a fruity laugh.

'You're just perfect,' is what comes out of my mouth, her temperamental forecast an All Clear!!

We ping-pong anecdotals at each other and skirt round one another's private lives.

'Do you live alone?'

More laughter. 'You Eenglish! I am in love, but nut married. And maybe wiz two people.'

'You *are* Anaïs.'

Relief is evident all round that this casting duet is a match. Wonder at the nerverack experienced by a director who, in addition to a multitude of technical demands and production pressures, has the risk of thesp personalities *not* gelling. Unlike the theatre, where a play might rehearse for anything between three and six weeks during which time you have a chance to get to know the other actors fairly intimately (depending on how emotionally exposing the play requires you to be), rehearsal time on a film is at most a week if you're lucky. Time is concertina'd. You have to get to know someone very fast and these initial meetings with fellow cast members, although apparently brief and casual, are *crucial* to your work. It is sometimes frustrating that just when you're getting to know people and want to spend more time together the schedule interrupts or their role is completed and they are off and on to another film. However, if friendship is often a snatch-and-grab affair, filming does spare you the potential nerve shredder of having to tread the boards with the same pain-in-the-arsehole *every night* for *six months*. Even the best friendships undergo a sea-change when you see each other nine performances a week. Or mine do, anyway.

As you rarely shoot more than a couple of pages of script per day, the absence of a long rehearsal period pays off in that you have to play the scene 'in the moment' and cannot be waylaid into surveying what happened before or will happen next or what can be achieved in a two-hour performance. Filming offers the real luxury of trying to get something right, and the opportunity to go back and reshoot it. (You can't exactly face the stalls and say, 'Excuse me, but I got this bit wrong. Do you mind if we start again?' It *has* happened, but to get away with it I suspect your surname would have to be Wolfit.)

American actor Kevin Spacey bounds in as Maria beams out. He plays Miller's best friend, an unsuccessful writer who constantly claims that *he* has actually written or at least inspired Henry's work. Kevin is garrulous and encyclopedically well informed about movies and everyone in them. He is also a brilliant mimic and launches into a cabaret of his specialities including Jack Lemmon, with whom he has worked three times, and Marlon Brando, with whom he hasn't but with whom he wants to. He is accompanied by his ancient dog, Slate, and moans that when he did a play in London Slate had to stay home in the States. No sooner in than he is out and off to have a costume fitting and it's starting to feel like *This Is Your Life* but with total strangers.

Fred Ward, playing Miller, is in next. Silent and contained as muscles. Head nod and monosyllabic and into another office for something. An assistant asks if I have any special requests. *Meaning what?*

'Well,' comes her reply, 'Fred is a karate black belt and we 'ave found him a gymnasium in Montparnasse and 'ave been informed 'e is a kickboxing master and that 'e is invincible.'

The final member of the quartet is Uma Thurman, whom I meet in the hairdresser's where she is having hair and makeup tests while an electric buzzard denudes my head in about five seconds flat. The mirrored reflection renders my features as those of an aged seven-year-old. Uma is nineteen, tall for ever and painted to look like Marlene Dietrich. Which gives her cause for complaint: 'It looks like a mask.' This induces a flurry of activity and fast French from the team of chain-smokers who hover, prod and paint. Everyone is decked top to toe in leather and chains and you could be fooled that this is some sort of bikers' convention. I opt for some biographia in Uma's direction to try to lighten things up a bit round here.

'I saw you in a teen movie called *Johnny Go Home.*'

'Oh my God!' She laughs. 'Oh, my Gooood. Nobody saw that movie. It went straight to video. Oh, my God! How could you?' She is laughing a lot now.

'Well, Oom, I can only dredge this one up 'cos I appeared in a flick called *Killing Dad* that played one week in the West End and was on the video shelves a record three weeks later.'

Sharing some SHAME pays dividend and, within a very short space of time, we are off and jabbering. We rake through the recasting brouhaha and get round to the nudity factor. Which is a big one on this movie.

'How worried are you by the nudity?'

'Well, Hugo reputedly had this donkey-sized dong so I'll be counting on co-operation from the Props Department.'

'Phil seems to have this thing about the lesbian-erotic element . . .'

We then traded family history awhile and I realized I had been earning a living of sorts for ten years which constituted *half* of her LIFE. Wondered whether she thought of me as some kind of pre-Galapagean tortoise lumbering towards the Middle Ages. Probably. Around my late teens I used to think thirty pretty advanced.

We are invited to have lunch with Phil and Peter Kaufman and the topic is resolutely sexual. They are a sort of double act, with uncannily similar voices, and assert that *all of Paris is bisexual and they kinda frown on condoms.* The likelihood of *my* father and me having such a conversation is as remote as my ever comprehending Albert's theory of relativity and I feel as if my upbringing has been Pastoral indeed.

Rose Kaufman arrives, having been scouting for *objets d'art* for the Nin interiors. She wears little makeup, flowing ethnic-Indian clothing and beads and exudes an air of Buddhist calm along with a quietly expressed *passion* for Miller and Nin. This is clearly the fruition of a lifelong project, with the recent publication of the book *Henry and June* working as the catalyst and *way in* to making these lives into a film. Rose speaks quietly and sets out to reassure me that although my character is the obvious outsider, cuckold and dullard of the quartet, it is INCREDIBLY SIGNIFICANT AND IMPORTANT. This is a line of persuasion that I could happily do without, for no amount of bluster can beef up my part. However, the Kaufmans' mutual care to accommodate and involve is sincerely intended and I remain mute. Perhaps they thought I might transform into a sidewinding Diva demanding more attention than the character requires.

With this placebo and *petits fours* downed we all disbanded, to meet again for the read-through a couple of days hence.

24th August

Instead of two free days being a *tally-ho!* into the streets and museums and life of Paris, I am immobilized, paralysed from the waist down by THE FEAR!

Maybe ... maybe there is just TOO MUCH ART out there. Nouveau, Rococo, Richelieu and *bateau-mouche*, go-go, disco and can-can? What has specifically precipitated this crisis is having heard my tape-recorded attempt at an American accent. The read-through of the script with *real Americans* to come sends the prospect of firings and rehirings rattling around my head. How can you let yourself be rumbled by such a small detail? Rumbled? Rigor mortified! Resolve to reach for the phone next to the bed and ASK FOR HELP.

Cindia Huppelaar, the American dialect coach on call to perfect Uma's Bronx accent, obliges my panic-stricken request and sets up an appointment. Shoo-be-doo-wah-wah ... Will my legs shift *now*? Steady the buffs, boy. Let's listen to that tape playback one mo' time. The dialogue sounds like a runaway train with a bad accent and I am now cringeing at not having learnt anything. *Don't talk so fast!* This accusation has haunted my head ever since I began acting. Mentally indulge in fifty lashes, followed by an eyeball roam all around the apartment. Tall-ceilinged and mirrored and wealth-ridden and stale-aired as if the oxygen has long since been sucked out and I and IT are dead. Faint smell of mothballs permeates the air.

Resolve to share my paranoia with a bona fide American and call up Kevin Spacey, who is mercifully in, and mosey down to his place, in Place des Vosges. Of course his apartment seems crammed with LIFE. Plants, music, windows looking out on to a small courtyard garden, access to restaurants. Picture-postcard Paris. The contrast underlines my feeling of isolation up the snoot end of town where everything is strait-jacketed by wealth – designer shops displaying a single item of clothing in a football-field-sized window and statued shop assistants within to match.

'You gotta move,' is Kevin's sage advice.

Sure! 'Dear Universal Pictures. I am writing to inform you that the vast wedding cake apartment you are so generously forking for *doesn't* meet my measly requirements. Please relocate me to some sleaze. Yours Ungratefully, Grant.'

Spacey steadies my derailed nerves with a trot down his very vivid Memory Super Information Highway. He names *names*: who did what to whom and when and how, and did you know what a fucker this name was and what a doll that one was? Actor yak.

Kevin is *waiting* to play leads in movies, having done them in the theatre including Broadway. His when-will-it-be-me? *kvetch* receives scant support from me. My nerves are all too grateful just to be enjoying a dose of fresh air. After all, what have I to complain about? Here I am employed on a movie, in Paris, in summer, well paid and well watered and YET. I induce my own nausea at the naffness of my ninnying.

25th August

Read-through: held in a conference room overlooking the Champs-Elysées above an Alsace-Lorraine restaurant, hence the vague nostril-assault from the cooking vats below, boiling up the pigs and sauerkraut.

Uma is doing a thick Bronx accent full pelt and I am blanched by her courage. Fred is mumbling along almost inaudibly. Maria is rolling her 'R' according to the recordings of Nin's actual voice. Come my turn to utter and every note and ounce of coaching with Cindia has done a Burton. My tongue is concussed with fear like so many jam doughnuts in a tight bag.

The whole thing is pretty deadly and lifeless, except for Uma. And this is the horrifying moment when you wonder how it is you EVER got a part or if you ever knew how to act. Eye contact is rare in these circumstances, lest your shame burns a hole in someone else's cornea.

Phil and Rose thank us for doing it and we're then driven out to the ancient Épinay studios outside Paris to see the sets and to mooch around long trestle tables laden with props and reference material from the period, everything from postcards to books, pornography, bicycles, fabrics, clocks, cloaks and watches of the twenties. It's all rounded off with a ride in a 1926 Citroën belonging to my character. This is PLAYTIME. And having something to get your hands on is a mighty relief after the piping verbals of the read-through. Unlike a playscript, where the dialogue reigns supreme, film scripts are very episodic and 'bitty'. Scenes are no longer than a couple of pages, with detailed descriptions of the action and visuals. It's not *that* unusual for it to sound dead when read aloud. We reconvene, having chosen personal props, in the tiny studio bar, complete with peeling posters of French flicks from the fifties and sixties. Everyone beats up on themselves about the tortuous reading, which makes *everyone* feel a fuck of a lot better.

28th August

Épinay Studios, pre-shoot finals. Chaos, with a big cha-cha. Everything from Mr Baldwin's withdrawal to the stifling heat, language barrier, foreign idiosyncratics and last-minute hiccups has *gripped* one and all.

Getting this whole shebang up and shooting has everyone on RED ALERT. Costume Department is in a sprint of stitching, seaming and fitting up to try to make it in time. Hair and makeup tests are still going *escargot*-slow and the lighting fiddle-abouts are painstaking. Phil is to be seen in a corner with his script, trying *not* to pull his full head of hair out with the frustration of working in a foreign country and not being fluent in the foreign tongue. The American Way is direct and bullseyed in contrast to the French, which seems to require a circuitous route via verbal foreplay and/or seduction.

Hot and humid as a hippo's rectum, I am trussed up in a three-piece tweed suit with overcoat and tweed hat, choking on a pipe for a camera test. *Sans* hair and wearing this tall domed hat, my reflection is that of an extra long condom. Am seriously considering asking Philippe Rousselot, the cinematographer, to use a Cinemascope lens to widen things out a bit. Ponder a Head-widening Contractual Stipulation when hair is shorn for Period Part Purposes.

Fred Ward has been shaved bald, save for a pudding-bowl edging of hair round his ears to affect the Miller Profile, which is completed by Henry's trademark round lenses.

Maria is clipped and gelled to achieve the period Marcel-wave style and Uma is 'NO NO NOOOOOOOO-ING' all attempts to cut a little more from her bangs. She is sheathed in a satin skin and is about to shoot a clip for a film-within-the-film sequence, a replica of Hedy Lamarr's *Ecstasy*. Which word best describes the faces of the assembled crew on seeing Ms Thurman's entrance. Murmurs of 'Venus', a part she has already played in *Baron Munchausen.*

Fred is smarting at the installation of blue contact lenses over his brown eyes. And, considering that most photographs of Miller are in black and white, it does seem to be pursuing authenticity too far.

Maria's authentic teeth, however, have met with objection from the powers-that-be who have declared them 'UNSIGHTLY' and ordered the fitting of caps to cover all skew and blemish. Which causes much giggling from Maria about her IMPEDIMENTA.

Fred has managed to get hold of Miller's cook to provide a first-hand account and get character info. Everything about Hugo Guiller refers to his innate grace, charm and longevity – he outlived the fornicating trio of Anaïs, Henry and June.

Costumed, made-up and coiffed, we are then shepherded into a dance rehearsal to learn the cha-cha, tango and foxtrot for later in the film.

Phil and Rose are using up all their diplomacy in trying to get the message through to the Art Department that, yes, they do want the colours of the Nin interiors to be extreme and dramatic and as dark as they are documented and described.

This causes many heads to shake. They feel *their* artistic input is being compromised/criticized, and opt for more 'tasteful' neutral tones. Phil has clearly had enough of this farting around and his voice is climbing the octave and finally settles for a full top C blast of 'DO IT LIKE I HAVE ASKED, PLEEASE. IT IS NOT ABOUT "TASTE" BUT ABOUT HISTORICAL ACCURACY. PLEEEEASE CAN YOU JUST PAINT THE ROOMS THE COLOURS WE HAVE DECIDED UPON. THIS SHOULD NOT BE PERSONAL. TRANSLATE!'

Eyes are hooding over and there is the audible muttering of 'Les Americains!' to accompany the shaking heads.

It's all too hot and all too close to the first day of shooting . . .

29th August

The first day scheduled is a scene between Maria and me, which we rehearse with Phil before the end of the day. 'This marriage is like a pot of boiling water. Monday [first day of shooting] will be the time to put in the spaghetti.' Hopefully sauced by an authentic Yank accent.

'It's yours now. I know you will both be wonderful. You are Anaïs and Hugo. Enjoy your weekend,' says Phil.

Invited to dinner with Jean-Philippe Ecoffey and Co. He is playing the bisexual dance teacher who also 'dangles' with the ubiquitous Ms Nin. We nod briefly into an eaterie that offers soup at forty dollars a bowl. Shoot out and settle for a restaurant whose clientele *all* seem to know him.

Someone called Belinda joins our table and declares she is in the middle of a nervous breakdown, hence her constant to-ing and fro-ing from the phone. Kevin does his impersonation cabaret which goes off like a bomb. But the shellshock of the night comes in the shape of a casual question from Belinda: 'Are Gary and Uma coming tonight?'

It turns out she doesn't know Gary Oldman or Uma Thurman, but asserts that 'They are an item.' I feel topsy-turvied. I did a television film with Gary a couple of years back and we both got married and had children at about the same time. This news didn't seem to fit. Surely Uma would have said something. Or maybe it's the last thing she would have said. Either way, I don't remember the rest of the dinner, capsized by this upheaval. Not my business, but any split is a raw reminder of my parents' divorce when I was eleven, and playing this cuckolded man and then hearing this news is a pin-filled jolt. Do I say to Uma, *I have heard*? I feel uncomfortable either way.

4th September

The first day of shooting is at a replica of the Nin house in the suburb of Louveciennes. They have found an almost identical replica further out of Paris. Pick-up is at ten a.m., then an hour's drive, and eleven a.m. start – unlike the usual dawn raid schedule favoured by English and American films. Unusually civilized.

A huge marquee has been erected and a five-course lunch with wine is on offer. Exclaim a couple of *Sacrebleu*s out loud and assume this is a French way of welcoming everyone. I have never seen catering on a film anything like this before. There is not a single baked bean or battered cod in sight.

The scheduling allows for *slow entry*. The first scenes simply require entering the front door/running up the stairs. But overhanging all this is the last scene of the day, which is a spat, pivotal to the breakdown of the marriage. All of which has to be conveyed in about ten sentences. None of which seems possible at this pre-feast distance, when we are all still relative strangers. 'You will just have to bloody well act then, boyo,' a Welsh voice yodels from some secret part of my medulla.

It being the first day everything takes double the time it would normally as everyone sorts out their function in the new hierarchy, and with the language barrier, translation nibbles away more minutes. The combination of costume and three-dimensional sets – the real house, finally painted to Phil's specifications – and all the background reading swirling about the cranium converges so that SOMETHING clicks. And whereas before lunch all seems chaotic and uncontrolled, come the moment to start, excitement and adrenalin have replaced the jitterbugs. Phil offers a key to the scene: 'I want no outward show of hysteria or snotty pleadings – all is repressed.' This is the moment when all your personal betrayals and demons are called upon to transmit into lines written by someone else.

I have read numerous doorstopping tomes about ACTING, but none have really conveyed HOW this STUFF works. But when it comes out RIGHT, you KNOW and usually the crew around you KNOW too. What it does not feel like is the SHOWING OFF you mistook for ACTING at school! The set-up is an absurdity: thirty-five strangers are crammed on a landing outside a closed door with lights, mikes, camera, cables and inconvenience focused on one actor having an argument about infidelity with an actress who is on the other side of the door. Alone yet surrounded.

You move through the action for a camera-lighting rehearsal and to give the camera focus-puller a chance to measure the distance between your head and the lens. He has marked the floor with tape, which you have to hit exactly *without* looking down, during which time everyone is talking and readjusting equipment. You *think* you know what will come out when the director calls ACTION, you *think* you understand what this moment of BETRAYAL feels like. And then the first assistant director calls, 'QUIET ON SET,' and a couple of beats later Phil says, 'ACTION,' and your head feels hot and the reality of the situation suddenly overwhelms you and the thirty-five pairs of eyes become background. Invisible. And a sound comes from your throat that sounds like someone else. And seemingly without thinking, just feeling, YOU ARE, at that moment, A MAN ARGUING WITH HIS WIFE ABOUT A SUSPECTED AFFAIR WITH A BEST FRIEND. And it IS painful. And it's just ACTING.

'CUT,' is called and, in the few seconds of silence, nobody looks anyone in the eye, or so it seems, and you feel SOMETHING has happened. And without saying anything you know you have passed the test. The sense that you have *done it* is momentarily satisfying, yet it also feels as if it's somehow *out there* and not really to do with yourself at all. Yet it has come out of you. Perhaps this is what those tomes mean when they talk about actors as vessels, conduits and every other variant of conductor.

Phil mercifully says little but seems satisfied with the way the first day has panned out and that the whole thing has begun.

I have a revelation of sorts on the car journey home: in costume and shorn haircut I look very like my father did when he was my age and he was treated like Hugo and similarly suffered. Twenty years on, I am re-enacting the same situation. The 'Holding a Mirror up to Nature' chapter heading in an acting manual is a-hovering. Having been so nerve-raddled at finding a way to fulfil Phil and Rose's James Stewart prototype, I realize that this connection is what I have been seeking. And once experienced, I feel I know how and why Hugo is what he is. I re-examine the photographs and swear I recognize the look in his eyes: tight-lipped, set-jawed, smiling, gentle and betrayed. All the fish flap and what-the-hell-am-I-doing-here evaporates. *This* is the *what*, the *why* and the *wherefore*. The discovery is exhilarating.

If any of this transmits on the screen remains to be judged by others, but it has given me a route.

Day two. Scene: dining room of Anaïs and Hugo. In theory, an eating scene is straightforward in that most of the action is relatively static: all the actors are seated in one position and it will be the camera's problem to move around and get everyone *in*. The usual problems are incurred with actors moving in one direction, the camera in a counter-movement, but weather, planes, traffic or whatever are not an issue in this controlled set-up. Plus, the mood of this scene is celebratory and *bon vivant*. In theory!

While getting our makeup done and costumes donned, we hear that the Art Department has been fired and it's PANIC STATIONS. Something to do with not painting the wretched wall the colour requested by the director. The dining room has been hastily repainted the right dark shade of blue but now the props boys' noses are out of joint because Rose has enlisted a Parisian friend to help find appropriate period pieces for the set. At which point Phil has to wade in with, 'Look, guys, I would much rather concentrate on directing and shooting this film but the set isn't right yet and we gotta get it right. So please just bear with us, whatever it takes. OK?'

Vague sulky mutterings ensue and the new *objets* are duly placed about the room. There is further delay while an assortment of blue bottles is brought in by the trayload and positioned in lines around the shelves and sideboard. It now resembles Dr Frankenstein's laboratory. Phil returns just as the last one is being placed and says: 'Fuck the historical accuracy, we cannot have all these blue bottles in here.' Some survive.

Now we have to get some garrulousness going among a bunch of actors who are playing best friends but who have barely met one another.

In this tense atmosphere, it takes concentration to try to jolly things along. One actor is having a very wobbly time of it and keeps forgetting his lines. The OUTTAKE bloopers or fluffs that find their way into *It'll Be Alright on the Night* come, like most comedy, from some human being in an acute state of distress. On every take, the more he tries the more he cocks it up. *Every* actor has experienced this horror and we sympathetically avert our eyes as the poor man's brains scramble and start frying. What renders the whole débâcle truly farcical is the added requirement that a perfectly risen soufflé be placed before him in each take. Now the Props Department is being tested for its culinary finesse and speed, and they are making soufflés in the adjacent kitchen as fast as they can. Getting the soufflés to coincide with the actor getting his lines all out in order and the dog not to start barking at the wrong moment has taken on the dimension of a Monty Python marathon, without the laughs. Assistants are running around like headless hens refilling the wine glasses after every duff take to keep the continuity accurate.

After about an hour, and a runway of collapsed soufflés forming a holding pattern in the corner, all sense has escaped the proceedings. When the actor finally manages to blurt his way through to the end of his speech the very foundations of the house are shaken by a low-flying plane. At which point the soufflé supply, film stock and everyone's tolerance have been exhausted.

There is a tea-break and the actor is now blaming everything around for what has gone wrong. *Concentration* and its power to blot out *every distraction* is an invaluable discipline and also a money saver. Every minute wasted costs big bucks. No one wants to fall behind the shooting schedule, especially not on Day Two.

During the relight, when camera and lamps are moved to the opposite side of the room to catch the reactions of the other actors to the soufflé speech, Fred unexpectedly opens up about his history.

'Yeah, I done a whole lotta stuff – lumberjackin', tomato picker, bouncer for a bordello, you name it . . .' All this history *perfect* for playing Henry Miller, and as far removed from my background as could be.

'Some guy turns up outside my house in Venice Beach one night, smacked outta his head and hollerin' and threatenin'. I considered waiting till he came through the door so I could legally blow his brains out. But after some consideration I decided to just get out there and kick-box him in the balls instead. Which I did— Where's Swaziland exactly?'

6th September

Uma Thurman begins shooting. Her *entrada* happens at night: she appears out of the mist and enters the Nin household for her first dinner with Anaïs, Henry and Hugo. The rehearsal for camera and crew happens in the early evening and Uma is wearing leggings and a shapeless oversized sweater, hair in a bundle and not a scrap of makeup. She walks back and forth so that the crew can work out how much camera track to lay and where the smoke machine should be set up. Uma, like a sleepwalker, is surrounded by the carpenters who are busily hammering and fitting wedges of wood beneath the track while someone checks it all with a spirit level. Lamps are trolleyed in and finally the camera is heaved on to the tracks by three 'heavies'. Philippe Rousselot, the cinematographer, is sharp-featured, with piercing eyes and pointy nose; there is something distinctly feral about him. He moves among his camera team pointing out what he wants and fixing and arranging lamps with incredible speed, creating with apparent ease a quality of diffused, romantic light that beguiles your eye. He has worked with this team before, and together they co-ordinate like a mechanical toy.

Later, once the shot is set up, Uma emerges again from her caravan as though she had just bust out of her chrysalis, such is the transformation. At something around six foot tall in heels, hair coiled and waved close to her head, vamp makeup with blood-red lips, and body poured into a sheath of black satin, she is nothing short of a Venus Coca-Cola bottle! The dress features spider straps and it's impossible not to cliché forth that she has wordlessly webbed us all in her spell. Such is the potent effect of her silent entrance, that you can hear the collective *jaw-drop* of the cast and crew – fifty of them!

Normally *everyone* is clock-watching by the end of the shooting day. Tonight I understand for the first time what *to be electrified* means. And by the expression on the faces all around the current has formed a complete circuit. Curiously, now that Uma is all done she is treated completely differently. Her beauty and its effect translates into a flurry of activity all around her as though everyone has to be careful not to knock into, bump or break her. The combination of genetic engineering and makeup and wardrobing pronounces out ward perfection, which probably has nothing to do with how she *really* feels. Her hand is shaking as she gropes for a cigarette.

'You look like a million bucks, Uma.'

'Your accent is sounding good, Rich.'

Fair trade!

Watching her enter from the dark and slinking towards the lit house is as potent a delight as my first ever sighting of Monroe side-stepping the steam in *Some Like It Hot*. No one is immune to her charisma and we quite happily watch take after take as they co-ordinate the moving camera accompanying her first entry. There is general disbelief that she is only nineteen. So apparently self-possessed. So much the personification of Hollywood Glamour with an MGM G. Like Dietrich and Garbo rolled into one. And, lest I thought I was throwing myself overboard, I looked round to see what effect she had wrought upon Phil and Rose. They have mega-volt smiles on their faces.

During our first meeting scene indoors, we raise again the Titanic topic of NUDITY and who is going to do what. I have signed a contract for the full frontals should this be required, hoping like hell that my fear-filled gonads will be spared. Uma says she will NOT be baring her breasts. This is out of the director's earshot, and I am wondering if he knows about this as the script clearly requires major dollops of flesh. Maria is fully aware of what is expected and seems totally unfazed. Fred has the hooded eye of grin-and-bare-it. Kevin declares boldly that he can hardly wait to get his kit off! So a full house of every variation.

Uma outlines her abhorrence of all things Hollywood and, at the ripe age of late teendom, says she is committed to making quality pictures, 'which really means Europe'. She exudes all the certainty and forthright clarity of the future that I remember having then, everything simply black or white, life an eternal stretch ahead with yourself at the centre pointed towards fame and fortune. And, for the first time, I am all too potently aware of time passing and that, within a decade, real doubt will come to roost and will be irremovable. I cannot help wondering what will happen to her, and her burgeoning film career, especially as she is now involved with a married man, who has a child. Although she is fiercely independent and grown-up, she is so young.

7th September

Not called the next day. Chronic flu has gripped my lungs overnight, it's pouring and Paris is all moody and misty grey. Peter Kaufman calls around midday to say that everyone is thrilled with the rushes from yesterday, which cheers things up somewhat. Having a day off should be a bonus, yet the reason for being here is to film and doing that is so all-embracing and involving that, come the day you don't work, there is this terrible void. Feel as if I have *never* worked and this grates the nerve ends.

Haul myself out of the nest and meet Spacey for a viewing of *Batman* in Les Halles. He is on a rant because he didn't get any close-ups during his scene and has been in heated consultation with his agent and manager. The irony is that he is playing a man who is ferociously frustrated with his artistic lot in life, in Miller's shadow, and I, like the all-patient and calmly listening Hugo, do the diplomatic soft-shoe shuffle. This is in complete reversal of our roles a couple of weeks back, when he was all *bon vivant* and cock-a-hoop, while I was stewing around in a dose of the doubts.

'When it comes down to it, let's face it, this is just another gig like any other and it's the same old fucking routine and bullshit there always is.' Kevin is *not* going to stop here, and carries on all the way to *Batman*. On the way back his rage is mercifully waylaid by *Batman*'s shortcomings, which he delineates with the precision of a neuro-critic, and which diverts me from my chestful of mucus and makes me laugh. Which spurs him on to even greater heights. I recognize this syndrome all too acutely and wonder whether having a brontosaurus-sized moan is common to every human or whether it is a particular speciality of actors. Whichever, it's a relief to be merely a spectator at this entertaining outpouring of bile rather than its purveyor.

8th September
Friday is a good one, the chief pleasure being the ease with which Maria and I work together. She makes everything fuss-free and is open to any suggestion, has a great sense of humour and has effortlessly inspired total devotion from the entire crew. Huge owl-like eyes, and endless patience and delight in playing this role. 'I get to fuck everyone in this picture' – more giggles.

My frustration derives from the impotence of the character I am playing. Hugo is so 'back-footed' and it's a challenge to suppress the impetus to 'drive' the scenes along. Passivity is *not* one of my attributes. Phil assures me this is A Good Thing. Oh, yeah?

9th September
Go to see *My Left Foot* and am floored by the performance. Daniel Day-Lewis is incredibly moving and quite brilliant. I blub all the way through from the moment the little boy writes a word on the floor with a piece of chalk stuck between his toes. Feel completely inspired, and swop eulogies with the Kaufmans, who had worked with him on *Unbearable Lightness of Being*.

12th September
Forest outside Paris. It's a smoky autumn day but still swanny-warm. Hear a load of swoon and gush from Rose and Phil about how marvellous the rushes are. And it's all woodland, dappled light, and Impressionist visuals and the four central characters riding bicycles and much Bonjour and bonhomie.

The camera is being set up on a platform on the back of a truck, which means some delay between the rehearsal and shooting. I peek in to see Uma, where she is in the middle of hitching on a headscarf, and plonk myself down.

'How's yer love life, kiddo?' blurts out.

'Just dandy, Daddy-oh,' she retorts.

I confess I know who it is and she says she thought so, but wasn't sure whether to ask and there is just relief that it is out there. Uma is keen to discover how I heard and intrigued when I tell that it was from someone in a restaurant who doesn't know either of them.

Fact and fiction collide like tram-lines; Uma's role in *Dangerous Liaisons* was originally played in the theatre by Lesley Manville, Gary Oldman's now estranged wife. Playing the cuckolded party in this picture, and revisiting my own childhood, inevitably stacks my sympathy on the side of the Betrayed Party. Trying to objectify or to accept that it takes two to tango requires a couple of deep breaths. And/or psychiatry. Lest you think I am now going to Couch Down for a heavy Oprah Winfrey 'Poor Me!' Special, *relaaaaaax*. It's just that in 'dealing' with this professional situation I have become all too aware of how much personal baggage I am carrying. I know Gary-and-Leslee and must now segue to Gary-and-Uma. And all I can think about is the little boy who is the same age as my daughter. Caught.

What has this to do with me, sprouting forth like Ye Olde fuckin' Curiosity Shoppe, you may ask. What it is to do with is how to conduct my merrye-self *without* being a TWO-FACE now that I am working with Uma. She unravels the story of their courtship and I am schizoided by her joy and passion in contrast to the pain and sadness that must be suffered by Leslee. The instinct squirrels around inside wishing it could *make good* somehow. But the rational *knows* that what is BROKE is not MENDABLE. These thoughts and feelings slosh around like so many milkshakes as we talk.

The whole plot of *Henry and June* revolves around the nature of fidelity and Hugo pays the price for his monogamy by being marginalized. He is the silent fourth, upstaged by the torrid trio. Knowingly cuckolded *yet* unable to stop loving his wife. This is a slow cruelty that weakens the spirit, though in Hugo's case didn't affect his longevity! Yet again I reflect that this character is frustrating and perhaps explains the sense of impotence that seeps into real life. Just as Hugo was *of* his world yet not *in it*, I participate in this film like a bystander, for all the real *meat* of the scenes and story happens between the trio of Anaïs, Henry and June. And while I understood this role at the outset, the *short-change* aspect of it I did not anticipate. But no stories or films are made about happily married couples who celebrate a century together, for without *conflict* there is no *drama*.

A journalist wants to include my face in an article featuring up-and-coming Brits for *Time* magazine. A group of us satellite *comers* revolving around the solar cover story of Mr Branagh's *Henry V*.

The Dwarf calls to say: 'You have an offer to play an evil cunt opposite Christopher Lambert in something set in 2092.'

2nd October

We have three night-shoots scheduled. For this, read late-afternoon arrival and get to bed after dawn. The scenes are a re-creation of the legendary arts carnival held in the streets of Paris by students and Bohemians in the twenties and early thirties. From the photographic evidence it looked like a fantastic excuse to get stark bollock naked, paint yourself blue and gold, get drunk and fuck as many people as you liked, all in the spirit of ancient bacchanalia. Only, with the departure of Alec Baldwin and the delaying effect of recasting and re-scheduling, what was to have been filmed in the swelter of August in the holiday-emptied streets, with government-permit permission, is now a NIGHTMARE. It's October. It's freezing. And there are big problems resecuring and cordoning off streets with Official Permission.

However, a street is located and the poor residents clearly have *no idea* what this all-night shooting is going to entail. You can see this from the smiling interest they are showing in the preparatory proceedings. Especially as the three hundred and fifty extras, mainly students, are divesting themselves of their clothes and being painted with blue and gold body paint. In the early evening of Day One Instamatics flash intermittently from apartments. The poor fuckers don't know that by four a.m. on the third night of their disrupted sleep they will undoubtedly be *throwing* those little cameras at us and *yelling* '*Merde*' and 'ALLEZ 'OME!'

Wine is provided in large quantities, as much to get everyone into the spirit of midsummer madness as to combat the freeze that is about to assault the collective unguarded and exposed gonads. The Wardrobe Department has aluminium blankets at the ready for between-take times as there is not enough indoor shelter to cope with the vast numbers. People queue up to be painted and powdered by the fraught, overworked Makeup Department, who have had to requisition distant relatives and anyone who can wield a sponge to get everyone painted up in time. As these are not hardened extras, prepared to put up with any amount of discomfort, the crew is being very jolly and whooping it up to convince everyone that this is GONNA BE FUN.

It is during this Bacchanalian hysteria that Hugo, disguised in blue paint and wearing a mask, follows his estranged wife and practically rapes her in a vain attempt to get her back from Henry Miller. The wardrobe mistress has taken pity upon my scarecrow physique and has given me a minute penis-pouch with a string up the bum like a go-go dancer. My flesh is pale blue *before* the makeup and is goose-bumping all over.

For the first time, Phil is visibly and audibly *freaked*. Massive crowd to co-ordinate, cajole and try to control and he is stalking around with a clutch of story-board drawings of what the action should be and how many shots and set-ups are required. Within a short space of time, *everyone* is arseholed, and rudimentary loin-cover has now been forsaken for full frontal assault and dangle. Swinging genitalia and mammaries painted blue and gold exert a hypnotic fascination for the first three hours after which curiosity palls – UNTIL a faction of revellers engages in drunken coitals. We are now having a good chortle at an extra leaning against a wall and inspecting his blue erection with all the wide-eyed wonderment of a lunar scientist. The crew are duffel-coated and, for once, the smoke coming from their mouths isn't Gauloise but *arctic* breath. Between takes, the wardrobe assistants rush forth with aluminium sheets and there follows a strange crackling sound like giant sweet-wrappers uncrinkling in a small cinema as each extra is *foiled*. Gold heads and blue feet either end of the silver. A Cecil B. de Mille crowd from the Video Age.

Megaphones are employed along with the usual walkie-talkies to *try* to control things and co-ordinate the camera-on-crane movements. Panic pervades and someone yells for more crowd, at which a phalanx of Blues and Golds are divested of their crisp-foil cover and shoved nearer the camera to simulate continued Bacchanalia. I am surprised that frostbite has not taken a grip, such is the ferocity of the gale coming off the Seine nearby. Just before dawn 'WRAP' is announced, concluding with the bizarre sight of hundreds of blue bottoms running away in every direction. Like troops of baboons.

After two more nights of this, I almost believe that the Blue Carnival will comprise at least *half* of the final film, yet no doubt watching it in its edited state a year from now, it'll pass by as just another short sequence – the Pavlovian penile frosties a mere twitch of memory.

10th October

With a few days free from shooting *State of Grace* in New York, Gary Oldman Concordes into town to see Uma.

'Hello, my darlin'' – as insouciant and charming as ever.

'State of Dis-grace, if you ask me!' is what jumps out of my mouth, and the expected thin ice of unease is broken by unexpected laughter. Relief of sorts. But guilt-edged.

'What d'you think of Uma, then?'

He is full of falling in love, fired with his new life in America, and is soon off and running through uncanny impersonations of Penn, De Niro, Brando and Ian McKellen, from which he seamlessly transfers into a lisping, campy 'South Lundun' monologue about why he 'just 'ad to give up livin' in Lundun 'cos it'd jus' got sooooooooo fuckin' booooooorin', d'you know what I mean, luv?' sashaying off down the corridor in caricature before turning round and giggling back as Gary. There is no doubting that he is an *acting magician*. And I am charmed from any vestige of *j'accuse*.

It's only when he has calmed down, fifteen stories later, that he quietly asks about my daughter and then is raw at what has happened to himself. And to his son. And to his wife. And then shakes his head and says, 'Just happened,' looking unflinchingly eye to eye. Finishes off with a silent, mimed pistol shot and whispers, 'Pop.' He gazes into space. Then, 'When are we gonna work together? Stoppard is gonna do a movie of his *Rosencrantz and Guildenstern* play. Be perfect. Goes in January. I'm gonna suggest you. Was set to go last year with Sean Connery, Sting and Roger Rees, but all collapsed when Connery had to have throat polyps removed. Now it's going with myself and Richard Dreyfuss and he hasn't got a Guildenstern yet. Be bloody great.'

This comes at me from left-of-field – and how quickly that carrot-call of work diverts my thoughts from his family dissolution. Maybe it's just a trick. The *maybe* brain scramble and scent of a movie, once initiated, is like a marble in a black drum: rolling and rattling and taunting and teasing every ambitious corpuscle in yer solars.

11th October

The Dwarf calls from a mobile phone on his way into London. 'Gary has suggested you to Tom Stoppard and I think you would be great together. They've got Dreyfuss. Shoots for eight weeks in Zagreb and would fit in perfectly after you finish up in Paris. I'll send you the script and set up a meeting with Stoppard.'

Another drama unfolds alongside the filmed one. Revved up am I about this damn thing. Too revved. Too 'wanting'. Would all work out just *too* perfectly. And how keen is Mr Stoppard? Can I stop fulminating about all this? Can I buggery.

The script arrives and my gut is now lurching about with each page turned. I WANT THIS LITTLE FUCKER! This is NOT the usual dross that passes for an excuse of a script where you read the first ten pages and *know* that a month in Belgium would seem an attractive alternative. Instead it's RED ALERT. Ambition going off like a SIREN.

And a warning: *Don't want it too much, boy. Step by step.* The problem, though, is that I have already packed and prepared for the eight weeks in old Zagreb, convinced that, of course, my meeting with Mr Stoppard will be a mere formality after which the contract will be whipped out and my pen *poised* for the *seal.*

15th October

Fly home for the weekend and have a date to meet Mr Stoppard late Sunday afternoon at his house. Sunday morning call and it's: 'Hello, this is Tom. Could we turn things around and I come to your place for a chat?'

Meeting on home turf is slightly wobble-inducing as the territory is no longer neutral, but I tell myself that the request is a good sign. Having been brought up without any religious infiltration or superstition, I am suddenly ready to read teacups, cloud formations and movements of local black cats and ladders.

The day passes with little more than a low flutter in the stomach. By five thirty I am beginning to feel like squelchy oysters and he is at the door and into the living room. He is smiley in jeans and tweed jacket, unshaven and undergrad-ish, unable to settle down, pacing about and speaking in his distinctive transplanted English. 'Tell me about *Killing Dad.*'

I am *very* glad to be in a seated position when this little bomb detonates. 'Why?'

'Well,' says Tom, 'it is my benchmark for all that can go wrong for a first-time director.'

As I played one of the lead roles, this does not bode at all well.

'I have to tell you I had never heard of you before, but I haven't heard of anyone under the age of forty.' Curiously this does not come as any consolation. Offer him a brief résumé of my previous efforts and am now ready to depress that ejector-seat button in James Bond's Aston Martin.

'How do you see this character?'

This question from the WRITER of an acknowledged theatrical landmark, in *these* circumstances, befuddles all thought. What comes out of my chops is a sort of 'dribble' about *George Sanders* and *Keith Richards* in a Moulinex. In answer to this offering, he suggests opening things up into a family occasion. Joan is upstairs bathing Olivia, whom he requests to meet. 'Great house you have here,' as we bound upstairs and into the bathroom, where Joan is nonplussed to have an uninvited audience. If this move has eased Tom in, it has now completely thrown me. Faff and fartle talk and he says he has yet to meet Tim Roth and Iain Glen and—

31st October
Back in Paris, all four of us shoot an interior-car scene. Uma is voicing her reservations about the sex scenes. 'Since I fell in love, I'm finding this stuff really hard to do.' Silence from us three, 'cos there ain't too much sway here to swing with. Fred ambles in with diplomatic words about accepting the script, which clearly states that there will be nudity and intercourse. Uma is undeterred and aggressively adopts another tack, talking about her newfound, but undisclosed 'love' as being an actor ... in fact a great actor, maybe the greatest actor of his generation. She seems poised to blurt out his name. And clearly wants to play opposite *him* rather than someone old enough to be her father. Fred handles all this air-twanging calmly, and resolutely refuses to be drawn into asking *anything*. Which frustrates her even more ... and I am now wondering how the hell they are going to transmit desire for one another in the scenes to come. Seems to me that Uma can hardly bear to contain this secret of hers. But I wonder how much of a secret it is when a lady reporter from the *San Francisco Chronicle* opens up our interview over lunch with, 'So has Gary Oldman been to visit Uma on the set a lot?'

'Well, babe, I may look like the *National Enquirer*, but I suggest you ask Uma,' I retort, but I am now wondering *why* they are being so circumspect, if a journalist from a 'respectable' paper is asking as though their relationship is common knowledge. Enough, already!

This morning I get a call from the Dwarf, a ghastly alarum that goes off before my actual wake-up call, with the dread-filled words, 'I don't think it's gonna work out. With Tom.'

'I know,' breaks out of my mouth, as though I might somehow salvage myself from the disappointment by saying this first. As if I'd already accepted this in advance of the call. Which I suppose I had despite the grain of hope that dwells eternal in the Optimism Department of the thespian cranium.

How awful to be an agent and to have to utter this dis-missive more regularly than the delirium of, 'Dahling! It's you they want! You've got the job!' Then again, they probably have to say it as often as undertakers offering their professional condolences. Your *shared* misery, the length of a phone call. My guts are plummeting. But hang on a mo'. The Dwarf is barrelling along with further news that Mr Stoppard would like me to come in for a reading next week, after he has had a go with Messrs Roth and Co. 'But you said you didn't think it was gonna work a minute ago.' 'I know. But looking at this note here, it says he wants to read Roth and Gary together – hold on, Iain Glen too, as well as you. So are you prepared to read some of the script for him?'

'Are you mentally retarded? Of course you bloody know I will!'

Most acting jobs are a to-do-or-not-to-do conundrum but this little fucker is a WANNA-DO-IN-A-BIG-WAY one. And not something likely to go to an American actor.

Meantime I have an answerphone message from Christopher Lambert to call about his futurist film. And why, I ask myself, while in the midst of *Henry and June* am I getting all cat-gutted over *any of this*?

Because ... BECAUSE that lurking goblin that forever asks, 'So what're you doing next?' has taken up residence once more. Just exactly when I should be enjoying what I am presently involved in, rather than wish-thinking away into the future.

CUT TO THE CHASE, KID! Tim Roth is cast in the Stoppard and I and the other contenders thrown upon the scrap-heap of RECALL.

And I am now feeling *very* sympathetic towards Roger Rees, Robert Lindsay, Sting, Iain Glen and whoever else *might* have had a twinge about this little episode.

6th November

A message to call Robert Altman.

'I'm editing *Vincent and Theo* downtown. Come by and have lunch. There's a project I think you might be interested in doing.'

I know this must strike as nauseating but the ego shift into EU-FUCKING-PHORIA cannot be too highly exaggerated. A drummer from a famous band I have never heard of is sent round to give me some bongo and tomtom instruction for a nightclub scene, and the pounding of these 'pods' is a small catharsis.

ALTMAN ALTMAN ALTMAN!

Saw *Nashville* twenty-seven times when I was a student and to be summoned by the man himself has transformed this fine and gorgeous, positive and hope-filled fabulously Parisianly Paris of days. Leg it down some boulevard, eat like a Dobermann, and generally feel as upright and sassy as King Kong's erection.

I had met Robert Altman the year before in London when he was casting his Van Gogh biog, at which time he had pronounced that we would be working together 'sometime', not this time but SOMEtime. It was just a matter *of* time.

When I arrive at his offices he is avuncular, charming and casual as though we had known each other for ever. No la-di-doody formalities or usual status-pull. He says, 'You wanna see some of the film?' I do, and we are in the edit room and he is at the Steenbeck and rewinding and explaining along as he goes.

One of his fleet of staff, all of whom seem to be women, comes in to ask if there is anything I don't eat and that lunch would be 'ready in about five'. No door is shut here. Nobody stands on any kind of ceremony. Everybody ranges in age from twenty to mid-sixties, with Bob, like Colonel Sanders (on account of the lookalike goatee), offerin' ya some Southern fried hospitality only he comes from Kansas. Like the Wizard of Oz himself. 'My wife Katherine is the reason you're here. She got me to see *Withnail and I* and thinks you're OK.' His eyes do not flicker from mine as he tests my sense of humour, irony, self-absorption – WHATEVER.

'Why, thank you, Katherine. She is clearly a woman of infinite variety and taste.'

'I'll tell her that. D'you wanna have dinner one night?'

'Let's see whether I make it through lunch.'

'What d'you know about Rossini?'

'Overtures.'

'Me too. Well, I got a script by this English writer, Julian Mitchell.'

'*Another Country*?'

'Right, and we've been working on this thing and it seems like it's gonna go in Rome as we got finance from the Italians and I'm wondering what you would be like as Rossini and if you'd be interested.'

Lunch never tasted so good. People come and go and I am completely seduced by the incredibly casual communal atmosphere he creates around him. His producer, and longtime associate, is a woman called Scottie Bushnell, chain-smoking in cowboy boots, with a voice like a smoked haddock and an immediacy that makes you feel you have known her all your life. I think her accent is Chicago – anyway her speech sounds like chewing gum and seems to have no commas or full stops: 'So-whaddya-think-of-the-idea-you-were-just-fabulous-in-the-*Withnail*-pikcha-you-Brits!'

AAAAAH! The merest snifter of a film in this team's company has me Tin-Manning and trotting like Toto up the yellow-bricked boulevards of Paris. Being in Altmanland was something I had read about in film magazines. And here I *am*, ready to scrawl some graffiti: SWAZI BOY WAS HERE.

All sense of impotence and isolation, playing the patsy Hugo role, is dissipated by this meeting and I feel poised to give this good news to Kevin, knowing that he will dispatch himself like an Exocet missile in Mr Altman's direction within a sec.

9th November

Bruce and Sophie Robinson are over to stay for a long weekend, and we proceed to ponce around Paris and be entertained by Bruce. For he is never anything short of a flagon of bilious humour. He speaks fluent *Français* on account of his having worked here on *Story of Adèle H* with Truffaut and subsequently setting up home with its star, Isabelle Adjani. As he is particularly virulent (especially after dinner) about nosing out any fascist tendencies, and is tonight *ranting* about one of his favourites, THE MARGARET (Prime Minister rather than Royal), he has decided to enlist the support of the French taxi driver, assuming the old prole to be Socialist *simpatico*. It transpires that the bruiser HATES Mitterrand, les Socialistes and les Communistes! Bruce opts for an immediate 'U'-turn into silence and wide-eyeballs Sophie and me as our charioteer gets *really* whipped up. Within nano-secs we're hearing our Maggie being hailed as LA REINE DE LA JONGLE!

This would normally have had Robinson reaching for his firearm, but the practical necessity of getting home unharmed at this late hour takes precedence. However, this stranger up-front is now gesticulating, or to be more precise is RAISING HIS ARMS to illustrate a point, thus allowing his armpits to let loose their nostril-paralysing TERRORS: an Old-Garlic-and-Unwashed-Nylon combination of secretions that about matches his verbal eulogy to the Maggie. We are now crippled with suppressed hysterics on the back seat and the imminent threat of a vomiting. All of which rids me of my resentment about the non-Stoppard.

Robinson is a Dickens fanatic but I have yet to hear him praise any *living* playwright or screenwriter other than his own BRILLIANT self! He is equally scathing about my current filmic endeavours. 'Impossible to portray a writer on screen. Especially someone as visceral as Miller. They'll never do it.' And he unleashes a rich diatribe of all the reasons why not, a lot of which I find myself in agreement with. Not since university have I met someone with whom I have so BONDED (to quote our American allies) and felt so Finitely that we will be Friends for Life.

I'm sad to see them go.

13th November

Paris by Night, Brassaï's photographs of the Parisian demi-monde, which are displayed in every poster and postcard store, are the inspiration for the brothel and dance-hall scenes. The casting director has chosen lookalikes and it is a bizarre *déjà vu* to find these black-and-white images, given flesh and blood reality in *colour*.

My discomfort comes from being fully decked out in black tie, standing among these extras playing ladies of the night, all of whom are starkers, middle-aged and tending towards the obese. Rubenesque, if you're kind. Although I am assured these people have come of their own volition and are getting paid, I feel ashamed. Which is *precisely* what Hugo is experiencing, having brought Anaïs here to try to break the Miller stranglehold on their marriage. While waiting for the camera set-up, I find it difficult to open up conversation about what's on in Paris with extras exposed in all these goose-bumplies. I suppose it's a question of Dignity and more *my* problem than anyone else's, borne out by the indifference expressed by a crew member who dismisses my discomfort with 'Zey are h'extras and very h'ugly'! Chortle, chortle.

The scene involves Anaïs requesting a SEXUAL EXHIBITION from the madame. She is offered a choice of the prostitutes and opts for a June and Anaïs pair of clones. Philippe Rousselot ceaselessly devises the most fluent camera movements around the action to such an extent that its mechanical presence has a sinuous life of its own. Period music is piped in and the set pumped with artificial smoke, all of which helps to dispel the abrupt nakedness of the whole.

After half a day I do manage some chat, although strong eye-contact is maintained throughout, lest mine absent-mindedly stray and end up staring at someone's minge . . .

And queasiness on my part vanishes with the arrival of Brigitte Laher, which sends a frisson round the crew as she is a famous ex-porn star and is playing the part of Uma's lookalike. Her face is a disconcerting mixture of Uma and Glenda Jackson. Hugo and Anaïs 'watch' the two women simulate sex, re-enacting Anaïs and June's liaison, with Hugo oblivious to this bi-way from the hi-way affair she is having with Henry.

The actress playing Maria's lookalike has never done anything like this before and is vociferous in expressing her discomfort, complaining about how long the lighting takes and how cold it is and how sore it is on her elbows, etc. etc. Ms Laher, though, is the epitome of the professional. And we are all under the Equity employment banner of Performer. I daren't imagine what it would do to my old psyche if I had to get my 'kaks off' and 'get it up' for 'ACTION'!

14th November

Ralph Brown, the actor who played the epochal drug dealer in *Withnail*, calls to make dinner plans. He is in Paris for the filming of *Impromptu*, a bio-pic about the life of Chopin, starring Hugh Grant as the famous piano-thumping cougher opposite Judy Davis as George Sand. We meet up in some seafood brasserie and I discover that Hugh's girlfriend is Elizabeth Hurley, with whom I had done a Schweppes advert a couple of years back. She was a Monroe-blonde back then and has transformed into a brunette siren wearing a micro-mini skirt, which she deliriously disports before the goggle-eyed punters every time she cruises off to the ladies'. She and Hugh are like gorgeous siblings, both speaking in accents that sound like old BBC recordings from the fifties, tossing their voluminous manes of hair about and being as funny and provocative about everything as they dare. Hugh orders a vast platter of oysters, which provides the cue for talk about aphrodisiacs. It is impossible to take *anything* he says seriously as *everything* is 'ironized'. 'Do you like anal sex? I bet you do. You have that "look" about you!'

'You *must* be telepathic,' I reply, trying not to choke on the poised oyster, which elicits great guffawings from both of them.

'I can spot an ex-public schoolboy from a mile off. Bum bum and buggery. You must be ever so rich?'

'Rolling, Hugh. Rolling.'

'Little bastard! Must be ma'v'lous to be as rich and famous as you are.'

'I wish.'

'Don't pretend to be modest with me. You are rich, aren't you? Out with it!'

'Loaded.'

'Bastard!'

'Hugh, do you *ever* talk and say what you mean at the same time?' enquires Ralph.

'Of course not, you stupid ignorant working-class person!'

Hugh manages the precarious feat of insulting you up, down and sideways, without your wanting to lay his dentals on a platter. Too busy laughing. Too busy wondering if he means anything he utters.

'I hate you! Always getting these jammy jobs. Getting even more famous and with the same surname. I've got better hair, though. Did you want to sleep with Elizabeth when you did that appalling advert together? I should jolly well hope so.'

'How can you even ask? Of course yes!'

'Well, I'm sure she wouldn't mind.'

Things are sounding increasingly like a skewed version of the Famous Five round here. When I ask about *Impromptu*, his reply is exclamatory: 'Euro-pud!!'

'Excuse me?'

'Euro-pud – the hurling together of a bunch of nationalities all trying to speak English and acting in totally different styles. Made for fuck-all money and destined straight for video. I met Elizabeth while making one of these puds in Spain. I was doing Byron and she was slaughtering Mary Shelley. Terrible stuff. But great fun. My career is a joke!'

'But you're playing the lead – Chopin!'

'Don't be daft. Euro-pud.'

Once we were back on track and talking about SHAGGING, Ralph suggested we look into a sex shop, which we did, followed by Hugh and Elizabeth offering a running commentary on the merits and demerits of the merchandise. I have never worked *anywhere* where the topic has so relentlessly revolved around the reproductive act and wonder if it's Paris that elicits this response or whether the subconscious is at fever pitch with the goings-on in *Henry and June*.

POSTSCRIPT

Uma succeeded in keeping her top on, and subsequently married Gary.

ROSSINI ROSSINI was shelved five weeks before filming was scheduled to begin.

And a note from Tom Stoppard:

> Dear Richard
>
> It was difficult! Thank you for bearing with me – I'm so sorry to have disappointed you and I hope something comes up which makes you [SOMETHING SOMETHING SOMETHING (indecipherable)] about this ill wind.
>
> Best wishes,
> Tom

AND AU REVOIR TO THE 1980S.

LA Stories

Lumière Cinema in St Martin's Lane. Sunday morning. Cast and crew screening of *How To Get Ahead In Advertising*. Imminent bowel collapse anticipated. Olivia is asleep in my arms. The movie rolls forth inexorably while my nerves quietly shred themselves in the back row. On the way out it's a TV-less version of *This Was Your Life* – most of the people you meet at a cast/crew screening you haven't seen since the film wrapped a year ago.

And the embarrassment of trying to remember everyone's name – a congestion of Daves, Joes and Kens all scrambled together in the aftershock of seeing myself poncing about on screen, magnified fifty times. Something unnatural about seeing a film so early in the day, with everyone standing about afterwards like loose farts, as though they're waiting for something else to happen. But what does happen next is a sidewinder.

An American man with silver-grey hair, baseball cap and a strong handshake is saying, 'Hi, I'm Steve Martin, this is my wife, Victoria, and I just wanna tell you we thought you were g-a-rate!' Shiver me old timbers, but it's the wild and crazy guy HIMSELF. To say that I am flattered is slightly to understate it.

'How come you're here?' trills from my tonsils.

'We're friends of Bruce and Sophie Robinson and he invited us. We loved *Withnail*. If you're interested I've written a script called *LA Story* that has a part you might wanna do. If it happens. Probably a year from now. Depending. Not the lead role. Wrote that for myself.'

He's *doing* that ironic *dumb* act I know from his records and tapes. Voice and all.

Spend the rest of the day prancing about saying, 'Hi, I'm Steve Martin. Hi, I'm Steve Martin,' like I've installed an Eveready battery up my arse.

14th March 1990

Fast-forward a year and I get the Call from the Coast. *LA Story* has been greenlit and is a GO project. It's being produced at Carolco by Dan Melnick, who first employed me on *Mountains of the Moon* in 1988, and is to be directed by ex-BBC Brit Mick Jackson, whose name I know from *Chatahoochee.*

26th April

Flight to Los Angeles but uh-oh, the ticket reads GATWICK–DALLAS–LOS ANGELES. I now compute that a direct ten-hour flight from Heathrow has been converted into an eighteen-hour arse-paralyser. Upon arrival at LAX my legs grasp the true impact of JET-LAG, this flight having rendered my resources around Gravitation X. Even the eyeballs are weighed down. A medium-sized limo hauls my tired-olds to the Château Marmont Hotel on Sunset Boulevard and the driver takes this as his cue to give me a run-down of everyone who has died in the joint, from Belushi backwards.

27th April

Messenger bikes round a fat envelope full of dollar *per diem.* A very good reason to get out of bed and test the Californian climate and cuisine. The hotel is one of the few really old buildings here and recognizable from those black-and-white stills of Hollywood haunts of the thirties. It feels as if you might just pass Fred MacMurray and Barbara Stanwyck in the corridor. Instead, sunglassed rock'n'roll bandits and staff dressed in Hawaiian shirts smiling a 'Hi!' is what you get. It is two years since my first foray into Lalaland and I have forgotten how disarming it is to be in a hotel and hear, 'Hi, Mr Grant, enjoy your stay,' from total strangers. It's all *sooo* friendly! The phone-line, which is 'life' in LA, connects me to various people I encountered on *Warlock*, many of whom I discover are remarrying, relocating, rewhatevering or just not speaking to people who were their *best* friends before. 'THEY'RE HISTORY,' I hear, which strikes me as ironic in a town that prefers to have none.

28th April

I am woken by a call from Victoria Tennant. 'Welcome to LA! Steve and I were wondering if you had already made lunch plans? Come by around twelve thirty and bring swimming trunks. See you later.' No fumbling and fruitling around here. 'Swimming *trunks*' has a sort of Julie Andrews commanding tone to it – friendly but forthright.

It's only when I press the button in the convertible to get the sun-roof retracted and take a right on to Sunset Boulevard that my old ticker accelerates faster than my foot. Sun blazing down, music Kiss FMing, and the red car is nosing towards Beverly Hills and I'm a-thinking, Blow me down, gals. This is the Swaz off to meet the stars!

A bored Mexican sits smoking beside a blue clapboard stall, which proclaims 'MOVIE STAR MAPS'. Being a lifelong movie buff, I cannot convey just what a stomach growling *thrill* it is to have an address in hand of *one* of them! Steady-the-buffs-me-boy, you cannot go in there like some gibbering fanatical half-wit. A moment to check out my sunglassed reflection at the traffic lights. YES, it *is* you, tomb features! Enjoy this moment because, chances are, reality will nose-dive in soon enough. You might never work in this town again. Alternatively you will become so blasé that nothing will charge your little batteries quite like this ever again. As I leave West Hollywood and enter Beverly Hills, the roads widen. The palms look 'palmier', standing like sentries on either side of the very wide boulevards. The 'houses' are mansions and their architecture a complete fantasy. Manicured lawns, and driveways displaying mega-buck motors. Foliage and flora like a suburban Babylon. Front doors that are three storeys tall, and architectural motifs that range from Fake Château, Sunshine Tudor, Santa Fé Adobe, Cotswold Cobble to Hansel-and-Gretel Disney. Side by vast-lawn-in-between side. No sign of any people except the odd truck piled with garden refuse manned by a Mexican gardener.

Pass the Beverly Hills Hotel on the right, which looks exactly like it's supposed to look: all pink and palm-fringed and presumably still polo-lounged within. A few blocks further and hang a left. Switch off the radio and glide noiselessly down a slow, winding boulevard, blue sky and swishing palm trees above, audible heartbeat pounding below. Swing into a driveway and stop before a white oblong bungalow. I am about to meet Mr Martin who, I have been told, can be as inaccessible as the Arctic. Engine off and I inhale a couple of deep ones, fixing on an image of Denis Lawson beating imaginary drums in the air when the Yanks discover oil in the little fishing village in *Local Hero*.

A totally anonymous, handleless door is spied upon by a recessed camera from above and presumably opened by a code punched into the numbered panel. Opt for a buzzer and wait. Door swivels open on a huge hinge like a hospital ward door and it's Steve in casuals saying, 'Come on in. Do you want a glass of Aqua Libra?' Victoria is equally welcoming, dressed all in black with straight blonde hair chopped at the shoulders, no jewellery and a skim of makeup. 'Let me show you some *art*!' (Steve.) 'I collect!' The interior is all white and open-plan with a long corridor and adjoining rooms, skylit like a private gallery. Bach chamber music wherever you go, controlled from a central panel that regulates the light, air and sound. Smell of freshly baking bread coming from an individual bread-making machine. And walls of *serious* art. These are the Big Boys of American Abstract Expressionism and I am drop-jawed at seeing them in a private house rather than in a gallery or book. I did a history of art course at university, which helped in expressing my response beyond the usual 'my gosh' gush. Steve is passionate about his 'hobby' and happily tours me round the vast canvases. 'Do you like Bacon?' As it's near lunchtime I pause long enough for him to point out the Bacon he means, which stands framed above the mantelpiece. Other Brits are on display – Freud, Hodgkin and David Hockney.

Being in this house is like being *in* a Hockney – everything clear-lined and California-coloured. Like the paintings, whose images are so familiar, Steve's face is equally so. Yet here he is unscripted and live and it is taking some self-control *not* to tour his features like that inquisitive pop-eyed professor from *Tintin*.

'We are so thrilled you're able to do this movie.'

'Believe me, the thrill's all mine.'

'But seriously—' and he catches himself 'at it' and riffs off into his All-Purpose Showbiz Schlockmeister routine, trotting out all the insincere platitudes that pile up around Celebrity. At the end of this we-are-so-excited schtick, he completes the 'loop' by reiterating, 'But seriously! I *am* serious! We *are* thrilled!'

His gush at me 'short-circuits' my gush at him – how do you respond to a eulogy beyond a humbled bunch of thankyou, thankyou, thankyous – which means that we are able to begin a conversation that has been depth-charged free of all flattery.

Victoria has barbecued up lunch and we manage to yak away some hours without the dreaded iceberg *longueurs* I had been warned might occur. Before long we are exchanging nicknames: I am given the title of Relentless, with which you may well sympathize if you have managed to read this far! Steve chats away all the preconceptions I have been fed and I am quietly relieved not to have made a complete *goombah* of myself.

There is nothing blasé about this mega-wealth. Or ostentatious. Just an incredible hushed quiet and ease that seems a signature of the very well bank-balanced. All gleams and is spotlessly clean and organized; shelved walls crammed with art catalogues, books covering everything historical, philosophical, artistic and mathematical. At my request Steve gives me a guided tour round his study and reveals himself to be a 'gadget maniac' with state-of-the-art computers, sound systems, lasers and a television screen that is the size of a family hatchback. I make no pretence at being *au fait* with any of this technology, and he is as delighted to show me how it all functions as he might have been were we seven-year-olds inspecting his new train-set.

'Let's go down to Venice Beach.' And we do. FAST! Steve motors down the freeway like it's the Grand Prix. I am briefly marvelling at the long-forgotten sensation of doing something impulsively *without* an itinerary of diaper and 'tot travel' requirements. However, no sooner has this bachelor memory surfed in than it's beached by sudden homesickness and dribbly-eye at the distance that separates me right now from wife and child.

Park and stroll through the Saturday afternoon throng along the sea-front, which is every bit the FREAK SHOW it is purported to be. In the land of the wannabe, here is Vanity and how it's *gonna-be*! A cacophonous contrast to the sanctuary-like calm of Beverly Hills. Snake charmers, robotic dancers on skates, muscle-builders busting their oiled veins, live but stock-still shop mannequins, bag-ladies, folks from Omaha – they have their jaws permanently dropped at O – knife-throwers and glass-chompers, mimes and live Barbies, along-side the Tribe of the Obese. Steve wears a cap and sunglasses and, for the most part, manages to pass through, offering a card-with-an-autograph-and-quip when approached. 'This is where the hippies come to die,' the man ahead of me informs his wife. And *yes*, this sunset is Technicolored, and the throng is people-thick, the Pacific Ocean so vast that maybe this *is* the Twilight of the Age of Aquarius? We detour left and go to a restaurant owned by director Tony Bill and Dudley Moore. All concrete grey with free-standing panels of pebble-glass and waiters who wear discretion in lieu of any expression – the kind of place in which my father would never have quite known where to put himself.

Quaff down a couple of gallons of fresh watermelon juice. The menu is a triumph of invention that manages to offer *everything* cholesterol-free, dairy-free, preservative-free and sugar-free at a GREAT FEE. I am intrigued by chocolate cake that is both flour- and sugar-free.

'Let's get outta here and get dessert somewhere else.' There is no hanging about with Steve. Up and off PRONTO-PRESTO! Whip back into West Hollywood and nip into a yoghurt-and-icecream parlour and the poor bepimpled server has been struck dumb at spotting Steve. It's as if he's seen a ghost and is a sudden reminder of how bizarre this celebrity-stuff truly is. A seven-year-old blurts out, 'Hi, Steve,' assuming that he *knows* him, and carries on eating as though Steve is as familiar as any of his own family.

After some watermelon-juice-relief in their loo, I get back into my car and head off into what's left of the night, lunch having stretched into dinner into 'Come by tomorrow if you feel like it.' Back to the Château. Oh, so 'lagged. And a chapter of Arthur Miller's *Timebends* and the sage advice, Never to Think About Any One Thing For Too Long. I wish . . .

29th April

Continuing where we left off, Steve gives an impromptu cabaret, which is a Liquorice Allsorts of his philosophy ranging from self-deprecation ('I am a selfish, hedonistic man of medium talent') to wildly bombastic mockeries, interspersed with musical numbers. He is a brilliant banjo player and has three on standby beside the fireplace. It strikes me as the perfect instrument for him, as its playing style requires the restlessness that seems to course through his veins – Let'sgo/d'youwanna/Bye/Seeya. Finger strumming FAST! – In contrast to Victoria's aura of maintained *calm* and control. He tells me how working in the magic shop at Disneyland from the age of ten was his escape route from suburbia – 'YOURS?' he asks me. 'I had a marionette theatre in our garage. Do you want to have kids?' His 'No' is unequivocal. 'It wouldn't be fair. I'm too selfish and move around too much.'

Victoria cooks lunch with deceptive ease, disclaiming her obvious skills with a throwaway that 'people make such a fuss about what's essentially very simple'. We eat outside beside the narrow lap-pool, painted black to retain the heat. Overwhelming perfume from the massed jasmine creepers – delicious. 'Christie's is having an exhibition at the Beverly Hills Hotel today – wanna take a walk over and look?' A walk in Beverly Hills is an unusual prospect, the only non-motorized human sightings so far are restricted to Mexican gardeners and the odd lone jogger, usually betowelled, betogged and behead-phoned to within an inch of his/her life. As the three of us set out, a white minibus lurches into view and Steve ducks behind a palm tree. I stare at him, then stare at the bus whose occupants in turn stare at me accusingly: *Who are you? Are you famous, and if not why not?*, their cameras poised for that photo-opportunity, for these punters are all aboard the Tour of the Stars Homes' bus. Once the coast is clear Steve re-emerges and we look back to see the vehicle dawdling in front of his house, and people snapping the all-white oblong 'envelope' frontage.

'We gotta move. Did I tell you about the "painting drive-bys" we've had? Guy runs at the house and throws a bucket of paint at the walls and runs off again. Recorded on the closed-circuit TV, but difficult to do anything about. Once they know where you are the only alternative is to move.' I am tempted to joke that the blank-canvas exterior could be mistaken for an invitation by some Abstract Expressionist but don't. Cross Sunset Boulevard and it seems incredibly wide and dangerous compared to the air-conditioned calm of a convertible. Once inside the hotel you could be forgiven for mistaking the exhibition as a gathering of Friends of Nebuchadnezzar, such is the vintage of the patrons. The Ancients are more fascinating than the Art. The jewel-encrusted ladies are of indecipherable age, their flesh landscaped and buffed beneath rigorously bouffanted hair! B-I-G hair. SCARY hair. Hair like REINFORCED CONCRETE. These old Mummies shuffle about like so many Dorianna Grays, arm-in-arm with their husbands – who haven't been 'lifted' and are as bald as eggs or wrinkling beneath orange-dyed toupees. I resolve there and then never to succumb to the Brillo-pad Charlton Heston 'rug' when my follicles have all finally flown. In the midst of this I am introduced to Marcia Weissman, doyenne of art collectors, still recognizable from the vast portrait Hockney did of her in 1968 titled *American Collectors*, although she is not in the fluorescent pink kaftan that my memory expects her to be wearing twenty-two years later. Her brother is the founder of the Norton Simon Gallery in Pasadena, which houses most of the Impressionists outside Paris. The prices quoted for each painting are in mega-multiples of nought and for a couple of seconds I can feel my head *nodding* and *bobbing* as if I *might* just be considering the *possibility*. But I content myself instead with computing the combined ages of the assembled wart-hogs.

We finally escape to the terrace, and my tongue lashing its way round the wrinkled contents of the just-vacated Pharaoh's Tomb gets a laugh from my hosts, which dispels any vestige of formal awe I might have clung to over the past two days. They mutually conclude that I am missing that cranial 'organ' which censors 'thought' before it hurtles out of my mouth. No doubt confirming my RELENTLESS-ness. On a GOOD day, this comes out as comedy, but on others turns me into a fucking five-act TRAGEDY. Indeed *A Suitable Case for Treatment*! In this instance it induced instantaneous blush and button up. My only consolation is the sense that *being yourself* is somehow welcome in a city where bullshit has been elevated into an art form.

I ask Steve if we can go through his script together, to which he readily agrees, making alterations and adjustments then and there to some of my dialogue. 'It's up to you to make something of this part 'cos it doesn't exactly jump off the page *so you'll just have to act it*,' he booms, widening his eyes like he's in a silent movie. All this *bonding* will no doubt help when it comes to playing Roland, the WHELP, who is his real wife's reel-life husband in the film. Am I to be forever cast as the cuckold in American films? Roland could be seen as the comic flipside to Hugo in *Henry and June*. 'Be grateful for the job,' squawks up. 'What can you expect with your comedy face? It's better than sitting in an ivory tower stroking your deluded reputation.' This is getting to be like a severe dose of the old *Joan of Arc's*, hearing the VOICES ... And now that scene from Spielberg's *Sugarland Express*, one of my favourites in any movie, has spooled itself on to my scanner: William Atherton has conned a couple of old-age pensioners out of their clapped-out car in the middle of nowhere and then drives off down one of those *North By Northwest* kind of roads. The wife is trying to quell the endless moans issuing from her old man – the two of them stranded in the middle of nowhere, with nary a car in sight – until she finally says in an exasperated flat Southern accent, 'HUSH! WILL YOU JUST ... HUSH!!'

Costume-fittings, hair and makeup look-over. The clothes are *Brits abroad* – Ralph Lauren flannel pants and striped shirts, and the ubiquitous baggy khaki shorts, guaranteed to render most legs like a Spike Milligan cartoon. The makeup test is a dose of all-purpose American TV orange-tan slap and heavy pencil on the eyebrows. These Joan Crawfords are easily rubbed off later. The hair person pulls her hands through my wig, and declares, 'Let's just leave it as it is 'cos there's no way I could make it look any dumber, right? You are playing the GEEKY husband, right?' RIGHT! This character assessment is oddly reassuring in its uninvited abruptness – in *total* contrast to what an agent or director might have to say, feeling it incumbent upon themselves to shuffle around what the part ACTUALLY IS ... a GEEK! I like it! Start shooting in a couple of days' time. Accept dinner invitation with the Kopelsons, who produced the as-yet-unreleased *Warlock*.

Dinner at Spago's. This watering hole on a hillside above Sunset Boulevard overlooks the flat endless stretch of Los Angeles below, twinkling into the far distance like a scene from *E.T.* It is reputed to be an 'A' list eaterie, with 'A' list tables. Where you are seated is an indication of your current status in the social alphabet of the stars – although I imagine that on a celebrity-scarce night you could well find some tired old half-recognizable nag in a chair normally occupied by someone stellar. On second thought this does not really seem possible: better to stash the half-knowns and the once-knowns among the unknowns round the back and keep the front tables empty, thus riveting the atmosphere with the expectation of WHO ... MIGHT ... SHOW. Once valet-parked, you run the gauntlet of the scrap of photographers permanently lurking outside the entrance, whose eyes ruthlessly scour every approaching face for signs of FAME. Which serves as an uninvited hors-d'nerve before you've seen the menu. My hosts are already seated at one of the 'A' tables along the window, flanked by James Woods to their left and Burt Bacharach to the right. Behind us, stretching back behind the pillars, an assortment of prune flesh encased in immaculately pressed designer suits, a lot of which have a distinctly military aspect – boxed shoulder-padded ladies with fake medals and insignia embroidered in gold . . . a mixture of Cowes meets Custer for one last stand. Gallons of peroxided hair piled up in every direction, accompanied by lorry-loads of lip-gloss, which has to be topped up between courses. Fingers encrusted with sparkling knuckle-clusters. Arnold Kopelson looks exactly the same as he did two years ago and has proudly come through a heart by-pass and liposuction, which he talks about with relish. 'Good ta see you back, kid. I told ya you would be. Just remember it was me 's gave you your first break out here. How's the family?' after which he runs through the variety of projects they have 'in development', about to 'go', about to be 'released' and he is clearly still revelling in the post-*Platoon* Oscar glow. Actor-talk hovers around the role and artistic aspect of it all but here, in producer territory, *everything* seems to be about the bucks. THE BIGGER THE BETTER. Without any apology . . . just straight down the BUCK AND BOTTOM LINE. As I am the sole thesp at the table I cannot help but discern an unspoken contempt that Money has for the Talent, which is regarded as a sort of necessary and costly INCONVENIENCE without which they cannot PRODUCE. I have sniffed the same whiff in the company of Agents, where THE DEAL is ALL, their client-lists like overcrowded herds forever grazing at their nerves. But bunch some actors together and invariably agents and producers are unceremoniously dumped down the same shaft. A bit like those political analysts who get shirty on *Question Time* when stupid Humans don't behave as they're *supposed* to. It is a great ego-leveller to earwig The Other Side, where you amount to a number in a dollar denomination.

Generously fed and watered I return to the hotel to find two bottles of Cristal champagne in my room, one from Dan Melnick, our producer, and the other from an agency trying to poach me from ICM; both flatter and induce guilt for even *thinking* that either branch of this industry was anything less than *gorgeous* and *honourable*. EVERY 'ACT' HAS ITS OWN AGENDA. I put myself cynically to sleep.

2nd May

The cast of *Henry and June* have a coincidental criss-crossing: I call Gary and get Uma, who is planning her twentieth birthday party; I see *Miami Blues*, which stars Alec Baldwin *and* Fred Ward; then spy Kevin Spacey on the cover of the *TV Guide*, then watch him play Jim Bakker to Bernadette Peters' eyelashed Tammy, in the HBO television film *The Jim Bakker Story*, then see him 'live' on Johnny Carson's show doing his Brando impressions. All in one day. And now here I am working with Steve, who once romanced Ms Peters. Totally irrelevant information, but it's what relays around my cranial fluids. Forever seeking CONNECTION.

3rd May

Ambassador Hotel in mid-town LA. This is the joint where in 1969 Bobby Kennedy was shot in the kitchens, after he had just made a speech. Sorry – 'kitchens' sounds like a euphemism for 'bollocks'. He was *killed* here. The hotel never recovered from the shame and closed down. Now it's an *ad hoc* studio, cheaper than a real studio, hence its popularity. There are *four* other films being shot here at the same time, one of which is written by Neil Simon and stars Alec Baldwin and Kim Basinger. Mr Simon is a friend of Steve and we all have lunch together. Looks just like Kermit the Frog but with huge owl specs and an incredibly thick New York accent, just like Eugene in his own *Brighton Beach Memoirs*. We are shooting the big LA lunch scene al fresco, which is interrupted by an 'earthquake' amid people getting their orders in for coffees of every denomination, from nuclear caffeinated to de-de-de-detonated mud. It is Victoria's first entrance in the film. We are all seated at a large round table peopled with actors playing a variety of LA *types*. Three are also stand-up comics, which means that they seem impelled to do their routines *at* Steve and the rest of us whenever they have the chance. Very funny at first; VERY tedious after five hours plus.

The set-up is taking time as it's a huge area to light and dress with props and people. There are life-sized swans sculpted out of ice, foliage and fruit to arrange, circular camera-tracks to be laid and rehearsed for 'focusing' around the central table, microphones to be hidden in flowers and up the insides of our clothes, hair to be bouffed and faces to be 'tanned'. Special effects 'boys' are playing with the rigging and pulleys to effect the earthquake 'interruption', to which no one will pay any attention in the scene. And now the extras are being placed. These poor fuckers will have to stay put in their appointed posts ALL DAY.

I am seated next to Iman, the staggeringly beautiful Somalian ex-supermodel-turned-actress. She sports a great sense of 'ironics' about the world in general and LA in particular, and tells how she was spotted by a talent scout while a university student in the streets of Nairobi and transformed into a cat-walk Queen. She has a nine-year-old daughter who is five foot eight (her daughter's father is a six-foot-ten basketball player).

Meet Marilu Henner, whom I recognize from *Taxi*. She's playing Steve's bitchy girlfriend. Marilu is like Shirley Maclaine – on speed. Tinkly laughs and talks her whole family history out – how she grew up in a vast household filled with kids and how they put on their own shows and had their own football team and how her burgeoning career in showbusiness was *every dream* she ever dreamt of coming true, and doing *Grease* on Broadway with her friend John Travolta and telling about her bizarre memory capacity. It turns out that she has one of those freaky brains that remembers *everything*. Give her a date five years earlier and she widens her eyes in concentration and is *back* there in an instant. Remembers *every* line of dialogue she has ever had to learn. Can name individual episodes of *Taxi* (there are over a hundred) and what dates they were filmed on. We put her to the test and there is a go-around from the actors asking what day of the week we were all born on. She focuses her eyes in the near distance, stock still, and then tells you, unequivocally, *what it is*. A dozen bullseyes. This is like *Rain Man* for real, except she's much prettier than Dustin Hoffman. Says it drives her crazy sometimes as she cannot wipe anything out.

'Have you tried Vegas?'

'I don't dare,' she replies, like someone 'spooked', then gives me a *diet check-out*, on a mission to rid my system of all that is toxic. Sadly this does not extend to my brain, where evil, toxic thoughts dwell and fester unchecked. 'You see these little shadow-puffs beneath your eyes? *Salt retention. Killer.* You've gotta stop! Don't laugh at me!' she admonishes *and* laughs. 'Look around you.' Cue for us to gaze at the assorted dietary disasters in our sights as she ruthlessly identifies what's wrong with their diets, and projects what they are likely to suffer either imminently or a couple of laps down the track. Her enthusiasm and charm in delivering this TRACT elevates it above the drear and drone of a fanatical BORE and I figure, 'Hey, guys, this is Swazi Boy in LA. Give your ears to whatever's comin' over.' Marilu is in vibratingly RADIANT health and good shape and tells me her early-morning exercise regime, which has my corpuscles collapsing at the *discipline* of the gal. Maybe she *will* live to be a couple of centuries old.

Steve and Victoria invite me to their trailer for the sushi lunch that they have ordered in and he asks, 'D'you play Boggle?' It's Scrabble played in two-minute games with an egg-timer and the letters on dice. Each person tries to write down as many words as they can fathom from the assorted higgledy-piggledy. Very competitive. Compulsive, fast and totally addictive. I have not played in a while and crack out about six tiddlers to their twenty-plus tallies. Again I notice the restlessness that whirrs inside the man. There is no HANGING or DAWDLING about. When called to the set, which is some distance from the actors' motorhomes, he cycles over. If not playing Boggle, he is *talking*. FOCUSED. Or on the mobile phone. Or playing with a computer. Putting on a CD with a 'Have you heard this? What're you reading at the moment?' Not purposeless *restless*, but restless all the same.

After lunch Mick Jackson, the director, assembles us all and calmly goes through a list of what lies ahead for the next couple of days and offers detailed ideas of what he hopes to achieve. I have never known any director so obviously meticulous, and his preparation is visibly appreciated by the large crew and company. Murmurings of 'Must be the BBC training, huh?' Steve is self-deprecating about his writing and invites people to improvise dialogue around the table, which everyone does. Sat for a while with my mouth full of teeth until some courage crept forth. The Americans have a stunning absence of *any* timidity and throw themselves into improvising funny lines without so much as a *flicker* of self-doubt. Which I find wholly liberating and welcome!

Back to the restaurant, and the earth-quaking mechanics are a good gallows laugh, with cables and platforms shifting back and forth, crockery and cutlery shuffling and all of us resolutely NOT reacting, as if such seismic activity is so commonplace as to be not worthy of note. Knowing we are not allowed to laugh starts up that rumble that erupts in your lowest nethers and climbs inexorably up to your tonsils, causing terrible jaw-tightening strain trying to contain it. When I was a kid in Swaz we liked nothing more than to have dinner with the Stewart family, which comprised a table of fourteen, including their granny, who was suffering from senility (Alzheimer's was some years yet down the definition line). Anyway, it provided the same cruel childish laughter. We all had strict instructions NOT to NOTICE, no matter WHAT was uttered by said Elderly Personage. But, without fail, she would suddenly trill forth in fulsome falsetto 'I'm only a bird in a gilded cage.' 'Twas her querulousness, and the ferocity of the silence that followed, which caused cataclysmic gigglings into the napkins, until we were all shooed out of the dining room in hysterical disgrace. The accuracy of her 'observation' flew way above our sniggering heads. But the quality of this forbidden laughter precisely matches that which a dozen adults are now trying to suppress.

In rehearsal Marilu improvises a whole riff about the etiquette of dressing, which Steve endorses wholeheartedly and asks her to reproduce exactly when the scene is shot. The camera never stops circling the table and the timing of your two-bits' worth of dialogue has to coincide with where the lens is pointed, all of which requires some patience, as they work out the speed and order of talk. Sam MacMurray, a regular on *The Tracey Ullman Show*, is competing with Kevin Pollak to try and get in as many comic put-downs as he can before 'ACTION' is called. By the end of the day joke-fatigue has set in. This earthquake action, which will last only seconds in the finished film, like almost every action sequence, seems to take a Technical Eternity to achieve.

9th May

Patrick Stewart, whom I had seen in various roles at the Royal Shakespeare Company, drops in for two days to play the imperious French owner of the restaurant, called L'Idiot, and is instantly besieged by extras and crew asking for his autograph, as he has gone MEGA playing the new captain in *Star Trek*. Says it has cost him his marriage – he works fifteen-hour days nine months of the year, on another continent. In true LA style, no sooner has the excitement surrounding Patrick subsided than it resuscitates for the surprise guest cameo appearance of Chevy Chase, playing a star on the slide. Hence his duff table placement. We have been warned NOT to mention his new hairpiece but no sooner has he howdy'd everyone than he is bending over and showing off his new rug to all and sundry with a 'Roll up, roll up, hey, guys, look at my new piece.' He swathes through the day, at six foot and counting, just as if he *were* Mr Grizwald himself on that *Animal Lampoon* Tour of Europe. Seeing this kind of thing makes you wish it could somehow be incorporated into the film, and confirms my increasing suspicion that the backstage goings-on very often turn out to be more dramatic than what is supposed to be The Drama.

Mick Jackson carries around a small pile of white note-cards to which he regularly refers and we are keenly aware that he intends to get this picture done on schedule and on budget. There is no farting around. When a scene or take is done, he drives everyone on, always conscious that the script contains many short scenes and visual jokes that have to be in the can by the end of every shooting day. It means that there is a real rhythm and urgency of purpose, despite the painstakingly slow process of getting the whole shebang lit, rehearsed and shot from all angles. Andrew Dunn, the director of photography, is brilliant at suggesting Steadicam sequences, whereby the camera is attached by a harness to himself, giving him free rein to move around the actors in a sort of choreographed dance. This is particularly effective when we are shooting a fourway conversation outside the LA County Museum of Modern Art. We have limited time to use the exterior location and as the dialogue is of the short and 'let's make dinner plans' variety, his one-man dance technique gets the scene done in 'real' time and therefore maintains *fresh* dialogue. Which easily stales if a sequence like this is broken up over half a day with multiple set-ups and lighting delays. Loose and liberating. FAST!

Meet Susan Forristal, who plays one of Steve's best friends in the film and also happens to be one of his real life friends. She is like a Texan Holly Golightly – her conversation an all-day *Breakfast at Tiffany's*. Was a model, was married to Lorne *Saturday Night Live* Michaels, is now playing small parts in movies and knows just about everybody you have ever heard of. Infectious giggly laughter undertows in her voice and she's forever truffling for the flip and funny side of everything. A Human Tonic! 'I feel like I've always known you and I'm sure we're going to be friends for life,' is her emphatic take on the situation. And I'm sure we will be.

Simon Callow, whom I have never met, has sent a script of *Ballad of the Sad Café*, which he is meant to be directing with Vanessa Redgrave. I don't believe for a minute that they will cast me as her lover, although it's a great Carson McCullers story. Maybe it's the over-six-foot factor?

11th May

I have noticed something that escaped me on my first film out here: how the exact same conversational weight is given to talk about one's nutritionist, masseur, publicist, manager, agent, favourite eaterie and Gorby's current invasion of Lithuania – 'D'you think there's a movie in *there*?' History is mere fodder for the next picture 'pitch', and Current Affairs means which famous person is fucking which other famous person. But then I suppose this is hardly surprising in a town where there is such a concentration of self-obsessed THESPIA. Everyone on their own step upon the Pyramid of Fame. The lower down you are, the more crowded and desperate the *slaves*. There is rarefied air for them up there on the Pinnacle, but everyone knows it can only be breathed for so long before they, too descend down the other side, finally making their stately way towards Forest Lawns, for those who *count*, or the nearest all-purpose crem, for those who don't. And to take this trail all the way, the land surrounding these Ancient Monumental Tombs is mudflats, populated by swarms of wannabes, gonnabes, have-beens and never-beens. Tidally washed in and out like the Nile itself. The geography of Los Angeles tallies with this Cecil B. de Mille allusion. There, for all to see, are the Hollywood Hills, Beverly Hills, Holmby Hills, Bel Air, Pacific Pallisades, all the way to the Malibu mountains, where the 'Pharaohs' dwell, above the flatland hell of anonymity. The higher you are, the more likely you are to be known. Knowing everybody's business *is* the Business. With fleets of publicists paid to let everyone else know your business. Within this cosmos, rumour is able to run rampant like a computer virus. Once 'out there', it seems impossible to quell. A current story that has achieved mythic proportions – aided by the wealth of new technology, fax, mobile phones, laser copiers, e-mail, and, of course, plain old-fashioned grape vine-ing – concerns a globally famous film star known for his sexual presence. And *the gerbil*. The claim goes that this star had to be admitted to the Cedars Sinai Hospital to have a gerbil removed from his bum (gerbil-insertion being a current sexual 'option' for some consenting adults and non-consenting rodents), opening up speculation as to *how* these unsuspecting creatures are 'inserted' and so forth. Every crew member, at some point, has tried out the latest jokes and variations on this theme since I got here. It seems that every other person knows *someone* who was either *in* the surgery, *at* the reception desk, or *handing over the forceps* when this Star was reputed to have been wheeled in. Damage limitation, requiring major counter-publicity tactics, is the proffered wisdom of one lobby. 'All Publicity is Good Publicity' is the other extreme. *Any which way*, the rumour is loose, and shows no sign of subsiding. There are cartoons in magazines and papers, asides on late-night chat-shows, comic riffs from stand-up comics. Even writing about it, with a THANK GOD IT'S NOT ME on my horizon, is perpetuating it. Poor sod! Perhaps it would be better to crack a joke publicly about it ... but then again ... silence is probably the most sensible option. And the actor's chosen course of 'action' taken at the time of writing. My wife's dad was a doctor in Aberdeen and reported that he was regularly required to remove light-bulbs that had *mysteriously* popped up the old Khyber Passes of a variety of gents. 'Oh, yeah!' intones the actress hired to play Woman in Gaucho Outfit. 'Yeah ... yeah. My pa was a doc, happened all the time. Specially at weekends. Guys comin' in with flashlights up their anuses.' This thrown away with tired disdain.

Lunch in the Beverly Grill with Steve and Victoria and we meet Tracey Ullman. She does an instant cabaret of *Life in y'UK*, bemoaning the rampant negativity. But do I detect a filament of longing in her groan?

Victoria is giving Steve a grilling about the billing, having heard via her agent that only *his* name will appear above the title of the film. He points out that it is a decision entirely based upon the harsh reality of commercial drawing power. Over and out.

I ask Mick Jackson if he is always this organized, to which he replies that this film, more than most, requires so many camera set-ups to achieve all the written visual jokes that he has no option. He is having to use two and sometimes three cameras simultaneously, with an optimum of two takes for every set-up. All of which is facilitated by the new technology. Well, new to me anyway. The rushes, or dailies of the previous day's footage, are available on a video transfer, meaning it is possible to watch them on any video playback without having to go to a screening room at the end of a working day and watch a marathon load of footage. The video monitor which enables the director to see the scenes as they are simultaneously being filmed is now as small and portable as a radio. These advances don't mean you're any more likely to be making a classic than with the old technology, but it does make it SPEEDIER! The sound guys are Robert Altman alumni, having pioneered the multi-track recording system 'invented' for *M*A*S*H*, where a multitude of actors were miked up which enabled everyone to speak simultaneously and to overlap dialogue. This is the set-up used for the earthquake Round Table chatter. They talk of 'working with Altman' like the man is God, and agree that, from their point of view, he is the most creative and exciting director they have ever encountered. 'Don't feel bad about your film with him getting cancelled. If he likes you he's loyal to the death and will use you some day. You'll see.' I wish . . .

Message in my hotel pigeon-hole from Emily Lloyd, whom I have yet to meet, saying that Paul McGann is in town and that we should all meet up some time. Call Paul, and he is shaved bald, having just played a monk in Spain. He is here to do the round of agents and meetings with studio executives, which he says are little more than five-minute humiliations. He asks if I've seen Amanda Donohoe, who has sold up in England and is out here to try her luck. So far with no squeak of employment. Reply that I haven't and feel overwhelmed by a sense of my own good fortune. This revolting cockiness lasts all of about two minutes before giving way to the all-too-familiar shared actor-reality of *There but for the grace of good luck go I*. It is a conversation killer as anything you say that is the slightest bit *understanding* or *assuaging* just sounds patronizing. Our eyes shift around the floor till we mutually divert the conversation to more neutral territory.

'How are your kids?'

'Great!'

'Fine!' I feel embarrassed for myself and for him. His unspoken vulnerability catches me short. Want to express compassion but what comes out is just awkward. For both of us. Sad . . . Resolve, there and then, while walking away, that I will *never* come to this place *without* the invitation of work or real prospect thereof. I know that my old psyche would not stand it.

12th May

Lunch *chez* Steve and Victoria. Glenne Headly, who worked with Steve on *Dirty Rotten Scoundrels*, is round along with Tess Harper, whom I have seen in *Crimes of the Heart*. Glenne speaks in this bizarre little-girl-lost voice, like she was in *The Perils of Pauline*. Only this is her real-life voice. At first I think she *must* be kidding but realize *just* in time that this is how she *always* speaks. Like a cartoon. However, my curiosity gets the better of me and half-way through a mouthful, I hear the following words come shunting through my salad: 'Glenne, did you always talk FUNNY?', causing her to look me dead in the eye, pause, then peel off a tinkle-load of laughter. 'I warned you he was *relentless*,' says Victoria, through my half-blush. Glenne is dressed in the LA version of Oxfam *circa* 1980, and has a vocabulary of skittish gestures to match. Hands and hair twirling like she was Annie Hall's sister. She tweets: 'I loved *Withnail*,' which rightly shuts me up.

Tess Harper, by contrast, is an ex-cocktail waitress from Louisiana, and as hoe-down and earthy as you could wish, with an incredible twangy accent that she hillbillies up for comic effect.

13th May
Social Sunday. Pick up Fiona Shaw and go out for breakfast. She is here shooting *Three Men and a Little Lady*, about which she says, 'I play a Joyce Grenfell-ish spinster with lustful intentions towards Ted Danson,' her groan of embarrassment accompanied by sideways headshakes. 'What'll it be?' chirps Kirk, our freshly baked waiter, yeast-filled with the optimism of another sunny day. 'Let me alert you to today's specials,' which all sound like 'Eggs over easy, sunny-side upsky with sides of fries or hash browns with a guacamole seersucker fillet de scrambled flambé, lightly broiled with a Key Lime drizzle.' With a 'Take your time,' he motors off to fetch up some drinks, leaving us both bobbing about in the wake of his froth and gush. Fiona looks more bewildered and declares that she cannot really be doing with *all this*.

'All this *what*?' I prod.

'All this enthusiasm ... All we want is some breakfast and what we get is the Gettysburg Address. Poor idiot. It's not his fault he has to perform like a trained monkey ... I don't know ... everything is so ... so ... unremittingly cheerful.' Which makes me laugh, for she is *never* short of words and to hear her hesitating about just how to delineate this experience is a simmering pleasure. 'You just love it. Don't you? I know you do so don't even try to deny it.'

'Of course I do, I'm a totally superficial little hedonistic ponce.'

'This place is like a kindergarten for grown-ups.'

'So what'll it be?' Kirk's back.

'Could I just have some plain toast and coffee?'

'Sure! No problem. Do you want wholewheat, rye, raisin, sour-dough or buttermilk bread?'

'You see? I just want ordinary toast . . . brown.'

'You got it. Cappuccino, filter, caffeinated, de-caf, espresso or Kenyan?'

'Caffeine.

'Atta girl. I also like it strong.' Upon which he turns and squirrels away.

'How are we going to get through this lunch?'

'Smilingly!'

'I was right! You do love it!'

We have been invited to lunch with the producer for whom we both worked on *Mountains of the Moon*, a historical epic about Burton and Speke searching for the source of the Nile, which sadly 'took a deep bath' at the box office. Fiona's performance, however, prompted various American critics to hail her as 'the next Meryl Streep', and she is understandably smarting at having to resort to playing a goofball in the *Three Men and a Baby* sequel. Our breakfast rendezvous has been fixed so that we can talk without being in the midst of a social hob-nob of strangers. 'How are you supposed to dress in this place?' Nothing is going to appease her mood this morning. Nothing short of an Irish downpour and fifty bolts of intellectual lightning.

Later, I accelerate on to Santa Monica Boulevard and vroom up towards her hotel, where we are due to pick up Sheila Hancock, who is also playing a part in the *Baby* sequel. While we're waiting in the foyer we meet Denis Lawson, just checking out. He's been out here at Disney's expence to screen test for the pilot of the TV series of *Dead*

Poets Society, but is being Scottishly sceptical of his chances. It feels very unreal meeting Brit actors amid all this sunny-de-luxe, a whole Continental remove from the reality of duffel-coated rehearsal rooms and Styrofoam cups in dark corners of London.

Sheila finally appears from her delayed phone call and the three of us roar up Sunset Boulevard, take a right up Doheny Drive and see our address before we get near: cars are queued up waiting to be parked by the Valet Servicemen. Then it's up the steep steps to the front door. The bell is a symphonic chime and plethora of entry buttons. 'WEL-COOOOME! Come on in!' It's our trusty host, sporting all his teeth with alligator charm. He is wearing a white silk shirt that floats and shifts like a balletic tent around his ample girth. 'Got this in Thailand, when I was doing a picture with Mel and Downey Jnr. In fact, I had eighteen of 'em made in all different colours. Perfect for LA. And so reasonable. Welcome to my home. What'll you have to drink?' We move through accompanied by a soft wall of Mozart. Flowers, pot-pourri and penguin-suited waiters proffering drinks, and canapés laid out on large palm-leaved platters. The house is a slanted high-tech gallery-type affair, perched up a steep incline. Off-white carpeting beside charcoal slate tiles, and Italian furniture that has room for air to move around it. The high walls are covered with vast abstract canvases and huge African masks lit by the sloping skylights. The black bottomed pool and Jacuzzi is part indoors partly in the garden, divided by enormously tall sliding glass panels. All in all it's like being in a pristine set of *Carnal Knowledge*, 1970. 'I know how curious you are. Come, take a look at this.' I find myself in the strange position of a guided-tourist in my host's bedroom. He points out the control panel beside the bed; it looks like a miniature lighting keyboard for a reasonably sized repertory theatre, all black and shiny like almost everything else in the room. Phone, intercom, music-control dials, air-conditioning, levitating television screen, electric window blinds and 'Press that button.' I do and there's a faint whirring noise which gets louder as a slightly shaky black ice-bucket, holding a bottle of cham-pagne, swivels up from a mini-trapdoor in the floor. Like that hand holding the sword that comes out of the lake in King Arthur. 'Neat, huh? Gets the ladies every time.' I dare not think how many LADIES have been 'buttoned' by this James Bond gadgetry and wonder if any of them have ever swapped notes. 'Needs oiling.' The pillow-cases and bed-cover look like black leather but I refrain from touching or enquiring. Warhol portraits hang around the walls with that dead-eyed look of oh-to-have-seen-what-these-eyes-have-seen. 'I collect ART,' gets us out of the boudoir and back into the throng.

'I'd like you to meet . . .' and here is Richard Dreyfuss, talking at rocket speed about the lack of government funding for Aids research, Neil Simon and his new wife, a man who wrote speeches for Kennedy, Carrie Fisher, various agents, Cheryl Campbell and Andrew Dunn, Mick Jackson and Sue Mengers.

Lunch is served at three tables on the terrace, with people 'butterflying' between, and is a sumptuous feast of Thai-Californian. Carrie is asking questions FAST. She wants to know who I have met and whether I know any of the actors she trained with at the Central School in London before she was whipped off and beehived into Princess Leia for *Star Wars*. I do. But what she really wants to know is what I think of 'Hollywood – not the place, but the state of mind?'

I begin with that swivelling levitating ice-bucket in the black bedroom. She is so fast, funny and ruthlessly self-deprecating that I wonder aloud how she has survived.

''Cos I'm fast, funny and ruthlessly self-obsessing. Look, I haven't! The news obviously hasn't reached your neck of the woods.'

'Don't be daft. *Postcards from the Edge* was brilliant.'

'Thanks. Writing has saved my ass. I see you're married. Are you in love?'

'That's *my* question.'

'I got in first. Are you?'

'Yes.'

'Lucky you. Kids?'

'One. Baby daughter.'

'Tell me about the birth part?'

'D'you have plans? Who would the father be?'

'You ask too many questions. Brian, who you just met. Gone to get

food. Blond guy, over there. I wanna know about the birth part first.'
And within a few sentences I find myself detailing the nightmare we
went through as if I have known her all my life. I suppose her having
exposed her soul in *Postcards* goes some way to explaining why this
should have tripped out so trippingly, rendering a public function a
private place. Her conversation is a beguiling mix of anecdote, irony,
unexpected vulnerability and straight-down-the-line jokes.

Fiona and Sheila are signalling for an imminent departure. Fiona is
doing *gasping* acting, saying she needs some AIR! Says she found the
whole thing nothing short of *sinister*. And accuses me with 'I noticed
what a *tough* time you were having of it, you wretched socializer!' as
we wind our way down Sunset towards the Pacific itself. 'Isn't there
somewhere we could have an ordinary cup of English tea?' – Sheila.
Fiona knows of a place back in town on La Cienega Boulevard, which
we double back to. Pull up and park at Paddington's, which promises
The Real Thing, with scones, jam and clotted cream. More English
than anything I ever saw in England but provides the necessary Earl
Grey resuscitation required. Though it turns out that the proprietress
is an Aussie. We finish off our brunch post-mortem and drop back to
their hotel. 'Could never live here. Like a madhouse. Don't laugh,
you little bastard!'

'Bye!'

'You'll get brain-rot!'

'Byeeeeeeeeeeee!'

See Emily Lloyd in the Château foyer and she says she is definitely
going to come and live here. 'Denholm is here, you know, you should
give him a call.'

'I will. How's it going with Faye Dunaway?'

'I don't have any scenes with her so maybe I'll survive,' she says,
cackling off.

It's midnight in LA. Eight a.m. in London, the next day. Like E.T.,
I phone home, all sleepy, while my family is just about 'wakey'. The
'sop and goo' is par for the course when separated for any length.

Woken up around three a.m. by pounding from above. Call the

operator to find out if there's something I'm missing out on, to which he replies, 'Nah, just a party in Emily Lloyd's room. G'night.'

16th May

Two legends are dead today: Jim Henson at the age of fifty-three, and Sammy Davis Jnr. Always seems a pity that all the landsliding eulogies are only for the ears of the living. I reckon those Beverly Hilton Lifetime Achievement dos at least serve to pep you up while trumpeting your imminent roll-call before popping off. The 'what a great guy' obits flow endlessly all day on TV, which I find riveting: you get to see all the other oldies you haven't seen in ages speaking out. Even the newsreaders' tag-lines at the end of their Globally Bad News adopt an 'aw shucks' familiarity about the 'just departed'. Sammy Davis's interment at Forest Lawns is a production of epic proportion, so much so that I half expected him to pop up and go into a *just kiddin', folks* routine as choreographed by Bob Fosse. I mean no disrespect, it's just that the hoopla surrounding one old man's burial is superseded by the theatrical razzle-dazzle that is unmistakably HOLLYWOOD. Part of the morbid curiosity is spotting those for ever young faces, from old movies, which now look like they're wearing wrinkled prosthetics and bearing cruel testimony to the nature of Time. As the camera pans along the starry pantheon, it is almost as though it is spying on WHO MIGHT BE NEXT? Childishly I vow that this decrepitude will never grope me down, and purposely flatten the accelerator on my way to meet some studio executives and casting folk on the other side of the hills in Studio City.

Having twisted and turned, up, over and down the other side of Benedict Canyon, my map-reading skills fail me, with a left on to the wrong motorway instead of a right. It is only when signs for Malibu loom ahead that instant stomach squalls set in as eyeballs search for an exit ramp. Due for two, get there by four WRECKED. 'No problem' is the placebo offered.

The Disney offices are pristine, vast and peopled by friendly looking men and women wearing crisp white shirts, ties and laundered denim. General 'meetings' of this nature are excruciating-beneath-the-smile diplomatic forays that I am convinced amount to nothing. An actor-unattached-to-a-specific-project seems to have as much use as a mannequin waiting to be dressed in an empty window. You feel just as naked. Not that it isn't all very friendly. It's just *too* fucking friendly. In the way that you can only afford to be when you know damn well that you're unlikely ever to see the same bunch of faces ever again. I go into the Beverly Center to shop for some extra luggage and come across Emily Lloyd and cohorts giving some bemused punters an impromptu recital on a gang of pianos in a department store. Emily is yelling out her signature 'haloooooo', while the shop assistants are silently expressing 'wish you weren't here', but also 'Hey! Maybe it's best not to interrupt a hot-flavoured fledgeling celebrity playing "Chopsticks". Could attract custom.'

17th May

The producer for whom I had worked on *Mountains of the Moon* takes me aside and lowers his tone to a barely audible *sotto voce* with the following advice: 'I think you should seriously think about getting yourself pumped up. I mean with iron. Could transform your career and give you a Hollywood shot at being a leading man. Think about it. You look good but you could do with some beefing up. Look at Arnie and Sly.'

Do I take this advice to heart or recall what happened before *Withnail* where, having spent a year weight-gaining and pumping, Bruce casually said, 'Oh, and lose a stone before we start shooting.' In the cool light of a London day this kind of question would not warrant more than a couple of seconds' consideration, yet here, in the State of the Barbie, such considerations somehow carry weight. If you let them. Decide to read a book instead.

Every time I cross paths with my producer, GUILT locks in and I momentarily resolve to try reading *and* pumping simultaneously. However much I dismiss this WHISPER, there is always an attendant devil that queries my disdain with a *What if he's right? Whaddya got to lose, kid? What's a little iron pumped between friends gonna do to ya, other than gooooood?*

18th May

I ask Steve why he doesn't do stand-up any more.

'Let me tell you about playing in Vegas and you'll see why.'

He does an instant replay of his stand-up comedy nights in Vegas. 'Aaaaaaaaaand, Ladies and Gennlemeeeeeeen,' picking up some knives and forks and beating out the noise of pre-show diners, 'Weeeeeeeee proudly preeeeeeeeeeeZENT, theeeeeeeee comedyeeeeeeeeeeee styling of' CLANKCLANKCLANK 'STEVE' CLANKCLANKCLANK 'MaaaaaarTIN!' CLANKCLANKCLANCKCLINKANDCLANKCLANK. 'The impossibility of getting people to shuddup! You cannot compete with crockery and hope to be funny. Also it's incredibly lonely. Plus it takes years to shape an act, and the minute it's recorded or on TV, it's eaten up and you've gotta try and come up with something totally new. Kills you. I played stadiums where the audience was doing my routines for me. Insane. Impossible to keep that momentum going. My first film *The Jerk* was really my act transposed into a movie and I've never wanted to go back and do that stuff again.'

While somewhat disappointed, never having seen him perform live, I found his rationale all too understandable. And those days seem a far remove from the calm of his Beverly Hills sanctuary. Part of the charisma of celebrity seems to be in trying to reconcile the apparently *ordinary* person you encounter one-to-one with the *extraordinary* other persona with whom you are so familiar. Initially, this is like having two channels transmitting simultaneously in your head, the brain intent on marrying the known images and info with the unknown and mysterious. Walking around with Steve, I often hear people say, '*Are* you Steve Martin?' testing *just in case* it isn't. Alternatively, synapses short-circuit so fast that a hugely familiar 'Hi, and how are you and what's up?' comes blurting out, suddenly followed by blushing embarrassment as the *unknown* realizes he/she is having a chat with a KNOWN. At this point, tongues get knotted and sentences become non-sequitur.

Rachel Ward, with her daughters Rosie and Mathilda, and I are invited for Sunday lunch *chez* the Martins. Rachel did *Dead Men Don't Wear Plaid* with Steve, and was an ex-pat contact when Victoria first came out to California. She is giving LA one last shot, fed up with the whole schmooze-fest and imminently off to Oz for good. It is somewhat comical to watch this calm and highly ordered couple coping with the invasion of these miniature terrorists. Rachel, having eschewed her blue-blood background, has resolutely reared two 'girls' that would do the SAS proud, were they to open up a junior division. She arrives in a battered old pick-up truck that looks like it belongs to one of the gardeners that service these Babylonian gardens. Her makeupless face and Oxfam couture defy *any* submission to star-status and even her once cut-glass consonants have an undeniable Strine to them. 'LA is a dump! No place to live. Gotta get out. People are just so much movie-fodder.' Rosie and Mathilda are now terrorizing the cats, who haven't seen this much action since the last earthquake. Steve looks dumbstruck and tentatively suggests they might like to watch some cartoon videos. This unleashes squealing and screams and they maraud their way into his immaculately ordered study, pounce upon the sofa and proceed to jump up and down. Tape in and they settle down. For about ten minutes. Rachel is undoubtedly *revelling* in the seismic havoc they have wrought upon this calm sanctuary, for these surroundings, despite all the sun, pool and sashaying palm trees, have *not* been designed to accommodate anything as irrational as children. No sooner have we got a drink in our paws and begun a conversational trawl through our *worst movie experiences* than the SAS duo is back, screaming for their 'cossies' and thumping one another.

'This the Australian effect, then, Rach?'

'You betcha, *mate*! No prissy-missy Laura Ashleys for me!'

'No chance of that!'

Clothes are ripped off each other's backs and they hurl themselves into the water like turbo-charged Donald Campbells. It's the first time I've witnessed Steve looking nonplussed. Which makes me laugh.

Spy the study through the window and the room resembles the burglary from *Pink Panther: The Apocalypse*. Rosie has just bitten her sister, who has let rip a caterwauling yowl. Rachel offers no sympathy and declares that they have to sort themselves out. Which they do, after a fashion, having walloped one another mercilessly. Even the lure of lunch is not enough to quell the exuberance of these marsupials, who, having stuffed down a couple of buns, take to running in and out of the carpeted house and into the pool. 'Girls! Tilda, Rosie!' Rachel's belated attempts at control are keenly ignored until finally even her Olympian cool is sapped. With a 'RIGHT! THAT'S IT. OUT – NOW!' she hauls each one out of the water, which they assume is just another game until they finally submit when promised a stopover at some Häagen-Dazs outlet *en route* to their next battle-station. I understand the full meaning of 'to bundle into' when they scramble for front-seat supremacy in the jalopy. We stagger back into some silence.

21st May

Calls from a couple of rival agencies *on the poach*. Flattering and unnerving as I feel that even talking to them is traitorous. But then I remind myself that they have as much conscience as ... fill in whatever Brutus comes to mind.

Fax of apologia from Simon Callow to say that Keith Carradine is to play in *Sad Café* but he hoped and believed we would one day work together. Over and out.

22nd May

Susan Forristal calls and says do I want to go to a sneak screening of the sequel to *Chinatown*. We drive over to the San Fernando Valley to a shopping mall where there are queues for a movie that no one knows anything about. Neither the title nor the stars. All that *is* known is that entry is free and all the punter is required to do is fill in a score card upon leaving. There is a distinctly raucous atmosphere, either to do with the absence of admission fee, or lucky-dip prospect of seeing something before anyone else has, or maybe it's because the opinion score-cards render everyone an active participant rather than a passive observer. Whichever, there is a charge of anticipation and excitement in the stalls. No forthcoming attractions or adverts to distract. As the lights dim, tribal 'Yo's are howled and echoed from another 'native'. When Jack Nicholson's name hits the screen the crowd goes Circus Maximus. Clapping and screaming and 'YO'ing. 'Jack, my maaan!' is lobbed out by a fervent one. Up rolls the title, *The Two Jakes*, and the promised return of J. J. Gittes tips everyone over the edge. They might have announced the end of tax payment for one and all, such is the cheering response. Susan points out the producer, Robert Evans, in the back row, who is understandably *beaming*. He presided over *Love Story, The Godfather and Chinatown* in the seventies, followed by the murderous infamy surrounding *The Cotton Club* in the early eighties, and his demeanour suggests that this response has been a long time looked for. However, it doesn't take a qualified seismologist to read the audience reaction to what unfolds. Faye Dunaway's character is dead. As is John Huston. Polanski is director *in absentia* as he faces criminal prosecution in the USA; Robert Towne is not credited with the screenplay, and fifteen years have taken their toll on the once slimline private eye immortalized by Jack. And the let-down is increasingly audible. Fidgeting and dwindling attention ensue as the film meanders along with an endless voice-over trying to clarify the plot twists. Studio executives are now back-and-forthing to the foyer. You can tell them by their suits and/ or determinedly casual Armani jeans and laundered shirts, like you are always s'posed to be able to identify a cop in mufti. Mr Evans is looking very furrowed of brow as the swell of disappointment roams around the rows. Come the end credits and people are throwing themselves through the doors, none too keen to fill in the questionnaire being proffered. Many scoot, not bothering to 'pay' their opinions. Muttering, 'More like *The Two Jerks*,' as they scarper into the night. The lady to my right has written a single word in bold capitals across her card: MENOPAUSAL.

Which is the collective expression upon the faces of the shell-shocked executive contingent. Millions of dollars, months of shooting, mega-star presence and the deadly desertion of the stalls signifying only one thing. Instead of battle-smoke drifting over Custer's last stand, the fart-like pall of pop-corn wafts through the empty foyer. Susan loyally hangs around to speak to 'Bob' and his handshake is horribly clammy. Mercifully he does not ask either of us for our opinion and is talking at speed about this all being a 'work in progress ... still requiring honing and polishing'. As we leave this scene of blight, a childhood image sifts and settles upon my seven-year-old self watching a landed fish, flapping and mouthing the air as if it were trying to say something until its flaps grew fewer and its gasp transfixed into a gawp. Glazed.

We drive away in silence, which slowly unwinds into another attempt to decipher *why* it doesn't work, with a refrain of 'But how could it possibly have failed?' incredulously fuelling our disappointment.

23rd May

Last day of filming and the panic of the bubble-of-it-all about to burst combines with the longed for return to my family on the other side of the planet. Buy presents and cards. Draw some cartoons. Hope that these new friendships forged will survive beyond the sell-by date of 'It's a wrap'. Do an interview for *Première* magazine, second costume fitting for *Hudson Hawk*, have a lunch meeting with Mark Rydell, who is casting a new Bette Midler vehicle titled *For the Boys* at 20th Century-Fox and arrange a farewell dinner with Steve and Victoria. The Fox studio lot is everything I imagined a movie studio would look like. The offices are hidden behind the façade of New York City *circa* 1900, which, it turns out, were the sets for *Hello Dolly*. My parents took us to see this on New Year's Eve, 1969, in Africa, when I was twelve, and I find myself standing still in the parking lot, twenty-one years older, in the middle of my 'dream' that has come true: I've just completed a movie; I am about to fly to San Francisco for the day to re-do some dialogue for *Henry and June*, and am contracted to do *Hudson Hawk* in the near future. I am hooted back into reality by an oncoming studio golfcart, transporting some besuited man to *his* destiny.

24th May

Dawn flight to Frisco and the city looks exactly like *Dirty Harry* showed it to me on a drive-in screen in Swaz. With a soundtrack of Sinatra eulogizing that Golden Gate Bridge, the driver is pointing out the aftermath of the latest earthquake, which has left an overhead motorway buckled and lying on its side like a toy, and here are those streets from *Bullet* and round that corner it's *What's Up, Doc?* with a little *High Anxiety* thrown in. Bits of Hitchcock scroll their way through my viewfinder until we arrive at the dubbing studio where I walk into another time capsule. *Henry and June* is nearing its final cut and, although we're on the other side of the world, it's as though the interim months have never interrupted. Here are Phil, Rose and Peter, as welcoming and friendly as ever and clearly thrilled with how the picture is coming together. Everything inside hopes for this to be true while the undeniable nag of *What happens when it faces an audience?* slithers through the side-streets of my brain. The looping is straightforward and simple and we drive down to a restaurant beneath the Golden Gate Bridge for lunch. Get the late-afternoon flight back to LA, cushioned in the compliments of their Friendship Pack. Flight to London.

26th May

Jet-lagged and tentative. These first few days are spent trying not to infringe on the Independent Territory re-mapped out by my patient spouse during my five-week absence. I'm grateful not to have had a row of READJUSTMENT yet! Getting myself realigned to not being the centre of my own universe. Everything seems miniaturized.

Baby wakes at two a.m. and is teething. Still jet-lagged, I stupidly complain the next morning about feeling exhausted and unleash 'YOU THINK *YOU'RE* EXHAUSTED?' and the inevitable domestic explosion that follows with a dose of 'DON'T TOUCH ME' and a half day of brimstone and glaring eyeballs in every direction, after which all is 'levelled off' and 'loved up'.

Went round to see the Robinsons. They have sold their house and the staircase is lobby to loft in boxes. Bruce is now paranoid about being homeless prior to moving out to LA, and spleens forth a comical diatribe about 'how much England has fallen apart since I last saw you!' Which is all of five weeks. I ask him how his new film script, *Jennifer Eight*, is coming along.

'Stuck on page fucking forty something,' he spits, cracking open a can of McEwan's finest export.

The man in the newsagent's asks, 'Got anything in the pipeline, then?'

Hudson Hawk

21st March

Oh, my sweet darlings, where, oh where, do I dare begin to tell this multi-million-dollar EPIC?, which, as defined by the Oxford Dic, means: a long poem in elevated style narrating the adventures of a hero; long novel or film; one containing adventurous episodes; heroic, majestic, impressively great.

Hudson Hawk is *all* of these but not quite in the order suggested. *Long?* Certainly! *Heroic?* Oooooooh, YES, but not quite what you might have in mind. The patience required would sorely test the most Olympian devotees of Prozac. *Majestic?* The mega-budget spirals like new stairways to heaven. *Adventurous?* With a cast including Bruce Willis, Andie MacDowell, Danny Aiello, James Coburn, Sandra Bernhard, and myself – what else?

In keeping with this Ancient Aspect, be warned that *this* modern-day tale is bereft of any Poetry and is pure Doggerel. For Homer's *Iliad* and the siege of Troy, substitute Bruce's *Hudson* and the siege of Rome. For Homer's *Odyssey*, detailing Odysseus' adventures in his ten-year attempt to return home after the Trojan War, substitute Willis's *Hawk*, a tale of thespian desperadoes attempting to return to Hollywood from Hungary, after an interminable 'shoot', to be greeted by boiling vats of critical vitriol and a *Variety* inquisition.

To begin at the beginning. In the year of 1990, on the twenty-first day of March, a Wednesday, my agent, he of the aforementioned dwarfish stature, makes it known that the deal has been done for *LA Story*. After which he announces that an American casting director,

Jackie Burch, requires me to meet at the Athenaeum Hotel in Piccadilly, London, with the director of *Hudson Hawk*, a big-budget action-comedy which is to star Bruce Willis and Isabella Rossellini. The script is being messengered to my abode as we speak, he says. It is. And it reads fast and funny.

22nd March

Seven forty-five p.m. assignation at the Athenaeum. Suitably attired in smart-casual evening armour, I charioteer my way thither and stand about the marbled entrance of the hotel foyer, awaiting the arrival of the unknown Caesar. I won't try your patience much further with this arcane idiom, BUT may return to this mode when things get gladiatorial. Michael Lehmann (the director of *Heathers*, a low-budget but successful teen-murder flick), is helming this 'biggie'. I scan the elderly clientele getting their coats on to cab off to see *Phantom of the Opera*, mostly rich Americans perfumed up for a night of Lloyd-Webber Colosseum spectacle. The doorman is dressed in livery and bowing and scraping all over them. PING – and this time the elevator disgorges two straggly-looking 'students' in the wake of the fur-coat brigade. Just as I am about to blip them out, the shorter one beams, 'Hi, so great to meet you. I'm Michael Lehmann and this is Dan Waters the writer. We did *Heathers* together. Let's go siddown and get a drink.' We do. They really do look like undergraduates rather than the usual Californian-casual look – that is, laundered and designer-labelled to perfection. I feel over-dressed. And over-aged. They are not yet thirty. Michael and Dan do a double-act description of their script, which they characterize as a tongue-in-cheek Bond film – 'It'll be kinda fun 'cos Bond is already a sorta parody which we are double-parodying.' The story is the dream of Bruce Willis, who has nurtured it since his days of being a New York barman before his career took off with *Moonlighting* on television, and went ballistic with his movie role in *Die Hard* and *Die Hard II: Die Harder*. Joel Silver produced both and is repeating the same duties on *Hawk*.

'We just loved you in *How To Get Ahead In Advertising* and think you might be just perfect for the part of the villain in this. Kinda like all the Bond Blofelds rolled inta one – on mescaline! As it's Bruce's baby, he has casting approval but we would love to work with you. What do you think of Sandra Bernhard for your wife?' This gave the clearest indication of *exactly* the kind of *tone* they were going for. Her Masha in *King of Comedy* was indelible. And convinced me that they were serious about going *to the wall*. So, a shifting-raft situation here: they have made their feeling clear but say that it is up to the Star to make his final decision. Could involve having to do a screen test.

5th April

Two weeks have elapsed and today the Dwarf calls to say I may have to fly to New York to meet Messrs Willis and Silver. In the interim fortnight a friend is diagnosed with a terminal brain tumour and there is a very emotional memorial for Ian Charleson, which puts this 'hanging about' into proper perspective.

11th April

'Waiting on Willis'.

12th April

DOMESTIC HARI-BA-DARI. Between the Blind Piano-Tuner, the man coming to mend the boiler, Joan having her legs waxed and my resignation to a 'no go' scenario, I receive a call that is an offer, *without* having to fly to New York or any-such. And oooh and ahhh, how sweet the news is. 'To be (wanted), or not to be, that is (always) the question.' It's enough to make you heave but the day they *do*, *never* ceases to shift some sherbert down my spine. Especially as I have *LA Story* to do first.

28th June

I film *LA Story* in the interim and get a call to fly to LA for a *read-through!* of the script at the end of June. My salary is a smiling 'flush-line' compared to the low-budget British standard sanpic 'rim'. Some distance and expense to go for a read-through, but *hey!* this is *big-budget-wonderland*.

I touch-down and am limo'd up into the Hollywood hills to Greg Gorman's photographic studio, where I meet Sandra Bernhard for the first time, as well as Mickey Rourke who is tinkering with his bike. He *looks* like Mickey Rourke *in costume*, for he is decked up in the full biker gear, with snakeskin cowboy boots, shades, scowl and pirate-style headscarf. Fag in the right corner and sliver of lip-space for words to mumble out. Movie-Star-via-Marlboro-Man. Tough, clanking and undeniably comical to these jet-lagged eyes. Being a real-life TOUGH-GUY and ACTOR-MAN is a hard ACT to reconcile. Meet Marushka Dettmers, the Dutch actress playing the female lead. I wonder what has happened to Isabella Rossellini, but do not ask. Sandra Bernhard is having her makeup applied when we meet and is about to be transformed into something AWESOME. Her auburn hair has been teased up into a frenzy, until it resembles one of those ice-cream whorls that whip out of a machine on to a cone. Her eyes crane to their right corners, as she cannot turn her head just yet and she twangs, 'HI, HONEEEEE.' She has an instantly discernible trademark *sigh*, which insinuates itself through her speech and loping walk as if *everything* is slightly exhausting and demanding, and that whatever she is doing *now* is somehow keeping her from something she would rather do. Whether it be hair rollers, mascara, the freeway, photo sessions, Reagan, Haiti, Madonna-questions, global warming, it's all a bit too much to handle. All of which is what makes her funny. She takes everything *personally* and while professing to *loathe* the whole Hollywood *thing*, I do not doubt for a moment that she is *revelling* amid her own moanings. She is perfect casting to play Minerva Mayflower, the world's richest, most evil bitch-villainess. While the manicurist is doing her nails, she entertains us with stories of her humiliations and hilarities when she was a struggling comedienne, doing Beverly Hills' nails to pay her rent. She *demands* everyone's total attention, and I can feel myself inexorably drawn into her orbit. Her neck choked with ropes of pearls, gold starfish earrings drooping down her lobes, hair sculpted in waves, and body swathed in a multi-coloured 'wrap', she rises to ready for the first Polaroid 'test' shot, looking like a tall version of Hermione Gingold: mouth permanently set in a full-lipped sneer that *dares* anyone to *dare* to 'lip' back. When she cackles her eyes disappear into slits and her two gapped front teeth come at you like a 3D film, *sans* the specs.

Greg Gorman's studio is also his house, which is all white and glass and light and music playing and assistants and help yourself to food and drink, casual. Marilyn, the costume designer, kits me out in the Cerruti gear and Greg snaps and lights and Polaroids and relights and confers and makes the whole process seem easy. These pictures are for a *faux Vanity Fair* style cover for a scene in the film. Added to which, 'our' dog is included. It is a terrier, a white and tan, rough-haired, box-faced canine that looks like an Edwardian toy – the kind that has straight legs and is mounted on a platform with wheels and a handle-bar. We pose with the imagined arrogance of the world's richest couple, with Sandra doing an Ivana Trump monologue during the snapping. Change outfits, hair quelled, hats on and the actual shoot is incredibly fast. Greg Gorman has what the magazines call *bedroom eyes*, forever searching and 'undressing'.

29th June

Nine a.m. Read-through at Warner Brothers studios. Fuckhot day. Meet Albert Brooks on my way in.

'Liked your *Boil.*'

'Thanks, liked your *Broadcast News.*'

'Thanks.'

'Cheers.'

This casual, sunny, open-plan atmosphere makes it hard to believe anyone really has a *proper* job. Everyone looks and seems dressed for a summer holiday. The offices are full of movie memorabilia, toys and posters. The read-through is an odd biscuit – no producer, no lead actor; Marushka, Sandra, myself and Donald Burton, who plays the butler. Writer. Director. Coke and doughnuts. Read in requested Texan drawl. By mid-morning this request is withdrawn and 'Why not try it in like a snotty British accent?' Done. My Texan is not what it might have been. My villainous authority is ZERO. Though I feel it is restored somewhat when barking in 'olde Bulldog'. I have the merest *inkling* that this somewhat rudderless start *might* presage what lies ahead but, at this stage, the galley is not yet in the water.

Four p.m. to Paramout Studios to meet Bruce Willis and Joel Silver. He is finishing on *Bonfire of the Vanities* today and we arrive too early. We wait around. Sandra is otherwise engaged. I am now being entertained by Suzanne Todd, the fast-talking blonde assistant to Mr Silver. In her early twenties, with a double-torpedo bust, which I admire out loud for which she thanks me, laughs, then says, 'Let's go on to the set and see if we can find him.' Which we do. (Suzanne is with Bruce's brother, David, who is also working on the movie and who looks like a slightly less beefy version of Bruce.)

Filming is mid set-up, and when we find Bruce he disarms me with a bearhug and 'gimme-five-brother' handslap. *Molto* friendly and I am instantly won over. He tells me how funny he thought *Withnail* and *Advertising* were, and says, 'Welcome aboard. We are gonna make one helluva movie! Have you met Joel?' I 'not yet' my way back to his trailer where he shows me a plethora of pictures of his baby and wife and does everything to make me feel at ease and relaxed. 'You gotta meet Joel.' Suzanne is trying to reach him on a mobile phone, and when she gets through takes notes *fast* and replies even *faster*. 'That's Joel!' says Bruce. And all our energy seems to be vacuuming towards the imminent arrival of this reputed Human Hurricane, forever the *eye* of his own *storm*. Suzanne is still talking to him on the phone as his car squeals up and he invades the trailer.

He *is* the *energy-field*. Full and fleshly furnished, bearded, curly-haired, with dark eyes constantly darting behind big-rimmed glasses, and the VOICE: a raspy runaway-train of command and cajole: Joel Silver. Bullet-spoken and possessed of EVERYTHING TO DO WITH THE MAKING OF MOVIES. I am at once transfixed and terrified, like a rabbit caught in the headlamp glare of his personality. This is NOT a man with whom you disagree WITHOUT risking a verbal fusillade. Find myself taking three deep breaths before trying to enter his fray. Which I do, giving him a replay of the photo-session-with-Sandra-as-fast-and-as-funny-as-I-can-muster-and-make-it-to-the-first-base-when-he ... LAUGHS! His laugh matches his verbals and ricochets out from him. Although he is probably only a few years my senior, I feel like guppy-bait to his shark. The buddy-buddy camaraderie between Bruce and Joel is of a distinctly different metabolic rate from that of the young director-writer duet I was with all morning. Joel tells me that he is a 'hands-on producer', which I don't doubt for a millisecond. Just how well the Lehmann–Waters combo will mix with the mercurial Silver–Willis will-power is a chemical equation that does not bear consideration just now. I can't think when I have ever met two humans so obviously BRIMMING with self-confidence.

Conversation is dollar-thick with the projected box-office prospects for their latest joint venture, *Die Hard II*, and something muscular with Schwarzenegger or Stallone. 'You coming to the première?' demands Joel.

'I'm booked to fly home Monday.'

'Nah. You wanna come? You gotta see this. Change your flight. Suzanne! Do it.' She does and I do. Not that I'm forced against my will, you understand, but there is something *unavoidable* about Mr Silver when he issues a command.

Food, phone, fast-talk and faxes scurry for his attention and just when I've begun to sink into some 'ease', he's up and off and on to the next wherever. 'See you Monday!' Bruce chuckles at the expression still affixed to my face. 'I told you, diddin' I? He's a lunatic, but I love the guy.'

'What does he do to relax?

'That *is* him relaxed.'

Nothing at the wrap party for *LA Story* tonight can dislodge this nuclear-charge, and everything and everyone seems supremely sedate by comparison. As does my calm weekend with Steve and Victoria, both relieved that shooting is complete. They eschew any celebration/ acknowledgement of birthdays or Christmas, in keeping with their unsentimental hellos and goodbyes. I imagine that were you guaranteed never to see each other again, Steve would still say ta-ta as abruptly and unemotionally as if you were just going round the corner for a newspaper. When I encountered this for the first time, I couldn't prevent a miniature invasion of my trusty paranoids, but he does it to everyone, and I wonder whether this kind of *emotion* is deemed too messy for a man so scrupulously fastidious.

2nd July

LA première of *Die Harder*, Westwood Cineplex. Eight p.m. Suggested orders from on high that Sandra and I go together as we are to play in the Team's next BIGGIE. Agreed, and Sandra arrives in a mini-dress designed by a friend of hers, parks her wheels in the hotel basement and we climb aboard the stretch limo that's been sent round. Ten-minute drive down Sunset and my antennae are popping with the prospect of a big première night out. The evening is still dusky and barracuda-length limos are congested outside the cineplex. The smoked windows afford the chance to 'nose' the glass and check it all out.

'What the fuck are you doing?' barks Sandra.

'Gawping!' I reply, which makes her laugh.

The routine is as follows – the cars are numbered and ushered into position by a combination of police and publicity assistants. All walky-talkying and arm-waving and checking, so that whichever celebrities have just been disgorged on to the red carpet are not crowded by more in their wake before they have had a chance to give the phalanx of press and TV crews their 'news'. Air-raid lights sweep the sky and look like over-sized teacups revolving in their own customized van. Police whistles, wolf-whistles for busty-babes, and the photographers yell the first names of their starry prey to get their shots. Sandra is a veteran of late-night chat-shows and has a sassy quip for every comer, blaséing her way along the press corridor with aplomb, fending the Madonna-mania questions coming at her.

'Who's the guy?' they shout.

'My co-star in the next big one from Bruce and the boys.'

It's only when I'm sent a picture of the two of us with Joel Silver that I realize JUST how dorkish I really felt, doodling along. There is no discernible dress-code, with everything from beach clothes and flip-flop sandals to Fredericks-of-Hollywood nightgear, and a stash of sequined matrons with big hair. Barrels of popcorn and Coke. And two cinemas to fill, for the A list and B list respectively, according to your colour-coded invitation. As the credits roll there is whooping and cheering and clapping and everyone is sixteen again. *Die Hard* we know, and we are grateful for what we are about to receive. Applause breaks out intermittently, and it's as if we have all been plugged into a high-voltage 'hit' circuit. The collective 'pulse' that bleeps through the on-screen mayhem is a rhetorical *How much is this goldmine going to nugget up?* It is the only time I have ever mingled among such a crowd of sure-fire thought. Joel says to us on the way in, 'This time next year, you watch, *Hawk* will be even bigger than this one.' Engulfed by this mega-hitmosphere, I am more than willing to entertain the idea.

Before the end-titles have rolled, before the lights have brightened, the stalls are ERUPTING. Human lava flows over the backs of seats, scrambling to get within reach of the volcanic epicentre of this HIT. Namely Messrs Willis and Silver Inc. Hands are clasped, cheeks kissed, tears mopped and it's like a revival meeting at Lourdes. Perhaps by *touching* the immortals you, too, will be blessed with fame and financial salvation. Popcorn is hurled in the air like confetti. Wherever you look, full sets of gleaming dentistry are on display. I meet the financial *and* physical 'muscle' of Tinseltown, in the persons of Mr Stallone and Mr Schwarzenegger, both of whom are taking turns to bear-hug Bruce. Both of whom are substantially shorter than six foot. Which surprises. Sandra demands we 'get outta here and over to the party before everything get's eaten up. I'm starved.' Which we do, escaping the hit 'hive'. On the way out we are given complimentary *party bags*, like you get when you leave a kid's birthday party, full of freebies, including a sweatshirt, monogrammed cap, video of *Die Hard* and assorted trinkets. The party is at Joel Silver's 'house' at the discreet residential end of Hollywood Boulevard. He is a collector of houses: those of architect Frank Lloyd Wright, and has invested huge amounts of both passion and greenbacks into restoring these 'sites'.

Our limo is one of the first to arrive and white-glove waved into position, our names checked against a guest-list, given walkie-talkie clearance, we trail up the candle-lit stairs hidden from the street below, and enter Mr Lloyd Wright's masterpiece.

Woody, warm, glowy and immaculate. Soft music, sashaying waiters with wooden leaf-shaped platters offering Thai canapés, and we are in the pages of *Architectural Digest*'s Celebrity Home feature, in 3D. Sandra and I shamelessly case the joint and marvel at the civilized splendours on display. All is restrained and symmetrically challenging, and before I get completely pseudoed up to my rafters, *one* question has lodged itself in my brain and will not budge: how does a man like Joel, who makes big noisy action-packed live 'cartoon' films, equate with this opposite order of things? These extremes see-saw through my head all night long. The house is crowded soon after and the beach-wear looks distinctly out of place among all that is so WRIGHT. Joel seems to enjoy my obvious astonishment and gives me a quick tour of his Obsession, pointing out where and how he has had everything restored.

'Jesus, Joel! This is the last kind of place I thought you'd be shacked up in. Forgive me if this sounds judgemental, but *nothing* could have prepared me for this.' He just laughs. He seems to revel in this 'contradiction', which is wholly endearing. Lest you think I have gone soft in the head, my terror of him remains intact. But seeing where and how he lives is like being a cocker spaniel standing within safe distance of a Rottweiler, who unexpectedly bellies up and woofs you into his architectural kennel for some Pedigree Chum.

I meet Bruce's mother, who is German and who married Mr Willis Snr when he was serving post-war duties in Deutschland. Another surprise, for Bruce seems so quintessentially American and fast with a quip. She is so immensely proud of him and quick to retrace the years when he was struggling, which remind me that all this gung-ho bravado is underpinned by years of anonymity.

'You ask a lotta questions.'

'I'm sorry.'

'No need. Most people in Hollywood only can talk about themselves or their careers'.

Susan Forristal breathlessly sidles up with wide eyes, and 'Can you believe this place! Soooooooooooo beautiful. But sooooooo full.' Susan the Ubiquitous. She truly does seem to be a walking Filofax and takes everyone for who they are, rather than who they might or could or should be – which translates into a fearlessness about speaking to *anyone*, regardless of whether they exude star status or are presently ranked professionally as *persona non grata*. By contrast, Sandra has invisible battle-lines drawn, delineating to whom she will, or will not, speak. The room is divided decisively into Winners and LOSERS, the latter filling her larger register.

'I gotta get outta here. This is too crazy. See you in Roma, baby. Ciao. Love you.' The possibility of a personality overload looms ahead. Sandra stalks her way clear of the crowd with the disdainful hauteur of a Roman empress. God forbid *her* thumbs-up or down should decree your gladiatorial fate . . .

Meet Danny Aiello, who plays Bruce's partner in crime, and blow some fan-smoke up his nethers about his great work in Spike Lee's film, *Do The Right Thing*. Danny talks A LOT. 'I'm an Italian, Rich! We like ta talk! What can I tell ya?' He has no problem finding something.

Followed by Demi Moore – 'YOU PRONOUNCE IT D'-MEE', she corrects my 'Dimi'. Her voice is extraordinarily deep.

'You sound like a ruptured carburettor,' which makes her laugh. She has those kind of bore-through-your-skull green eyes that kick-start male-hormone circulation from nought to sixty in a couple of seconds. 'Bruce and I loved *Withnail* and *Advertising*. Funny stuff. Have you met everyone?' She takes my arm and wields me round the throng. It is their big night and she is in no way obliged to hoick me around, but I am more than delighted to have her introduce me in her throaty vocals. Talk is not the usual, will-it-won't-it-be-a-hit? but how-big?-how-much?-how-soon?

I stagger out, stunned but sober, and am ferried back to my hotel. Where a tidy pile of message notes is waiting beside the phone. At home every ansaphone bleep registers someone else to deal with. Out here in LA I am grateful for the human connection, glad to have every remaining hour booked and appointed prior to the mid-afternoon flight home.

*

Real Life in between. A friend got married. Another friend died. Devastating. Lists and schedules and bookings for the summer. We have bought an ancient little pile in Provence and prepare for our first holiday there. I am contracted to *Hawk* for a total of twenty-two shooting days over three months. Plan to commute between Rome and Nice. Meet Kevin Reynolds, director of *Robin Hood: Prince of Thieves* the day before flying. EN FAMILLE EN FRANCE!

The first sign that something is awry is signalled by a phone-call from the Dwarf. 'Your start date in Rome has been delayed. Shooting in New York has not gone according to schedule so you're on hold for a week or so. Enjoy your holiday.' Nothing TOO unusual ... although it does seem very early on to fall behind.

31st July
Flight from Nice to Rome. Delayed by a day.

1st August
I take the two p.m. flight to Rome, then a taxi through the pouring rain and arrive at the Excelsior Hotel to discover that I am not booked in until 6th August. 'No, no, Signor, Mr Grant, he no arrive before sixth.'

'I am *he*!'

'No, no, not possible.'

'Si, si, Signor. Here is my itinerary, passport. Do you have a room?'

'Yes. But Mr Grant he no come till sixth.'

I have no Italian whatsoever, beside *stronzo* and reckon it's a bit early on in the proceedings to be flinging *shit* at anyone's fan. I decide to phone the Dwarf. However, this simple action is thwarted by the cashier's refusal to change foreign currency as I am not a registered guest. 'But I very soon *will* be a registered guest' (you MORON). He waves me off to where I might find a bank. I wander wave-ward to find that it is closed for the next couple of hours. And it is raining canines. Which may explain why the desk-bound little mother was smiling as I went looking. Why haven't I arrived with pocketfuls of lire coinage? Because I am usually handed an envelope of *per diem* as I hit *terra firma*. Forsake the nanny-mentality of being on a movie and let an independent thought torpedo through. *Reverse the charge! That's it. You can do it! You are already in your thirty-third year! For Chrissakes.*

Get the Dwarf who harrumphs and steams and yells for one of his minions to call New York. His tone is that of a man talking down someone preparing to jump off the Empire State. 'Hold on, we'll get this sorted. Don't move. Don't panic.' I get a room and locate Ms Bernhard, who is in the Hotel d'Inghilterra below the Spanish Steps. We arrange to have dinner with a director friend of hers and two jerks. No matter, because Sandra is firing on *all* cylinders. ENRAGED. Turns out she has been alone in Rome for more than three weeks to *bond* with the dog that is her constant companion in the movie and to practise some tennis-ball throwing and catching tricks with the four-legged one. She speaks no Italian, feels TOTALLY isolated and neglected, but, worst of all, DUPED. Why? She tells us, with bulging eyes and steaming nostrils: the pink-tracksuited Italian dog trainer and expert – 'EXPERT? MY ARSE!!!!!' – is merely the owner of the terrier and has convinced someone that he is a bona-fido *animal trainer for films*. Hence the high-tech tracksuit complete with whistles, zips, dog chain and cellular phone. The dog is supposed to be called Bunny, and Sandra has been Bunny-ing the mutt every training session and flinging balls about for two weeks. With no discernible result. Bunny is as recalcitrant as *she* was on day one. It now turns out that Bunny is *stone deaf.* Sandra is half-way between hysteria and throwing in the towel. She manages to be very funny and very serious at the same time and is clearly happy to have Friends, Romans, and her own Countrymen lending their ears to her BURIAL of Bunny AND Rome. Neither of which she is here to PRAISE. It's August. Every Italian has left town for the holidays and those who are left behind don't want to know. Only ten per cent of eateries are functioning and then at 'half-mast' with a skeleton staff. Packs of tourists hording about. Groups of Japanese Nikon-snappers scrutinizing pasta bowls and Roman ruins with the same apparently quizzical incomprehension. And it's lung-stoppingly hot and humid. I resolve to leave the Titanic Excelsior and move to the Inghilterra where there is some Life.

La Bernhard reveals that she was the only kosher-gal in her home town of Scottsdale, Arizona, and was persecuted with the nickname 'NIGGER-LIPS'. She is *totally* fearless about singing or saying what she thinks, and berates Romans in general and those in her immediate vicinity in particular for their rampant sexism. 'Can't you guys stop scratching your fucking balls for one second? Leave your cocks alone and give a girl some service round here. Jeeezus!' The all-purpose expression of disdain for Americanos flickers across a couple of faces and I suspect that our chances of getting a bowl of pasta will keep us slim. Once Sandra has bitten the bullet she's unstoppable. The little-girl remorse comes later. Mostly too late ever to dare venture back into the same restaurant. Her trials and tribulations make it feel as if I, too, have been in Rome for three weeks rather than a few hours.

2nd August

Eleven a.m. rehearsal call. Bruce and Joel *et al* have arrived and we are going through the dialogue and camera set-ups for the interior of a stretch-limousine scene to be shot tomorrow, circling the Colisseum. Hot as a hell-hole. Rome all gorgeously ruined and terracotta homogeny. A deep-purple 'fifty-six Chrysler saloon has been especially customized into a stretch and shipped over from New York for filming. Cream upholstery, electric windows, phone and fax machine and shredder. It's the setting for the first meeting between Hudson Hawk and Darwin Mayflower (my character). Lots of discussion and general farting about. One thesp (and there is always *one*) has taken it upon himself to act as interpreter between some of the American crew and the newly incorporating Italians in his pidgin lingo. He is a chain-smoking old guinea-fowl who finds his own stories windbagfully hilarious and is today's front runner for Bore of the Century. I clock him *en route* to rehearsal when he takes it upon himself to give me an uninvited guided tour of the ruins. Shut my eyes and think of Brutus, suspecting that Equity specializes in a whole sub-species of these farty-pants old reps, forever prodding the air with their cigarette holders.

Some mildly obscene comfort to be had from encountering him being *iced* by James Coburn in the makeup van. Coburn eyes him up, bares his *Magnificent Seven* fangs (familiar from childhood visits to the drive-in), and grunts some dismissal. With his voice, gallon-deep, and the requisite cigar jammed into the corner of his mouth, he is as Movie-Icon-Cool as it's possible to get. Only, his hands are arthritic and he explains that the agony of this disease has kept him from working these past few years. But he is in love with Paula, who is his constant companion and as charming and drop-dead-gorgeous as you'd expect of this cinematic gunslinger. Lassos the lot of us with his silvery-haired CHARM. Goddammit! Sandra has yet to meet him but has declared him her Rome-appointed HERO. 'Worship that man. Worship him!' – she DARES you to challenge her TOTAL CONVICTION! I never really thought of RAGE as being sexual but, as displayed by Sandra, it somehow seems to be: her frustration with the world is expressed in hyperventilating *statements*, and opinions are accompanied by flaring nostrils that *hiss* vixen-like at you. Like she might just DEVOUR you at any moment. Eyes bulging like Godzilla. Redeemed by laughter. She trips herself up with her extremism every now and again, and being with her is as close a return to the intensity of adolescence as you are likely to get. Her worship-filled passions are precisely fixed at sixteen. Or thereabouts! And the penalty of her 'alchemy' is the hovering possibility that you might be cast out AT ANY MOMENT. I am a willing lamb to her sacrificial style of friendship. For I have already 'heard' her bleating beneath her wolf's clothing. She *is* vulnerable despite the SPITE.

Bruce has two bodyguards in tow; ex-Israeli-Army-ites who shadow his every move, plus his own makeup/hair person, and a best friend from his New Jersey schooldays, who plays a small part and is involved with the production side in some way. Bruce is constantly quipping and 'gimme-five-brother'-ing about. I have no first-hand experience of the music business, but there is a distinct rock'n'roll flavour in his loose-limbed let's-get-it-oooon! attitude. Though Bruce is not the director, he has conceived and co-written the original story and has an untouchable King Midas aura about him, buoyed up by the box office bonanza of *Die Harder* which has taken more than a hundred million bucks in the USA alone. This is HIS movie and what he says goes. The campy, cartoonish style of the script demands a somewhat over-the-top attitude. 'Go out there, man,' encourages Bruce. 'Don't hold anything back.' I know what he means but also suss that the more ridiculous we all are, gooning around him, the more laid-back and cheeky-chappy he can be.

3rd August

Ring-road round the war memorial in the middle of the city. Camera crew are pissed off about the purple Chrysler as they claim that, while 'customized', it has not been designed to accommodate a crew PLUS actors. Worst of all, it has no air-conditioning. With lamps, windows closed for sound-recording, generator, cables and eight fully grown men all breathing in close proximity, things get VERY sticky VERY quickly. Hand fans, water, constant stop-starts, background problems with curious Roman motorists, ALL combine to cock things up. Bruce is demanding I go 'stark raving mental' despite my reluctant excuse that if I start this 'wigged-out' there will be nowhere left to go in my subsequent scenes of dementia. 'You can't be insane enough in this movie.' During a break, Michael Lehmann, the director, sidles up to the window and says to ignore this advice and to 'do less'.

By late afternoon our collective brains are scrambled in this four-wheeled microwave, and nothing seems capable of stemming the perspiration that is pouring down Bruce's face. They decide to loop his dialogue later (as I have most of the talking to do), open the windows and mop him up between short takes. Things get real speedy when news comes through that the private jet standing by to take

Bruce and Joel to Nice for the weekend has to leave by eight thirty p.m. As I do not work again for another week, Bruce and Joel generously offer me a free flight. Madonna is on tour in Nice and they want to go to see her. How Sandra will respond to this getaway plan might best be described in military terms: she'll go ballistic. Especially as Madonna is involved (about whom she is territorial), especially as she has now clocked up some weeks in Rome and not yet worked a day. Especially as she HATES being left out and can locate a thread of 'rejection' in a yard of welcomes. Joel says mid-flight that I am the best fake-Jew he has ever met! Which I take as a compliment. 'What drives you to wanna act?'

'REVENGE!'

This makes him laugh. 'Why?'

'To prove to all those little fuckers who said, "You can't, you'll never make it," that I could.'

'Me, too! It's the same for me!'

This is not the common ground I had anticipated sharing with Joel. Maybe *his* laughter is similarly surprised, for the kind of actors he usually works with are heroic avengers in perilous action epics, rather than skinny English nancy-poms. Have a sense that we are skirting around liking each other, despite operating on totally different tables. Yet the very instant he reveals his underbelly, the hatches come down. FAST. I am fascinated by this man, reputed to be ruthless, lethal, INSANE even. Hyper-charged boy-man is my experience of him. So far.

I do not generally get to fly around in private planes, and understand the true meaning of that old sixties epithet *jet-set* as we 'Ready, set, go!' through customs, security, unhindered. Speedy Gonzales. They are met by a waiting car and sped off to St Tropez for the night. I rent one, which takes almost as long to organize as the flight from Rome, and drive out of this high-octane speedway for a familial week in Provence where all this intensity recedes as fast as their tail-lights into the night . . . *'It's only a movie'* blips through my head.

8th August

Iraqi troops have invaded Kuwait. My lawn-mower has conked out. Bathetic. Call to fly back to Rome. Get there and am told that I'm not needed until Monday. Book a flight back to Nice for the morning. In the meantime go to dinner with Bruce, Joel, Sandra and the gang. No one goes about in pairs or trios but in a phalanx, invading a restaurant and ordering most of the menu. Bodyguards, friends, assistants, actors, babes, *tout le monde*. So while Saddam insanes his way into Kuwait, red-alerting Western troops to action, we hear the doodle-bug news that Marushka Dettmers is being 'replaced' and that the reason for Desperately Seeking Madonna was to ask if she would take over. Impossible as she is mid-tour. Followed by a run-down of all the possible alternatives, beginning with Joanne Whalley-Kilmer, and then a ruthless canter through the ladies of the Screen Actors Guild, a verbal casting couch. Have a farewell lunch with the French makeup man accompanying Ms Dettmers, with whom I worked on *Henry and June*. He's pissed off that he has lost a long gig. Fly out of this sticky 'ointment' till Sunday.

12th August

Ten thirty p.m. return to Rome. Everything shut. Sandra comes round and says she went to a party the night before at Bruce's villa. 'Not that I really wanted to go but I was desperate. In fact so fucking desperate I gave one of the guys a hand-job and do you know something, the fuck couldn't even come. What's worse, though, he never even touched me!! This place is just too fucking insane. I tell you, I am on a one-way outta here!'

If you are thinking this is a little intimate and out of order to write up, rest assured. Next day, Sandra turns this incident into a running cabaret, entertaining the entire crew with her *Hand-job's Tale* (which the recipient takes with surprising good humour). Then she *publishes* it in the form of a short 'poem' in her second collection, titled *Love Love Love*.

13th August

Mussolini's old headquarters, located in what remains of Benito's New Rome. As Sandra and I play Darwin and Minerva Mayflower, the world's most obnoxious couple, the Fascist architecture is deemed appropriate. Formal gardens, wide driveways, arched white skyscraper and enough steps leading up to it to stage a couple of Busby Berkeley extravaganzas. The Mayflowers are lunching on their first-floor terrace with the double-crossing Coburn. Messrs Willis and Aiello burst through and fling themselves over the balcony, land below, LIVE! and roll down the endless steps, still *fighting*. THIS IS A CARTOON.

Endless delays in setting up a long camera track down the steps to cover a page length of dialogue between Bruce and me. The white steps only increase the already soaring temperature. What might normally take three or four hours to complete ends up eating eleven. The problem is threefold: Bruce, Joel and Michael – all have differing ideas. As Bruce has conceived this whole story he reserves the right to rearrange the dialogue, add jokes, watch the playback of each take on the TV monitor, suggest different line readings, discuss the Art of Comedy, *all* of which takes time. Joel is especially concerned with the technically slow process by which everything operates here and is clearly ready to ram sticks of dynamite up any arse that seems to be slacking. Translation into Italian and back again takes time. The heat is such that if you move at anything like normal speed you are apt to dehydrate and keel over. The Dettmers' departure hasn't helped any, and the schedule is now seriously up the crock. With new bulletins printed daily. Michael is attempting to get his opinion heard and things feel uncomfortably on the boil. Joel's personal chef provides culinary relief in the sanctuary of his trailer, to which Sandra and I are invited. And for which we are extremely grateful. You can tell just how off-kilter things are today by the degree of vibration in Joel's leg. He is on the mobile phone to the States and his leg is jumping before he has even made the connection. Frustrated by the eight-hour time difference, he looks ready to levitate. 'WHAT THE FUCK IS FUCK-ING WRONG WITH THIS COUNTRY THAT IT SHOULD BE

EIGHT FUCKING HOURS AHEAD OF EVERYWHERE ELSE? ANSWER ME, YOU FUCK!' For one bone-shattering second I thought he was asking ME, his eyes just happening to flick my way for an instant. 'ANSWER! FUCK!' Someone picks up the phone and the wake-up call he gets is a CLASSIC. As in a five-act classical opera sung at full *Aida* pitch by Giuseppe Silver. ATOMIC. My fork has fixed mid-way to my mouth, my jaw is gaping and heart POUNDING lest this INFERNO redirect itself towards my pasta-filled chops. This is the Silver from which Legend is mined.

'YOU TELL THAT FUCKING DICKBRAIN TO STICK HER UP HIS AGEING ASSHOLE, YOU FUCKFACED WASP. THAT IF HE HAD ANY DECENCY HE WOULD HAVE RETURNED MY CALL INSTEAD OF ACTING LIKE HIS SHRIVELLED OLD DICK WAS ALREADY IN THE METROPOLITAN MUSEUM OF FUCKING! WE COULD HAVE HAD A DEAL. WE COULD HAVE DONE THE FUCKING DEAL. NO, YOU LISTEN TO ME. YOU GET ALL OF THIS? PROBLEM IS HE'S JUST TOO FUCKING OLD. YOU GOT THAT? FINE, FINE! FADE IT!' All of which hurtles out on one angry breath. As his finger stabs the *off* button he's already all sweetness and light, and I could swear he has hugely enjoyed this. Followed by pasta which he hoovers down with equal ferocity. Nothing he does is by half measure. I have never seen this kind of human explosion first hand, misguidedly believing it only really exists in Marvel comic books. But this is 'KA-POW, ZAAAAAP! SPLAT and KABOOOM!' for real. Lichtenstein brought to life. It provides the revelatory key of how to play Mr Mayflower, who is given to verbal eruptions. 'This could give you a heart-attack, Joel.'

'This is what prevents one,' he counters.

At the end of this forty-degree day, the German director of photography unleashes a full-frontal argument with the director at the base of the steps. German blames American for the endless delays. American counter-attacks, saying that this is not the time or the place. German is not to be quelled. Insults bazooka back and forth. Bruce muscles in and says, 'GET THE FUCK OUTTA HERE AND ARGUE SOMEWHERES ELSE,' as he's trying to get his reverse close-ups completed before wrap-time. Then he retreats. Joel charges forth and the three of them hiss and fizz round the back of a trailer, the protagonists emerging *all* purple of face for the remainder of the day. For once Sandra is rendered speechless, jaw dropped, lips twitching till finally, 'What is it with guys?' queries out. (The scene in question never made it to the Final Cut.) Meanwhile Danny Aiello is doing a one-man cabaret outside *his* trailer as he has been hanging around since six a.m. and has said not so much as a scripted line. Though he makes up for it by telling endless stories, one of which I intercept about a famed Broadway actress renowned for her legendary farting. Her trick being to bang one out just as she is exiting a scene, leaving hapless actors to stagger about the stench-filled stage trying not to laugh and/or gag. 'How does she do it? I'll tell you how she does it. The woman lives on a diet of Greek-vegetarian pulses 'n' all, with a little gastro-enteritis thrown in, is how she does it.' Danny has a habit of asking and answering his own questions.

Amid this furore stands Flint himself, James Coburn, as calm and collected as those car adverts for which he does the voiceovers. He and Paula take Sandra and me out for dinner and he talks us down from the hysteria of the day. 'This is a big budget movie, with big budget egos. Enjoy.' His smile widens a couple of toothy miles. Maybe it's to do with this day being the thirteenth? However, I know that when excuses run to superstition it's time for bed.

15th August

All Saints' Day in Rome – which, ironically, could be the theme tune for what is happening to us, as 'All (our) saints go marching ... home'. The German cinematographer and camera crew have left. As has the first assistant director. Today Dante Spinotti is taking over the photography, and Andie MacDowell flies in to save us all! 'Oh, when the saints ... go marching in ... oh, when the saints go marching in ...' Sandra's girlfriend also flies in and transforms the gal with some love. But theirs is one of those Campari-and-soda affairs, very bitter and very sweet by turns. During dinner she reveals that she is part of the LA Art circuit scene, chain-smokes (which

Sandra abhors), sports a fakish Italian accent (but comes from Cleveland), complains that her perfect figure is *fat,* and before dessert arrives is giving Sandra some Heavy Duty about what a huge sacrifice she has made to come here. Takes up her 'Devil's Residence' two doors along from me and begins seriously 'torturing' the all-too-vulnerable Ms B.

How do I know all this? Around midnight there is 'activity' in the corridor and a syncopation of slamming doors and lift-button buzzings. Silence. Then tapping at my door: Sandra – sobbing and swollen-eyed, resembling one of those Chinese bulldogs. The girl-friend has stomped off into the middle of the Roman night. 'She'll be back, you'll see,' dribbles lamely from my mouth, half-choked with her hair as she hugs and holds on to me, shaking, but finally finding her voice to condemn the demon as 'a fucking witch'! I give her a bit of the 'now-now' and suggest that if only *half* the off-screen dramas were to match what was on film we would all be home and dry. Unfortunately the mention of home at this juncture is less than fortunate, eliciting a fresh gale-force of wind and water. Sandra angry is one thing. Sandra vulnerable is something else. Tears are reservoir deep and, having experienced this side of her, I feel very protective when people dismiss her as just so much mouth.

16th August

All clear. The return of 'Miss Martell' in the early hours; this pseudonym is the result of her posing about like the dame in the Cognac advert. 'Miss Martell' reveals over breakfast (we are not working today) that rumour in LA has it that the *Hawk* budget has spiralled to forty-six million dollars. 'Which explains why so many executive suits have flown in,' surmises Sandra. 'To assess the mess.' At least *she* is cheerful, while Rome crumbles all around.

Get a formal offer to play the Sheriff of Nottingham in *Robin Hood: Prince of Thieves* today, it having been 'passed' by John Malkovich and then John Cleese. I have three weeks clear ahead, according to the present schedule, but know all too well how stable that is, even though the director of *Robin Hood* claims that things are 'flexible' and he could shoot all the Sheriff scenes in a batch. He needs a guarantee of five free days in October. I know that this is asking the impossible but go to Joel anyway. He says he will see what he can do. The chances of jig-sawing both is remote. Yet knowing I will almost certainly not be needed for filming on those days is frustrating. Dates dangle in the air, waiting to be shot. Or not. Welcome to my very own *A Midsummer's Nightmare*.

17th August
Cinecittà Studios. Joel Silver's office has been decorated with *faux* Roman frescoes and columns and drapes. It is the setting for a photo-shoot involving Mr and Mrs Mayflower and their psychotic butler in *sado-masochistic* poses and leather-wear. These pictures are to be a 'joke' for a later scene during which we are showing Hudson Hawk slides of our goldmaking activities, which have been inadvertently mixed up with scenes of our proclivities. Standing about in 'Vargas-girl' high heels, crotchless leather panties, brassière, stockings and lipstick, like a lost member of some touring *Rocky Horror Show* is the *exact* moment that I know – beyond all reasonable doubt – THAT THIS MOVIE IS A ONE-WAY TICKET OUT OF MY MIND.

Fly to France. Fortnight free to wait . . .

12th September
Despite a flurry of phonings back and forth, I've had to bow out of my chance to do Sheriff duty opposite Mr Costner.

Fly to Milan. Picked up and driven to Rimini on the coast. Grand Hotel di Rimini. Corner suite overlooking the sea in this art-nouveau hotel, all fin-de-siècle and *Death in Venice*-ish. End of the season. None of the film unit about. They're shooting at some castle location an hour's drive away. Pink-mauve sky hushing into night. Sit atop my bed, lonely as a cloud, Wordsworthing up some diary while all is still and calm. You can hear the water below lapping along the endless stretch of very flat beach. Now you can see the transvestites flashing passing motorists along the esplanade. Mosey down into the marbled, bepalmed lobby and unexpectedly meet Demi, baby and nanny, who ask why my little tot is not around. Demi as direct, warm and funny as when we first met and coping with the all-too-familiar syndrome of being separated from her husband for long stretches by work. We joke about the tabloid EXCLUSIVE PICTURES of Bruce kissing Andie MacDowell and the accompanying SCOOP that it was Demi who said about Ms Dettmers, 'Either she goes or I go.' All of which is so much hog, as she has never even met Marushka, and this is her first visit to the set since we started seven weeks ago. The EXCLUSIVE kiss pics, taken with a telescopic lens, suggest some clandestine clinch. If the lens had not been so EXCLUSIVE in its focus, it would have revealed a wider view that included about seventy-five technicians and camera crew in the immediate vicinity. 'Happens all the time. Part of the deal.'

'Doesn't it drive you nuts?'

'Since the day we got married they've been printing stuff that we're on the brink of breaking up. The hard part is for our families, 'cos we have to phone around and reassure them that it's all bullshit. Hard for them when the stuff is on every newsstand and people keep asking.' Andie MacDowell and her husband and two little ones are also here and this influx of family induces instant home-sickness. Especially being at the seaside. When the crew returns, everyone is invited to go out and eat in one huge party. Bruce is transformed and exceptionally cheerful to have his family here. Being in a new town and all staying in the same hotel makes for a much more cohesive atmosphere. However, the schedule is like a veritable Hydra: every time a day is lopped off here or there, two others seem to grow back in its place and we are now seriously behind. There are rewrites. New pages, new schedules. The script resembles a Crayola colour chart as every amendment is committed in a different hue. Not that this is unusual. It's just that this film has more than I have ever seen before. My death-scene in the original version involved a fight between Bruce and me in the back of the purple limousine, ending in stand-up fisticuffs through the sunroof. This reveals that the car is hurtling down the interior corridors of the Kremlin before it crashes into a vast statue of Lenin, which topples forward, resulting in the decapitation of Darwin Mayflower by Vladimir Ilyich himself. Hence the plan to shoot the last part of the film in Budapest, which would stand in for Moscow, but be cheaper and closer. For a variety of reasons, all of this has been kiboshed and the finale rewritten to take place atop the Mayflower castle in Italy. Hence Rimini (the closest big town to the location). But the seriously insane news is that we are *still* scheduled to go to Budapest, to shoot ITALIAN interiors inside a HUNGARIAN studio owned by a producer living in LOS ANGELES. This seems like the logic of a deranged baboon, but I know that everything is dictated by the dollar and as I have never understood even elementary mathematics, I surrender my sceptical self to the coming derailment. An assistant asks why I am here already as I am not due to work until Friday. That *LA Story* producer's advice flickers through my brain as I ponder the possibilities of going body-building to ease my frustration, or to opt for sitting on my shanks to read *One Hundred Years of Solitude.* I attempt to console myself with the thought that this weekend, *Henry and June* is screening at the Venice Film Festival, and Universal Pictures have offered my wife and I a weekend at the Cipriani Hotel to attend the festivities. Schedule permitting . . .

The schedule has switched to night-shooting, meaning you leave for work late afternoon, drive to the location in San Limo – the castle perched on a lone tooth of rock – which takes close on an hour to reach, rehearse, set up and eventually start, finishing as dawn breaks. Back to Rimini, and then try to sleep during the noisy day until you're due to leave again. Whichever way you try to do it, night-shooting is a guaranteed strain for everyone. Exhaustion takes hold and tempers shred FAST. By midnight on Saturday the mainly Italian crew are mutinous with fatigue and anti-American sentiment. The much touted 'chemistry' between Hawk and his sidekick, played by Mr Aiello, is suffering industrial fatigue.

As the film now climaxes in this castle setting, there are stunts to shoot, fights to stage and the purple Chrysler to be detonated, all of which are to be filmed outdoors, all at night, and all will be bitterly cold. A second camera unit is added to the already large crew, crowded in and around this medieval fortress built on this finger into the sky. They do not get round to my 'scene' and I'm released at midnight. Suzanne Todd and David Willis kindly offer me a lift to Venice and, with Joel's approval, I set off for the 'sinking city'. The fog is that SOLID. What should be a two-hour journey turns into four red-eyed hours before we get a taxi boat to this fabled place for which we are fleeced an Arabian night's worth of treasure. My wife is surprised to see me bleary-in before dawn. 'You must be mad.'

'INSANE.' At breakfast she tells me about the screening of the film the night before, and that she'd met the other members of the cast. 'How did it go down?'

'Down.'

'Oh, shit.'

'I'm afraid so.'

Meet the gang, stroll through the streets, float along the water and leave six hours later. Depressed. Back to Rimini, nightshoot-shocked.

With the latest rewrite, the Hawk–Mayflower confrontation in the purple Chrysler has been altered. It's now a 'semi-finale' involving a fight between Danny Aiello and me. The actual finale where I get my comeuppance (electrocution and immolation in molten gold) takes place in the Gold Room inside the Italian castle. However, the Gold Room set is under construction in a studio somewhere in *Hungary*. Go figure.

The second camera unit, directed by stunt supremo Charlie Picerni, is assigned to cover this new fight, which starts rehearsals at around three a.m. We are all semi-catatonic by now. Without our actual director, Danny takes the opportunity to exercise some directorial muscle. With the result that what seemed on paper to be a simple punch-up and scrap-in-a-car scene has ballooned into an Orson Wellesian epic of motivation and varied possibilities. Added to which, the butler, driving the car, with no dialogue to speak, 'motors' in with a ten-minute monologue about what kind of look he should be giving in the rear-view mirror while Danny and I cosh each other on the back seat.

It is now four a.m. Mr Picerni is under severe pressure to get the scene done before daybreak. 'You're driving the limo, it's pitch dark in here, chances are we ain't gonna see your eyes at all, the scene is to do with these two guys fightin' in the back, we gotta get this fuckin' thing in the can before Joel comes down and busts our asses and before the fuckin' sun hits those hills. LET'S DO IT!' Pronto-presto, head punches are choreographed with Danny thumping just past each of my ears, me jerking my head left to right, the camera wedged close behind and at an angle to give the illusion that I'm having my brains pounded out. After which I manage somehow to hurl myself out of the car as it careers over the mountainside with Danny and the butler inside it. This fight takes place in a stationary position, the movement simulated by out-of-shot crew members rocking the car. I am now awestruck by the patience required to complete an action sequence that will last seconds on screen but which requires multiple angles and shots so that it can be edited to look fast. No sooner is this completed than a stunt double has to leap out of the runaway vehicle and roll away to safety. How anyone willingly attempts this brave madness for a living is beyond my wildest terrors. The common complaint from the stunt guys is having to hear actors boasting on chat-shows about how they do all their own stunts. They point out that the insurers will not allow them to do stunts even if they are able to – the cost of schedule delays from injury would be prohibitively high. Everyone is out to watch the car double going over the clifftop and being detonated by remote control. Multiple cameras cover to make sure this one-off stunt is captured on film. It also means the death of the Aiello character, as he is trapped inside the car – but not before my character taunts him on the car phone for one last demonic cackling: 'Arrivederci!'

However, the prospect of not being around for the Happy Ending has set Danny a-thinking and a-scheming. Just how his character could possibly survive an exploding limousine plunging over a cliff would defy most logicians. But hey! This is a movie. ANTHING CAN HAPPEN. And happen it does. Danny has concocted a plot-line in which his character is secretly kitted out with a hidden parachute, the idea being that once he has said his goodbyes on the phone to me, he will fling himself out of the by-now-airbound vehicle, pull his parachute cord and land safely down below in them there old Tuscan hills. I assume this proposal is a joke. The ramblings of any actor who might have become deranged by the experience of an endless shoot and being far away from home 'n' all. But, clearly, he has given this a lot of thought and actually succeeds in getting this 'suggestion' legitimized. Ditto a new green page added to the Crayola script. Having escaped the nuked-limo-inferno, we next see him astride a donkey, joining the hero and heroine for one last cappuccino before the credits roll. My jaw is now well oiled and accustomed to the drop-and-retrieval motion it regularly enjoys – like a marionette mouth.

Come the Big Day comes the Blow Out. Which goes something like this ... Our protagonist emerges from makeup and wardrobe with appropriately post-car-explosion smoking clothes and black-patched-face ready to mount the unsuspecting Donk. However, Danny's hairdo is still, as the Italian hairdresser would say, 'Rossano Brazzi' (fully blow-waved and set). Joel, upon seeing this 'oversight', marauds into the makeup trailer to berate the ladies therein for not giving him the Electrified Topsy look, in keeping with the rest of the post-explosion apparition. It transpires that Danny feels this would be Over the Top. At which point, the last vestiges of sanity surely take flight. Discussion ensues between director, producer and star and, within a short overture's worth, La Scala's fiercest notes are screaming through the air, culminating in a command that HAIR MUST BE MUSSED. This causes something to short-circuit below the 'Rossano Brazzi' and Danny is OFF and SCREAMING. 'INTEGRITY' bobs up and down among the flotsam and jetsam of his tirade. NOBODY has the right to challenge his hair decision. This is surely the result of many weeks' frustration and instead of punching live flesh, a lighting truck is preferred for the actual 'fisting'. First aid and bandaging follow, as does remorse and follicular 'compromise'. (Half a 'Brazzi'.)

His wife has arrived for a visit and leans over a lobby armchair whispering that 'Danny has always been funny-like about his hair. In all the years we've been married, it's the one area that is outta bounds.'

As it is not the last day of shooting, there is the pasta-strangling reality of having to carry on filming. Whereas I would doubtlessly require Full Institutionalization in such circumstances, Danny is made of sterner stuff and within no time, his good humour and equilibrium restored, he has transformed this débâcle into an 'epicdote' worthy of a guest-spot in Vegas. In the retelling, he punches the air with both fisticuff and guffaw.

Despite Rimini's reputation as the resort where Fellini grew up and to which he returned for his nostalgic *Amarcord*, it is with night-shot relief that I leave for London.

17th September
Fly back to Rome to the aptly titled Minerva Holiday Inn, as the d'Inghilterra is full till next week. Cooler than August! But only just.

News arrives that the Budapest schedule has been delayed until the end of the month as there is still so much to complete in Rome. I'm taken to Cinecittà Studios to find that I am not required until tomorrow. Ho and hum back to the Hotty. Messages from Sandra. The kind you might normally expect to find in a bottle washed up somewhere remote, the bleep for *help* long dead. But these have a terrible insistency. What now? Quo vadis? Before I have had a chance to unpack and call up, she's on the blower. And *how*. Hysterical! Ready for the little-white-coat brigade and in dire need of 'the comfort of *any* strangers'. Turns out her New York agent is still quivering from the 'explosives' detonated in his ears by Joel Silver. 'WHY?'

'Why? 'Cos he got to hear stuff I'd said about the movie in LA these past three weeks and he's threatened to fire my lily-white gay ass.'

I rally round fast to her hotel and it's a scene straight out of *Valley of the Dolls*. She has lost nine pounds since the departure of Miss Martell and looks distinctly stick-insectish. She gives a garbled replay of her agent's version of events: 'You tell that effing Bernhard bitch she can go fuck herself and I will fire her if she says another word about this movie while it's still shooting and who the fuck does she fucking think she is?' Having witnessed the Silver-Express first-hand, there is no denying the gravitas of this info impacting itself like so much dry ice around her. Her having been Court Jester before, and returning to this Jacobean Court in disgrace, is going to require *some* shuffling. Stranded in the middle of her bed and giving old Vesuvius some heavy competition in the lava-flow of things, she vainly tries to deny that her mouth has got the better of her these past free weeks. But mid-whimper there is grudging acknowledgement that she has not been as discreet as she might have been.

Strategy: her first big scene is tomorrow. 'How can I work, honey, when I look like shit, feel like shit and am gonna get treated like shit, by that shit?' This *is* a *problemo*. I suggest she call Suzanne Todd to establish the extent of the damage. She does and has her worst fears confirmed: YES, Joel is LEVITATING. Back to the middle of the bed 'n' blub. Inevitably a dose of the paras creeps up my guts at the prospect of Silver-plating due to my close proximity to the perpetrator. 'Abject apology required. No real alternative,' is what trips somewhat lamely from my mouth. *This is a fucking all-time nightmare!* Agree to meet for Damage Limitation dinner later with Lorraine Toussaint, who is playing one of the candy-bar-named 'flunkies' in the film. Sit about like Chekhov's Three Sisters, feeling spectacularly depressed.

On my way to bed I run into the twin Martin brothers, playing another set of goombahs, who have just got back from a four-week break in LA and are chock-full of the latest industry revelations and rumours about the runaway budget and goings-on. Two rumours defy belief, the first being that a first-class plane seat was booked to send over fresh chocolates, the second one, worthy of Hedda Hopper on hashish, is that the George Lucas special effects team at Industrial Light and Magic had been specially commissioned to paint in more hair optically for Bruce in a scene where the back-lighting was too strong! Terrible sink-gut at hearing all this as we still have a long way to go, and the time committed charges up your sense of loyalty to the project, *despite* the general craziness. They conclude their duet of doom with 'The word on the street is baaaad' – like we were in some schlocky episode of *Dick Tracy*.

Just when I think it is safe to go back into my hotel room, lo and behold if there is not a large envelope stuffed with faxes. Reviews of *Henry and June* from the States. All bad. All in opposition to my enjoyment of seeing it for the first time. All annoyed because the film is NOT what they wanted it to be – *The Henry Miller Story*. None really acknowledge that it is all seen through the romantic and self-conscious eyes of Anaïs Nin, rather than the raw and ribald Miller. This has not been a good day! All the news has been BAAAAD – first-hand, rumoured and faxed. Giving the ceiling some scrutiny, having channel-flicked to no avail, it is hard *not* to wonder just what horrors await the actual release of *this* flick. 'It's only a movie' does not do the required right now and I feel as nailed to the wall as the all-purpose Hunting Prints affixed around my room. Who do they think would *want* to steal *these* fuckers? I swear I can TASTE this box-office poison and resolve to look into the possibilities of retreating to Africa to brew some pineapple beer at a farm stall . . .

The 'conference scenes' with Sandra have been delayed till Thursday. I am called out of my pen for reshoots on the car-fight scene with Danny and the second unit at Cinecittà Studios. At this point I don't even ask why, and when told, instantly forget anyway. One of *those* days.

8th October
Sandra does some Prostration and Bandage work on Joel.

11th October
My dad died nine years ago today at the age of fifty-one. We buried him in the mountain-top cemetery in Mbabane, down in Swaz, with a view of the Ezulweni Valley, meaning Valley of Heaven. Which it is. Our house, on the adjacent hilltop, has the same sweeping panorama that stretches for forty miles. To the right runs a mountain escarp-

ment that 'ends' with Sheba's Breasts (named after the fabled treasures of *King Solomon's Mines*), and they do look like a mountain version of a fifties pointy brassière, aimed at the sky. In the far distance, the hills are hazy-bluey and there is not a day that goes by that I do not think of this place and always travel with a six-picture stick-together-blow-up of it. Expecially today. My father had been Minister of Education during the English colonial jurisdiction of Swaziland until Independence in 1968 after which he was made an honorary adviser. He resigned, and went into management. Swaziland, nicknamed the 'Switzerland of Africa' on account of relative economic stability, was a single tribe population and single language status. No horror stories here of inter-tribal war, starvation, drought or despotics that have so blighted other countries on this continent. However, when he contracted cancer, much of his looking back was riddled with self-doubt about his not having contributed anything of lasting value to the country, and he concluded that perhaps *any* white man in Africa is inherently a paradox. His funeral proved otherwise. I wish he could have been there! It would have delighted him and made him proud.

His grave was dug on the slope of the mountain, with the best view, among people he knew, all of whom had lived much longer than he had. As he resolutely refused *any* religiosity in his life, there was no church service although an Irish priest he had known offered a blessing and a short reading from the Good Book. My father was fluent in Siswati and honoured with a Swazi name, Mathlaganipani, which translates as the 'man whose thoughts ran faster than his feet'. All doubts about his relationship with the Swazi people he had known, befriended and worked with were laid to rest, for as far as you could see there were crowds of Swazis, interspersed with the remnants of the Colonial Old Guard, all here to pay their last respects. This is what undid me almost more than anything else on that quite extraordinary morning. A brilliantly clear-skied day and a location that felt like being on the top of the world.

At eleven a.m. his coffin was already six feet below in the as-yet-unfilled grave. Pat Forsyth-Thompson gave an oration that charted his life, and managed to be both funny and profound, which was followed by an address from a young Swazi priest, fresh from an Evangelical course in the USA. (His father, Dr Gumedze, had succeeded my father as Minister of Education. His son was my contemporary at school.) What happened next was Monty-Python-meets-Joe-Orton. After an incredibly emotive speech, the Swazi priest suddenly leapt down into the grave, on top of the casket, and began to unscrew the bolts, while chanting in a near trance-like state that he was 'GOING TO RAAAAAISE THE DEAD. I AM GOING TO RAAAAAAAISE THE DEAD.' This caused somewhat stupefied pandemonium to shock-wave through the crowds. Nobody knew what the hell to do. My stepmother staggered sideways. People crammed forwards and, within no time, he had the lid off and was commanding and beseeching that his faith and power resurrect my dad. A terrible curiosity forced my eyes to look below and see what I did not want to see. And what I saw was the near-skeletal remnant of my pater, waxen and 'gone' – as unlikely a candidate for Resurrection as ever there was. After I don't know how long, young Gumedze, now weeping and wailing uncontrollably, gave up his evangelical quest for a miracle, and had to be helped out of the hole and consoled for what he felt was his 'failure of Faith'.

At that moment I knew just how much I was always going to miss my father, for it was exactly the kind of idiosyncratic event that made life in Swaz that bit different from anywhere else. It would have made him laugh. As it made me laugh then and as it still does, if somewhat ruefully ... today. I couldn't bring myself to scatter soil or lift a spade. Or even weep. That came later. We had what would in other circumstances have been a Garden Party, now a Funeral Lunch full of apology and 'could you believe it?' exclaimed all over the place, which amused more than it hurt. It was only while sitting, reading through the cards, that I was undone. Not so much by any of the effusive, retrospective canterings down Memory Lane but by a crumpled scrap of paper, written in a barely legible hand that simply stated: 'GOODBYE BABA "MATHLAGANIPANI" – DON'T FORGET US.' This inversion of the usual 'We will never forget you' pinpointed exactly the feeling of having been left behind among the Living. Death somehow given the aspect of a destination to which we were denied entry. Six months later I left for England, my past quite literally Another Country. I discovered this scrap in my diary, nine years later in Rome. Everyone told me that 'Time heals everything'. It doesn't. Just goes numb.

I am grateful for the elixir of work on this anniversary day. Finally a proper scene to get the gnashers out for. To Cinecittà Studios, where once Fellini reigned omnipotent. Today it appears run down and the visible remains of Terry Gilliam's extravagant sets for *Baron Munchausen* compound this image. Within a huge soundstage, they have built a monumental conference room that feels like it belongs in *Diamonds are Forever* or *You Only Live Twice*. As it is the Mayflowers' headquarters, the table is a vast three-dimensional 'M'. Everything goes just tickety-smoochy and the atmos. is relaxed and productive. Joel, Bruce and Michael give their approbation by saying every now and again, 'You two are funny,' as if mildly surprised by this discovery.

What takes time is getting Bunny to perform. The pink-tracksuited Dog Expert is forever blowing his little whistle and prancing about, trying to get the wretched canine to follow instructions. Which seem quite simple: to run off and retrieve a yellow tennis ball thrown by Sandra. After much coochy-cooing in Italian and many trial runs with the pooch, he does his best to assure us that the dog is now Primed for Action. Convincingly. His trepidation, fuelled by Sandra's total disdain for *anything* he suggests, manifests itself in his twitching forehead, while the sweat circles around his armpits increase their diameter by the minute and threaten to flood when 'ACTION' is called and the dog is expected to fetch the ball. Something quite ridiculous about seeing nigh on a hundred adults, lights, camera and ACTION concentrated on the activities of a four-legged creature. I need hardly tell you that Bunny clearly feels the pressure of this moment and upon hearing 'ACTION' bolts for the nearest exit.

Roman scrum as *everyone* scoots after him. Once traced and reset for further starting orders, it does everything but what it is supposed to do, at one point chasing its tail round and round. I know the feeling. Finally Joel bawls something to the effect of, 'LEAVE THE FUCKING THING FOR LATER. SECOND UNIT. WHATEVER. CAN'T WASTE ANY MORE FUCKING TIME SHOOTING THIS FUCKING THING.' All of which exonerates Sandra's continued gripe about the pooch. A dog possessed.

Playing someone richer than Messrs Willis and Silver and carrying on as though I own the universe is unavoidably underlined as mere ACTING when in the company of two REAL mega-rich men, who have the confidence and outward bravura of cosmic buccaneers. Attempting to act Mayflower-power in their company gets panic a-pacing my arteries and I can feel my reserves of MANIC being sorely stretched. In fact it is the one thing they openly admire as, like a performing poodle, I get up on *my* hindlegs and prance about, suggesting that I conduct some of my speech stomping on top of the M desk. 'GO FOR IT!' they encourage.

When I get back to the hotel I can't escape the nag that it all feels too close to the kind of high-school-play set up in which any insane suggestion is instantly cheered and endorsed. Except that this *isn't* school. And everything, including new jokes and suggestions, translates into schedule delays and big bucks burning fast. The whiff of budgetary hysteria is ever present. What would surely induce a coronary in any other man seems to FIRE JOEL UP. Unless I am not reading his signs right. He *challenges* the executive panic with the bravado of a seasoned gladiator. After he'd had one particularly heavy brawl down the phone, I happened to be in his flightpath and was slipstreamed off to an ice-cream parlour with him and Suzanne, his assistant, in tow. He does something I have always fantasized about doing, which is to order EVERY SINGLE ICE-CREAM CONCOC-TION ON THE MENU. 'Don't bother to choose something, I've ordered the lot.' My disbelief is exactly matched by the waiter's. He wrongly assumes his smattering of English has failed him until Joel stabs his finger at each and every little drawing of what is on offer and has the chap RUNNING to the sorbets. Our table of three is STACKED with every variation of banana-split and sundae while Joel scoops and tastes each glass like a man condemned. This binge cools him down and I sorely wish the script went half-way to capturing this sort of FRENZY. For he is simultaneously frightening and very funny and, above all, FAST. Which has a hypnotic effect.

Late-night argument on the phone with Joan. One of those thermo-nuclear domestic explosions that are as much to do with exhaustion as anything else, for a few days later neither of us can recall what it was about. Maybe some heated argy-bargy is the substitute for denied conjugals caused by being apart for so long. Problem, though: on your own, far from home, the instant eye-to-eye patch-up potential is lost and you have to cope with different time zones and hotel operators that formalize and intrude upon the battle. What I really mean is that when Joan has slammed down the phone, thought better of it and redialled, she is forced to decelerate mid-rant by having to ask the operator politely for my room. This has been known to cause Apollo 10 jet-thrust towards marital meltdown. But, then, it *is* Friday night. She is at home in London with baba, at the end of a hectic working week, and hearing my travails about where and with whom I am having dinner *does not* have the same 'cachet' as *her* night in. The possessive conundrum of wanting your 'other' to be watered and tended but somehow hoping this can happen in 'solitary'. For any socializing merely underlines that you are leading separate lives, held together by phone lines.

The weekend exodus is upon us again. Bruce has gone via Paris to catch the Concorde to New York. Joel has gone to Paris and suggested that Sandra and I come too as 'Madonna is going to be there and we can all hang out.' 'Are you paying, Joel?' asks Sandra. 'Are you kidding me?' retorts Joel. This challenge for a freebie floors my politesse, especially as it seems that only a couple of minutes back Sandra was in a state of palpitating prostration before Joel.

'No harm in trying,' is her response to my slack-jawed gape. 'Gotta hustle, honey. It's the only thing they understand.'

All this travel flurry creates a kind of mild panic, making you feel left out of the club if you're not bound for somewhere, *anywhere*, other than old Roma. Two days in this circumstance have a way of suddenly LOOMING up at you, like a couple of months in solitary. At this desperate juncture Sharon Stone – 'Shaz', as she was instantly nicknamed – blonded her way into our orbit. She is here working on a thriller flick with a title like *Moving Target* or maybe it's *On the Run*, whatever, and is an old friend of Joel's. Turns out her plan to fly to Paris with him has been aborted at the last minute so she, too, is at a loose end. She is incredibly stylish and sophisticated in a somewhat self-conscious way, as if she has watched a catalogue of Grace Kelly movies a little too closely. Voice sounds all the time as though she has a slight cold. Sandra and I meet her in her rented apartment before going out to find some lunch. It's as hot today as the stage directions of any Tennessee Williams play, which provokes Shaz to beg our patience while she finds 'something else' to slip into. Sandra is on to this tactic FAST. 'Dame wants an audience, for Chrissakes!' I dismiss this uncharitable thought, momentarily, until Shaz slinks back in like a cat on her own tin roof, sporting something purry and pouts the question, 'What do you think?' To which Sandra unceremoniously replies, 'I think I'm starving. Let's get outta here.' Which we do. Only, our timing is all up the jacksie and it's nearly three p.m. by the time we hit the restaurant trail. Near the Pantheon we attempt to lasso the attention of the about-to-close restaurateur. Sandra motors in first and her protestations of febrile hunger are met with a tut-tut no-no. With an 'Oh, fuck,' she slopes round and says, 'So what do we do now?'

'*Watch this*,' says Shaz, with the winky glint of a seasoned assassin. And in she swishes to lay on her 'deadlies'. Sandra is not easily impressed and says we're wasting our time. No sooner has she uttered than Shaz emerges with the beguiled and smiling proprietor in tow, who is now concave at the prospect of cooking us up *anything* we desire. She is bristling with her triumph, but manages an air of *sangfroid* Kelly-cool, as she fingers her way down the menu, then flutters an eyelash or two upward to the mesmerized male before giving her order, which he scribbles down without taking his eyes off her. An ancient ritual worthy of David Attenborough's documentary scrutiny. Eyes down to 'us' for the *coup de grâce* of 'What'll you have?'

From here on outward, and into various shops, we are in her control. And we are her perfect audience, going with every whim and flow of her fancy, including visits to her favourite stores. This may sound innocent and ordinary enough, but the Lady has an Agenda. And the Hitchcockian connection is not entirely fanciful. For now we are being guided into a cut-glass and cutlery joint that is for the seriously loaded, one of those stores where you practically need to be finger-printed to get through the bullet-proof glass doors. Not that big an ordeal, once you're used to the vacant stare of the human wardrobe guarding the exit, and we're truly grateful for the arctic air-conditioned relief from the swelter outside. We gaze like Method devotees at the sparkling shelves of priceless glass, while Shaz works the grizzled old nanny goat who presides over all this luxe. She, being a crêpey ancient no-neck, sniffing out our collective credit-entials. I twig that Shaz has cased this joint beforehand and is trowelling on the charm about her movie work in Rome and how she has to try to make a choice about which dinner service she wants. So convincing is her spiel, especially when she seeks my opinion about which handles and style I would choose, that I am lockjawed when I finally hear her say that she will be back ere long to make her final choice and intones, 'Hey, guys, let's get outta here.' It's *all* a game and she delights in playing it, with us as innocent punters along for the ride. Next we are in a leather shop and she is trying on coats and sashaying up and down before the mirror, and the assistants are quietly preparing themselves for a big commission, such is the conviction of her shopping technique. Having exhausted their repertoire we leave yet again, empty-handed.

'Would you wear fur?' I ask.

'Of course. Don't give me that animal rights crap. Mink is farmed just like leather.'

Now it's an interior design emporium and Sandra is starting to lose it. Shaz yodels about a large terracotta column-top that she thinks would be perfect in her dining room with a glass table top, 'and some foldaway black canvas director-chairs'. No doubt covered in the just-seen cutlery and cut glass. She is now enquiring of the owner how much and would it be possible to ship this loot to California? The afternoon is passing by like some bizarre rehearsal for superstardom and I suppose this must be the hidden engine. Along the way I ask whether she has had an affair with Joel. To which she demurs, but says that she likes a 'cuddly producer'. Our final pit-stop is the Versace store, where she is now choosing jackets for *me* to try on, for all the world as if we were old marrieds. 'So good for your eyes, this suit. Perfect match. You must have it.' It is with some hot-flushy discomfort that I escape the store without being fleeced or forced into clothes I have no intention of buying. This form of 'shopping-foreplay' is something in which she clearly revels and is amused at my incredulity that it is something to do to while away the time. Of course, I could have refused, but such is the sheerness of her 'slithe and tove', that before I know it I am poncing about in clothes in shops that I do not generally frequent. Sandra is not so easily taken in but as she says later, 'What the hell? Had nothing better to do anyway.' Like a scene from *Chinatown*, Shaz tells us the 'story' of how she got to have a substantial scar slashed around her neck. I say 'story' because of the way she told it. It is true, I'm sure, but in the recounting of it she again appropriated that Chandler-blonde-fatale persona that left me feeling suspiciously as if I was in a scene. (By the end of the week three versions of 'The Scar' were going around, as gleaned from various sources. Rather than challenging her on any of this, I enjoy this 'on location' mystery, happy for the diversion.)

15th October
Cinecittà Studios. Second Conference Room Scene. After the energetics and work satisfaction of Friday, today is all torpor. All activity has been torpedoed by the absence of Bruce, who is still in New York. We shoot *around* where he should be. The scene is parcelled up into a variety of bad options. We do the dialogue to a 'double'.

Cruise into Joel's office at lunch-time to borrow *Variety* newspaper.

(Sandra and I are keeping tabs on all the films-in-production listings and a run down of who *is* working around the globe and who isn't.) Seeing our own names listed is the level to which we are now stooping for reassurance. Of *any* kind. Like kids staring at their first school nametapes, and nodding in silence. Mmmmmm, yes, I DO EXIST. HERE IS MY NAME. Which aptly prepares me for the headmasterly bombshell that detonates in my face.

Joel says, 'Come in, come in. *So I hear you were asking what it's like to fuck a fat old Jew?*'

My knees go first, followed by the rest, slumping fast into the sofa. Eyes dead ahead. Ears ringing. Nervous system approaching meltdown. One word dries out of my mouth: 'SHAZ?'

I don't know if he says yeah or you betcha or what, because I am retracing my afternoon with Shaz at *Road Runner* speed, coming to a standstill at *Have you had an affair with Joel?*, which are the words that come trotting out of me, as past and present simultaneously combust. He starts laughing, and says not to take it so seriously.

'ARE YOU KIDDING? I asked if she had had an affair with you. Not "fucked a fat old Jew".'

'I *am* a fat old Jew,' he roared. 'She's history. Over and outta here.'

I never spoke to Shaz again. I also wonder whether these were her actual words, or whether Joel was giving me a dose of the *fear*, knowing I would nuke on cue?

We all troop into a screening of *Pacific Heights* that night, courtesy of the distribution company, but I am in no fit state to be affected by celluloid scaries, having collided with the Real Thing at lunch.

Bruce is back. We shoot all his coverage and reshoot some of the already shot stuff to suit.

17th October
Cinecittà Studios for the Rutherfords Auction House sequence. This is supposedly in New York and features all the main characters bidding for equine antiquities. Bernhard and I attempt to outbid each other before making a hasty exit, after which the auctioneer explodes, followed by the entire room. All the usual delays and tediosity

involved in rigging falling columns, explosions and non-English-speaking extras, plus the wretched Bunny and its human 'trainer'. About as close to incarceration in an Italian lunatic asylum as you're likely to get. For two days.

23rd October
Last day at Cinecittà. The usual HURRY UP! and wait all day while explosions don't happen and I count myself lucky that I wasn't in *The Poseidon Adventure* having to do everything upside down, with everything sinking or exploding.

Today the extras really have to be whipped up to convey the speed and terror of the bombed auction room. Having 'fled' so many times now, some are practically sauntering through collapsing columns and flying debris. A rapid relay of orders passes from producer to star to director to assistant directors, to crowd controllers, via interpreter to the befuddled ears of the bored extras: '*Move your fucking arses.*'

Nino's restaurant for a farewell dinner, presided over by Joel, who is on top form at the prospect of finally leaving Rome for the final 'push' into Budapest. Every pasta invented is brought forth. We are all charged with the prospect of the *move*, and Joel takes charge of the crippling bill for the meal. As usual. I attempt at least to pay my share as he is always forking out but, as usual, he flatly refuses and says the Shaz Episode alone was 'entertainment payment' in itself.

25th October
Unit exodus to Budapest. I fly to London for a week's break. Theoretically this is my final day on the film, according to my original contract. The reality is another month to go in Budapest. Which now holds about as much attraction as a night out with Attila the Hun or Hannibal the Elephant Man. No, it's *Hudson Hawk* in Hungary.

What follows is something that I suspected might unhinge my brain. And it did. There are diary entries to prove it. Be warned.

Ten a.m. to Budapest, 13.35 arrival. If the Roman summer and Rimini had nigglesome moments, they are now instantly upstaged by the goings-on behind this recently lifted Iron Curtain. Nothing works. Three and a half hours east of London and it truly is the Eastern Bloc. My luggage is lost. The airport staff resemble left-over recruits from the Luftwaffe, with attitude: that FUCK YOU look that transmits messages to your legs to U-turn and bound back into the aircraft. No one seems used to the idea yet that people can enter and leave of their own volition. My passport proves to be of inordinate interest. People look as ugly as Belgians. Eye-contact is fish-eye dead. The onion spires and sharp Slavic cheekbonery are in scant evidence. Everything *is* grey – in every possible variation. High-rise upon high-rise block after block of grey municipal housing, with single naked light-bulbs straggling down from the ceilings. And it's not even night yet, just a blood-draining, bleached afternoon. The buildings are decrepit and dissolving from the acid rain – factories belch in the middle of the urban sprawl. Roads are a potholer's delight. Air is visible and dense with smoky pollutant. The BLUE Danube is a slow sludge of industrial waste. There are endless queues of potato-faced humans in nylon flares, imitation Nikes, man, woman and child smoking in chain-gangs. The Ramada Hotel where we are impounded is, appropriately, on an island in the middle of the Danube, between Buda and Pest. People cough a lot. I start too and fear I have contracted lung cancer. Call Sandra – and the room-to-room phone 'service' has clearly been installed by a company of Inspector Clouseaus. This does not bode well for calling home. Sandra finally crackles down the echoing line, which she swears is still connected up to Bugging Central. She merely confirms that, yes, it is every bit as bad and worse than we ever anticipated. Bruce is back in New York, Joel has yet to arrive. In other words, things are in the hands of us lesser mortals.

The menu in all but one eaterie seems to consist of a catalogue of goose-liver variations. Cooked, they proudly announce, in its own fat. Hot or cold. Someone kindly elucidates just how *foie gras* is 'produced'. The birds are caged and their webbed feet nailed to the floor. A length of pipe is forced in to the gullet, down which they are force fed every few hours. When fat enough they are slaughtered and their obscenely enlarged livers are exported for the ecstasy of gourmets everywhere. We have discovered a lone Italian restaurant that serves *fresh* vegetables. Fifty American dollars is the current monthly wage. We are Midas-like, easily paying twelve bucks for dinner, which induces a conscience strike until James Coburn advises, 'Let this old swine cast you a pearl – compassion but no guilt.'

The town square is like a Breughel painting come to life, with medieval faces selling recently skinned fox furs on the pavement. The hotel is all First World pomp and frontage, giving way to an embarrassment of ineptitude that makes me feel horribly spoilt and loath to order anything. For when you do, it arrives with all the brouhaha of Dolly Levi swanning down the stairs of the Harmonia Gardens.

The silver-domed 'helmet' is lifted with all the pride and *élan* of an amateur magician, the waiter as surprised as yourself to find anything beneath the dome. As curry is to India, so paprika is to Hungary. I have a horrible suspicion that it is a spicy plot to blow out and cover up all ingredients unmentionable and/or inedible. At surrounding tables German businessmen grin at platters of steak, uniformly covered in a phlegm-coloured blanket of cheese, sprinkled with that trademark red pepper, along with lashings of goulash. There is relentless violin-sawing, electrically amplified no matter where you sit. Now I like a dose of Paganini. I like to hear the tarantella of Transylvania or Bohemia of an evening. I DO NOT like the lift-Muzak version, tortured by a snaggled tape recording.

Stupidly I attempt to phone home but might as well have decided to pile the Ceaușescu-style furniture in my bedroom on top of the curvaceous Dolly Vardin three-way mirror and strapped it to the curtain tabs *E.T.* style, such is the likelihood of ever getting connected. The TV incongruously offers MTV, whose images and sounds seem extra-terrestrially alien here.

Our hotel is connected to the adjacent thermal baths by an

underground passage. Fluorescent lit, it is the hunting ground for terminal cases of old Germans. Three large pools of varying temperatures and hippo-sized humans infusing their flesh with the sulphurous mineral waters. Bunions galore and bullfrogged eyes bulge as blood pressures rise with the steam. Along the damp corridors white-coated 'Zsa Zsas', smoking profusely, offer 'Massage and Dental Care' in a variety of cubicles. The window displays exhibit grotesque before and after false-tooth plates and dental fixtures. The female attendants seem to be in a moustache-growing contest and, oh, how overwhelming is the overall sense of sickliness and incontinence. The menu in the Health Bar seems to consist entirely of cabbage, boiled, in one of two colours: bright purple or the more popular bleached grey.

1st November
My fourth wedding anniversary.

I'm picked up and trekked out to the far-flung Mafilm Studios, an hour's-plus drive out of the city, to shoot interiors set in Italy. The studios are located in the middle of wasteland, in a barely heated jerry-built dump. Within, all seems indecisive, incapable and akimbo. While the cats are away, the mice will play. The rewritten scene is cue for everyone to offer an opinion. Michael, the director, has one idea, James Coburn another; Sandra's eyes are rolling around the rafters; David Caruso, playing Kit-Kat, another of the candy-bar flunkeys, and up until now, *silent* (his character has had his tongue bitten off and Caruso has been observing this *out* of character as well as *in*), has released himself from this self-imposed Method Act, and is offering *his* idea of how we might progress. I have not had any significant interaction with him so far and I am completely taken aback when he confronts me in the makeup room, saying that I have been 'ignoring him'. As 'apology' trips forth from my tongue, my head somersaults around the real insanity that has begun to prevail. '*But, David, we have hardly ever spoken on account of your playing this guy who has no tongue, right?*'

According to the front page of *Variety*, the budget has now racked up costs of sixty-one million greenbacks. No one openly talks about this stuff any more. Bruce is increasingly Mata Hari-like; now we see him, now we don't. We have shot almost entire scenes with his stand-in or stuntman, but are very glad when he's back, because *something* gets done. Albeit slowly. Frank Stallone is here to play a small part and talks of pursuing his singing career. Uncannily like his famous brother, but without the muscles. Very friendly and a welcome new face among our all too familiars.

8th November

Bruce is back. The set is the vast and impressive Gold Machine Room, where the Mayflowers' da Vinci alchemy plans are reaching fruition. Even to mention old Leonardo in the present context induces rectal cramp.

Our dressing rooms are on the top floor of this 'studio' and are appropriately bare to the breezeblock, confirming our sense of incarceration. Lurch below for Bruce's close-ups for the off-camera dialogue, originally shot without him present. Bruce's close-ups come in three sizes: the full head shot (Adam's apple to crown); chin to lower forehead; lips to eyebrows. This requires lens changes, lighting readjustment, makeup finnickitings, followed by the delay of watching the replay on the video playback. Leaving no one in any doubt as to who rules this precinct. What Bruce wants, Bruce gets.

He is incredibly energized when it comes to bullying a scene into action, and seems to thrive on staying in his trailer until the last minute, when a scene has been set-up, lit and worked out. Then he bounds in, joking and back-slapping everyone along the way, and rejects the lighting, moves, floor marks, and redirects the entire shebang, which means starting all over again. I am wondering why he doesn't just short-circuit the whole process by doing it his way in the first place. But maybe it is easier to replace an existing version with your own idea if someone else has already originated a version beforehand.

A variation of this tactic is even more frustrating. The formal mechanics of the studio bell ringing, followed by a shout for SILENCE, SOUND, CLAPPERBOARD AND 'ACTION' is aborted by the increasingly familiar intrusion of 'WAIT A SECOND ... Wait a second ... Howsabout if we try doing this? Or maybe doing that? Or maybe if I do it like this then you can ...' A hundred people ready and galvanized; stare, mute.

This is then followed by the refrain of 'LET'S GET THIS FUCKING SHOW MOVING. I DON'T WANNA SPEND THE REST OF MY LIFE EATING GOULASH, GUYS!' To which there are always enough people to offer some ha-ha, but, at this juncture, my laugh muscles have gone slack.

Yet, as exhausting as this all gets, when Bruce chooses to spotlight you with his charm and attention it is difficult not to be won over. He exchanges *bons mots*, stories and unexpectedly quotes Shakespeare. Whether he does this regularly or only in proximity to a tame Brit matters neither way. He is charismatic and totally accessible. Until he is back in the arena where contradiction rules.

We have been here a week, and the overall atmosphere is underwritten by verbalized Countdown Syndrome. That is, Counting Down to your last day here. Yet the climax of the story has yet to be completed. Joel is noticeably preoccupied and seemingly obsessed with getting the pre-Xmas trailer for the film cut to entice the punters with just the right Ker-POW and guffaw quotient for this epic. But even he seems to have that end-of-term enervation about him. Gone are the communal feasts. Gone is the air of Swash and Buckle. Bruce declares: 'I'm gone. Getting outta here! I ain't staying in Budy longer than next weekend.' We are issued with yet another revised schedule to accommodate this command and resign ourselves to the prospect of shooting the rest of the scenes once he has gone, by repairing to the thermal baths and lowering ourselves into one of those stinking pools; the overwhelm of sulphur – like wallowing in a wet fart.

Lorraine Toussaint, the African-American actress playing a double-agent, is along for the dip. To our acute embarrassment, the herd of old schnitzels, upon seeing her enter their Aryan-occupied waters, scramble out and into their bathrobes audibly muttering, 'Schwarze.' Sandra is having none of this and loudly announces, '*Jawohl*, and I'm Yiddish, you shameless old Nazis.' When Sandra is MEAN, her face and lip-curl are some sight. Within seconds we have the place to ourselves as the geriatrics cripple out and give vent to her trademark exhalation, 'JEEEEEZUS!'

Lorraine is released the next day, as are James Coburn and David Caruso. Seeing them off makes the internment ahead seem all the more lengthy.

10th November

A squadron of Sandra's friends fly in to relieve the tedium, the first of whom is New York fashion designer Isaac Mizrahi. Dumbly I assumed he must be Japanese but instead he is a witty black button-eyed non-stop talker and verbal cabaret, given to Liza Minnelli impersonation to cheer things up a bit. Sandra has been approached about doing a revival of *Funny Girl* on Broadway, and between the two of them (returning from yet another restaurant in Pest, crossing a Danube bridge), they break out into a medley of Liza and Babs' *Greatest Hits*. 'Don't Rain on my Parade' is belted out against the squall of taxis, drizzle and orange street-lights. Isaac recharges Sandra's depleted batteries with his high-octane presence, reminding us that there is life beyond this movie. He inadvertently kick-starts her already well-developed kick-arse instincts, which she unleashes upon one and all during the Gold Machine Room scene. Things are particularly sluggish and confused today. And Ms Bernhard has had ENOUGH. She is now standing on some raised bit of the set, like a demented Boadicea, telling *everyone* just what she thinks of the way things are going. No one is spared, and once she has wrung herself out, Bruce, having silently listened to this harangue with the rest of us, goes over and puts his arms around her and offers some console-and-stroke. Just as that Celtic queen's revolt against the Romans in Britain was unsuccessful, Sandra has to acquiesce to the Mightier Force. Our troops are saggy too – Andie MacDowell has some sort of virus, and the rest of us are hoicking up grey matter as a result of the polluted air.

12th November

Isaac leaves. We stayed up most of the night talking as though he was the last human contact we might have before being sucked into some Black Hole in Outer Space. Or Hungary.

Sandra and I have a fresh copy of *Variety* newspaper with which to torture ourselves and on a flit down the production listings we take comfort from the intelligence that Karen Black is currently shooting a film called *Aunty Lee's Meat Pies*. We swear to each other that if we ever get out of Hungary we will both seek out this flick, if only to reassure ourselves that we've made it out of *Hudson Hawk*-land ALIVE.

Joan calls from London. Exhausted. Olivia is ill and not responding to antibiotics. Pulling my hair out. Or what's left of it. HELPLESS!

17th November

Bruce's last day. He is as puppy pleased as I am Dog-of-Jaw. Gives Sandra and me a stash of verbal notes about the remaining filming before fast-footing out of here. Having secured the services of a priest in Rome to bless the production and its crew with full Catholic pomp and swish, the Hungarian Exeunt is swift and sharp. No champagne corks popping here. Just a bitter after-taste. Star and producer despatched.

Charlie Picerni is directing the second unit camera team to cover my electrocution. Means getting wired-up and taped with a variety of special effects and being very patient. Right now, I feel *this* close to saying, 'Come on, guys, fuck the effects, do me for real. Give me five thousand volts!' Spend the day jolting and jigging about.

19th November

FINAL FINAL FINAL WEEK IN HUNGARY!

The first unit crew return from their weekend in London, where they have gone to shoot a sequence involving the miniature postal train. The End is in sight, and energy erupts. Briefly. I am told by the director that tomorrow, Tuesday, will be my last day. I cannot wipe the smile from my chops. ALL DAY.

20th November

Sandra has become a one-woman travel agent and knows every detail of every flight currently networked out of Eastern Europe to New York. Today is the day I get to be smothered in molten gold and killed off. *And* shoot my final world-dominating speech to Bruce Willis. Only we shot his reactions last week. Now I am giving an Ethel Merman-sized rant to his stand-in. Which is never the same as having the real thing. Don't care right now. Anything to get this over with.

By four p.m. we have completed a total of three camera set-ups and the prospect of completing is nigh impossible. 'WHAT'S IN A DAY?' asks some goombah. Now, I may not yet have adequately conveyed to you the minute-by-minute excrucia of being here, but at this moment I have a profound inkling of what prison and parole feel like. The day they *say* you will leave looms so significantly that come the flip-and-flop casual of 'Not today, after all', followed up by a lazy 'Maybe tomorrow or the next', it is enough to tip you over the edge. Sandra goes first upon hearing this news and, despite all her warrior instincts, she breaks down and blubs her heart out. But not before telling the harbinger of this bad news where to go do himself. Olivia is vomiting in the middle of the night. The makeup guy is in the middle of marital heave-ho. Work is, as per, suicidally slow. Tuesday dribbles into Wednesday the twenty-first and someone very stupidly declares that Sandra and I will 'BE OUTTA HERE BY LUNCHTIME. ONLY A HALF DAY, GUYS.' To which Sandra retorts, 'YEAH! AND THE PYRAMIDS WERE BUILT IN A WEEK!' Which at least forces a smile on to my beak.

Our HALF-day is a FULL day of the usual disorganized, direction-less bollocks. I am covered in molten gold and kitted out with a milky contact lens. However, the Makeup Department are threatening a work boycott as they have been working thirty-six hours non-stop on these effects. Dollars are wheel-barrowed in and, like parking meters, once *paid*, they *displayed*. Feel numbed today. Just numbed. Numb. That this final day has finally arrived is, predictably, *not* the cathartic release and relief that you imagine it might be. Nay nay, just the exhausted, spent, bleached dull relief that it has come to its end.

Buy the crew a crate of Hungary's best champagne to toast and thank them for the ride, which they drink from plastic cups. The best costs fourteen pounds, or twenty dollars, and rather than this feeling like a bargain it merely underlines how tacky the whole thing is. Olivia is on the mend.

Final drive from the Stalag Studios back to Budy and a farewell dinner with Ms Burnt-out. Eat in semi-silence like we had already left each other, and experience that strange sense of seeing this person opposite – who has been in such intimate, blurry close-up till now – as they looked when you first met. Having been through this together so intensely it is already receding as our real lives encroach and mutually exclusive agendas invade this territory. An odd unease. A formal tone. A 'take my address and number and call whenever you're in town' politesse. Over and out. Streets of Budapest, the Danube, the Domes, the whole place seems neutral and framed by the window of the taxi.

Just when my brain had begun fully to endorse these non-judgemental, rational revisions of my recent history, a note at the hotel presaged further doom and delay. At which point Sandra and I were instantly reunited like a couple of SAS commandos ready to firebomb the entire contents of the Ramada Hotel. We read: 'MONDAY'S FILM FOOTAGE HAS BEEN LOST AT THE AIRPORT. WILL NOTIFY.'

Our moods, having eased into a Pinteresque state of oblique calm, have now somersaulted into an acute state of *panic*. How long? How long can this go on?

Sandra is 'dumb'. Our eyes glue to each other in a freeze-frame, which probably looks like the lightning of LOVE AT FIRST SIGHT to the hotel receptionists. I am wondering what the Hungarian word is for strychnine.

Some phone-calls later and someone, somewhere, has located the cans of footage.

22nd November

Final indignity: another note at the hotel. 'GET YOUR OWN TAXI TO THE AIRPORT. FILM UNIT DRIVERS HAVE BEEN LAID OFF.' A lunatic in a Lada is my charioteer. He embarks upon a diversionary route that promises to take in the Russian steppes and possibly the outer Ukraine. What he does not realize is that I have checked out the going rate for the trip to the airport, and spend the journey trying to imagine what expression will cripple his glee-filled features when he discovers what money I don't have to hand over. Finally, farting and belching smoke (the Lada, not me) we jerk to a halt at the terminal and get my bags on to a trolley. When he points to his meter of multiple numerals, I stuff the *exact* true fare into his paw and utter what I hope will be my last word here: 'KURSE-N-IM' (Hungarian for thank you). A torrent of abuse issues from his face, to which I calmly shrug and repeat the one word I know and now relish: a 'KURSE-'N-'IM' indeedy!

The plane is delayed. No matter.

To top this day of release, upon landing at Heathrow, the euphoric headlines smashed across every London paper declare that 'THATCHER IS OUT'. Me too, Margaret. And none too soon. She, no doubt 'out of her mind', and me, equally unhinged with JOY to be FREE! OF HUNGARY, *HAWK* AND HER!!!

More LA Stories

Fly to LA for two weeks for some casting meetings and to attend the première of *LA Story*. Two-hour delay for security checks due to the Gulf War, during which time I ponder this *folie de désert* and conclude that it would be inconceivable for Mrs Saddam Hussein and Mrs Barbara Bush to be bombing one another with the support of two hundred thousand female troops. Somehow think negotiation would have resolved the dispute. Perhaps if men could be impregnated, we'd be less frisky about shipping off our littl'uns to blow each other's brains out in the name of whatever cause. I was about to test this theory on my neighbour, but reconsidered in case he was in the FBI, was a war veteran or merely topped to the toes with testosterone.

Sandra Bernhard has invited me to stay with her in the San Fernando Valley but as all my meetings take place in LA I decide to stay in a hotel in the city. This does not go down well with Sandra, who is never one to take *anything* too lightly and I am cast in the role of the Betrayer and Treasonite. Until she simmers down. She retaliates by informing me that Isaac Mizrahi has seen a preview of *LA Story* and 'HATED IT!'

A strange phenomenon invariably overwhelms me the moment I touch down in LA, which is best described as Phone Withdrawal Syndrome. Nowhere else on the planet have I been afflicted by this, but it takes hold, as usual, within seconds of landing. As the plane approaches the runway, the houses below seem reach-out-close, stretching every which way as far as the eye can see. And somewhere amid the sprawl I know there lurk all the actors, agents and directors I've ever heard of, *all here.* All out there. Unseen. This induces the first stages of suppressed panic and with it my in-flight plans of where to go and what to do. All my resolve is suddenly vacuumed away and the sense of isolation, and especially anonymity, looms like a particularly awesome aspect of the Himalayas. The paranoid snowy peaks. The purple prosed outer reaches of *aaaaaaaaargh.*

Everywhere you care to look famously smiling faces are advertising their latest offerings which, of course, you are not in. I mean *I* am not in.

While trying to control my anxiety with assurances that it is all merely jet-lag, my hand has other thoughts and is riffling through the list of names in my Filofax, as I am hoping that, before long, that little set of numbers will be close at hand for some fingering. Some SERIOUS dialling and 'dahling' work. Though it has to be said I don't ever remember movie folk using this theatrical term. This is probably because you can usually remember the names of the mega-famous without resorting to the 'dahling' standby; a euphemism for 'I haven't a clue who the fuck you are'. Here, you *always* know who *everyone* is. And the folks you don't remember meeting *never* seem to mind. They are *happy* to reintroduce themselves and recount their briefest brushings with you; *you* being, to someone else lower down the pecking order, a Somebody.

I check into the hotel and, moments later, suitcases barely crushing the carpet, I am propelled to the bedside, cradle gripped, fingers punching in, hoping to catch a 'live one', rather than a bleeping answer message. Inevitably most are 'please speak after the tone' jobs, but it does serve to quell the fear. Stretch out on the bed and channel-surf through the multiple options. See a trailer for *LA Story*, which now seems as remote as Pluto. Maybe . . . maybe this is all to do with not knowing . . . how it has turned out. Scenes filmed almost a year ago retread through my memory, and it's a what-will-be-in-or-out-of-the-final-cut? crapshoot. I tell myself that, whatever the film is like, it is now an edited *fait accompli* and, whatever its reception, some serious *smiling* will be required.

Phone wakes me some hours later and it's my agent, Steve, saying, 'Hi, kid. Welcome to town. Got some meetings for ya and some scripts for you to read and let's see if we can find a window in our programmes to have dinner and catch up. Bye.' All this on one breath, which implies the man is busy beyond reason, the 'Bye' like a last gasp.

4th February
Phone wake-up. 'Hi. It's Steve Martin. Wanna have lunch? One p.m.'
'Sure, where?'
'Indigo. OK? Bye.' This is typical. He talks in telegraphese as though he last saw you five minutes ago.

We meet and talk. He is all 'kitten on the keys' about the movie, its first reviews and its box office prospects. 'Pauline Kael ... so-so, *New York Times* and *Rolling Stone* trashed it.' This bad news is coming through in Morse code blips between mouthfuls of salad, and punctuated by gulps of iced tea. 'I've shredded most of them already.' I know the feeling. This won't stop the stuff being 'out there', but there is the hands-on sensation of at least having done *something* in return for being DUMPED on. He is totally preoccupied and vacantly waiting for this week to pass by, with its cast and crew screening, première screening, press duties, chat-shows and, finally, the opening in cinemas across the country on Friday. Which, from today, seems a fair old obstacle course ahead. Concludes with the lunch check and, 'I think I'm gonna retire at the end of this year.' Which makes me laugh. Which just about makes him laugh. We dawdle and dangle through the afternoon, treading water, lolling about.

Victoria comes in from a meeting and seems unprepared to indulge in any gloom. She obviously has not read the early reviews. Or has steel girders for nerves. They drive me down to the old MGM Studios for the cast and crew screening, but don't attend themselves. 'Pick you up after.' Which means I have to TAP DANCE no matter what MY response. Feel somewhat nauseous going in.

Most of the crew are here and few of the cast, who have already seen it. 'Howdy, howdy-doody' my way through familiar faces and having waded through 'So what are you doing nows?', the lights go down, credits roll and the atmosphere of watching a home movie engulfs, buoyed up by the enthusiastic applause that greets each credit, no matter how obscure. The laughter, too, is that indulgent kind – in other words, NO MATTER WHAT ANYONE DOES, hey guys! this is, like, family – GOTTA LAUGH, GOTTA DANCE, GOTTA ENJOY! The opening credit sequence with 'La Mer', nostalgically crooned by Charles Trenet, tenor-ing his way alongside witty, lush images of Life in LA, is inspired; a guaranteed cue to sit back and enjoy. Andrew Dunn's cinematography is Hockney-in-Moving-Pictures. Usually, the first five minutes of a flick give you a gut feeling about what's to come and this opening *totally* dispelled Steve's lunchtime unease. WHAT'S THE PROBLEM? Film is up and running, especially with this crowd. BUT, and this is going to be the hard part, the whole caboodle starts to sputter and stutter when the romance gets underway. Between Steve and Victoria. Between my hosts. Between real-life husband and wife.

No sooner has this dawned on me than the horrible stomach-wrench of seeing just what *I* have produced blows ANY concern for anyone else out of the water. The rictus of seeing what has *actually* transmitted or passed for a so-called PERFORMANCE. Try as I might to say, 'It's only a movie,' it feels not unlike stepping on to an underground train, warned to 'MIND THE GAP' over the Tannoy, and absently wrong-footing it and plunging down. Down down down, like Alice into the cinema seat. Terminal – there is nothing you can do about it. Save blush and wish someone had some Invisible Powder handy. If deep-sea divers get the bends, I suspect actors watching themselves are equally entitled to go a little doo-lally.

Huge applause at the end, handshaking and 'you were greats' and through a side door and into the car, where Steve and Victoria look a bit stretched about the gills.

'SO WHADDYA THINK?' This is the hardest part, because I'm still trying to retrieve my guts, which seem to have been left behind in the popcorned stalls, and I hear the following come off my tongue: 'You were great and the movie went down a storm. But I'm hardly in any state to be objective, first viewing and all.'

'C'mon, you were great. So funny.' The journey has as many 'No, but you were greats' as there seem to be traffic-lights. At the end of which I don't think any of us was convinced. Becomes surreal. Steve is despondent and predicts that 'business will be dull'. And it does seem to be all about *business*. A film having either to make or break itself in its opening weekend. One argument goes that the country needs a comedy in the middle of the Gulf War. Or the reverse. No doubt either theory will be used come next Monday to 'explain' *LA Story*'s box-office fate.

The other film in competition this weekend is *Sleeping with the Enemy* starring Julia Roberts. The same question prevails: does the nation want to see a thriller in a time of war? Will people turn out for Julia's 'comeback'? (She is barely twenty-four.)

5th February

Esquire magazine interview in the morning. Meet Sandra Bernhard for lunch in the Valley, on the other side of the Hollywood Hills. She is incredibly depressed. Attempt an 'at least you're back in the States. Just remember Budapest, my dahling, my angel.' She is having none of this and my U-turn for not staying with her is clearly not forgiven.

'Have you heard any word about *Hudson Hawk*?'

'Are you kidding me?' and she's off and frothing. This is a tough lunch. Neither of us has the common-movie-denominator to talk about. I am preoccupied with the launch of *LA Story*, which is excluding, and exclusion is one thing Sandra is probably more acutely tuned to than anything else. In fact, she is the Chairperson of the Board, her catalogue of Exclusions vastly extensive.

Go for a casting meeting at three p.m. The film is *The Hand That Rocks the Cradle*; the agent pitch goes 'Baby-sitter from Hell in Suburbia – a thriller'. I am being considered for the husband. Role requiring solid, white-collar nine-to-five family-man charm. With a beard. Can they be serious?

LA Story Première. Only it's not called that. 'Industry Screening' is the term. My partner is Natasha Richardson, whom I have known since my stint in Regent's Park Open Air Shakespeare season in 1984. Swing by to pick her up at her father's house off Sunset Boulevard. Her dad is Tony Richardson, the celebrated sixties director of *Look Back in Anger*, *Tom Jones* and *Taste of Honey*. It's a Hollywood Hillside home overlooking the Los Angeles 'flats' below, with vast floor-to-ceiling double-storey windows, and birds. Parrots, in cages and out of them. Tony is flamingo-tall and thin with swooping beak and chin – like man, like bird. His gestures, voice and persona are instantly imitable, such is their distinct outline. Like a boldly drawn cartoon. Everyone I have met who knows him falls into doing an impression of him. He is full of jibe and irony and drawling dismissal and manages to plant seeds of doubt about why we are even bothering to go to the screening in the first place. 'You KNOW it can only be AAAAAAWFUL!'

We go. To Beverly Hills. To the Martins'. To have a drink before a shared limo ride. Natasha is all smiling, all supportive, the perfect friend at this kind of event. And I am deeply grateful to her right now. The stretched car is not unlike the state of my innards. It manoeuvres sedately into Westwood towards a red carpet, spotlights and press phalanx, and we step out into a cacophony of police loudspeakers, walkie-talkies, a screamy, shouting chorus of 'STEVE!' that resounds from the crowd identifying the silver-topped man himself.

Slow shuffle past the assembled TV crews and photographers who require 'soundbites' ranging from 'What do you eat for breakfast?' to 'Who is your date?' to 'Who are you and what role do you play in the movie?' I can feel a slight paralysis in my smiling cheeks. A ventriloquist's doll 'moment'. Once through this section, there is some milling about and introductions and handshakings with Oliver Stone, Michael Douglas, Tom Hanks, Paul Mazursky, Bob Rafelson, Teri Garr, Chevy Chase, Susan Forristal, Sarah Jessica Parker, Robert Downey Jnr, Marilu Henner, Iman and on and on. Into the theatre. Ninety-five minutes pass by and people laugh! Sausage out the other end and the adjacent shopping arcade has been transformed into a food arena. My agent, Steve, sidles up as if he was about to pass on some Cold War secret and quietly says, 'This movie is weird?' I am not really equipped right now to discuss his prognosis and fall into dummy-smile mode. Eat some pizza and willingly believe Tom and Rita Hanks' generous appraisal of my comic talents.

As this is British director Mick Jackson's first experience of this kind of hoopla, I recognize *his* expression from the one I can feel pasted across *my* phizog: benevolent stupefaction – totting up everything and everyone in order to decipher it later. Limo back to the Martins' for some immediate post-mortem. If only I could have liked their movie as much as I liked them.

6th February

Go to a casting with director Michael Mann for *Last of the Mohicans* – to consider me for the part of the British officer and mortal enemy of the Mohican, to be played by Daniel Day-Lewis. On my way over I attempt to reconcile the man who gave the world *Miami Vice* with a historical Epic. I hope he has not seen my poncings in *LA Story*, which are clearly at odds with anything militaristic. An extraordinarily *intense* man is Mr Mann, talking and firing off for a full twenty-five minutes' worth. 'Can you come in tomorrow for a test reading?'

Sure.'

'Have you ever been blond?'

'I can be a tomato,' is the Dustin Hoffman *Tootsie* dialogue that scams across my brain but which mercifully trips itself up before being uttered in favour of 'I could be,' as I retreat out of the door.

7th Februry

Call Hugh Grant and Elizabeth Hurley. He is playing Julie Andrews' gay son in a TV film and is full of self-mock about his present lack of career momentum, cast as Son of M. Poppins von Trapp. More meetings – including one with Patrick Johnson, who did special effects on *Warlock*, has written a script titled *Dragon Heart*, is setting up production to direct and speaks about my playing the Villain.

Then see Sandra, who is breathing her own fire at *LA Story*. I am tempted to temper her fusillade with the likely critical fate awaiting *Hudson Hawk*'s release. Stay shtup. Gnawing sense that no matter where she is THE LADY IS FOR GRUMBLING. Funny but sore.

Go alone to see *Godfather III*, not wanting *any* interference in this longed-for 'return', not anticipating the unexpected wet eyeballing as the screen goes pitch black and that mournful theme music horns and haunts its way through my head and catapults me back to the Cinelux Cinema in Swaz seventeen years ago, where and when I determined seriously to pursue this dream of becoming one of Them who acted in stories in a Never-Never Land called Hollywood. Now, you would be right in thinking this is so much syrupy gloop, but it is this single dream that has silently kept me going. Which in some smallish way, but more biggish than I dared hope for, *has* been realized. It induces a quiet load of blubbing in the empty front row, midnight showing, for the past, for the dead, even for a dream come true. The elegiac tone of the film, with its operatic set-pieces, moving menopausally along, seems a perfect conclusion to the trilogy, despite the barracking of the critics about there not being sufficient story left to tell. Just being in the company of this screen-familiar family again is worth the entry fee. Perfect Pacino and Keaton. Wobble out of there like so much exhausted jelly at three a.m.

8th February

Steve and Victoria invite me to go to Santa Barbara for the weekend in order to be out of town for the national release of the film. Drive off at ten thirty. LA reviews are mostly favourable. New York – dire. Lunch in Montecitto. Nod, nod, chit-chat with Michael Douglas, who is at the next table as well as a neighbour in this country retreat for the very famous and very rich. When I say a neighbour, I don't mean the over-the-hedge variety for round here whole mountainsides separate 'estates'. Despite the country air, there is no escaping the pollutant of anxiety. We three go to the matinée of our opposition *Sleeping with the Enemy*, which might more aptly be titled *Watching the Enemy*.

It's packed and Steve dolefully declares, 'It's gonna be huge.' We peek into the *LA Story* screening about to start next door. Sold out, which cheers us up immeasurably.

11th February

Another casting meeting, this time with director Ron Howard for a film provisionally titled *The Irish Story* and starring Tom Cruise, for an upper-class landlord-type. Steve Martin has called him on my behalf, as they had done *Parenthood* together, which is extremely generous of him and very embarrassing at the same time. 'Please believe me, Ron, I did *not* put that bastard up to this.' A misjudged moment of jokey familiarity and I know then and there that I have pressed my own ejector button.

Meet the *LA Story* cast at the Burbank Studios for the taping of the *Donahue Chat-Show*. Depending on who you speak to, the weekend box office takings of $6.6 million indicate a hit, while others deem it a so-so compared to the doubled takings of *Sleeping with the Enemy*. Chat-shows theoretically boost business. All parties understand that this is the *raison d'être* for being here and we line up on the stage, fielding whatever questions are thrown out by the audience, smiling like they were the most original questions ever thought up. My particular favourite is one posed by a particularly *huge* person with a tiny voice enquiring, 'Tell us, Marilu, where do you get yer sweaters from?' Followed by Victoria being asked, 'What's it really like being married to Steve Martin and is he as funny at home as he is in the movies?' She is so incensed by this that her answer scrapes out barely audibly, hardly disguised in its disdain, causing Mr Donahue to crank out some instant warmth and diversionary charm. Being an adjunct to someone this famous is clearly an ongoing dilemma. Another member of the audience says that she was at school with Steve and, mid-reminisce, he a-hums that 'Well, actually, I was at school in a different state' in his I'm-just-a-wild-and-crazy-guy persona. Saved by the theme music and a 'That's all, Folks.'

12th February

Mohicans meeting on the fifteenth floor of a glass building on Sunset Boulevard. I was advised to wear black by the casting director. The office has a single Anglepoise desk lamp on and the blinds are down. Mr Mann says to go for the read. Bonnie Timmerman, the pixie-sized casting director, reads in the other part – of a man. I'm given detailed direction and suggestion after the first go, and for once brain and feelings seem to be in tandem. Mr Mann is getting even more excited than he was at the outset. Which is pretty high octane. How long you are auditioned for is something gone over and over again after you have left unless you have literally been herded in and out. The longer always *seems* better but doubt kicks in and informs that maybe your twenty-minute stretch was to exhaust all your possibilities. I still don't know. No rules. How they end things is usually some indicator, and this one ends better than usual. Bonnie is avidly writing down phone numbers and dates of when I leave and where I will be and Michael is pacing and shaking hands with torturous intensity. No mention of being a blond, though. Pass the waiting room, which is loaded with ex-pat Brits, one of whom is Rupert Frazer who says to me in the elevator, 'You were in there some time? In and out like Flint, was I.' Cheers me up no end.

Meet up with Hugh Grant and Elizabeth Hurley and during the meal am debriefed in Hugh's trademark *Boy's Own Adventure Book* style of mock and tease. Turns out we have been up for all the same parts, along with the other five thousand Brits currently lurking in LA. 'All bloody righty for you, dahling. You're in there with them all, everywhere you bloody look, mocking your lowly namesake with all this work and publicity. It's got to stop.'

'Going up for *Wild Sargasso Sea*?'

'Yes, *yes*, yes.'

14th February

Phone home. Lunch with Steve and Victoria. Sandra has invited me to a Valentine's Night party at Madonna's home. Meet Sandra, and we drive up into the hills above the Spago's–Tower Records junction on Sunset Boulevard. Suddenly feel self-conscious about what I am wearing and feel an attack of the *wallies* coming on. 'Will there be lots of people?'

'Who knows? Relax, honey.'

Wind endlessly round and up the hillside and up a cul-de-sac that ends with a large solid metal gate, beside which stands an equally solid human built like the proverbial, with hand up in 'Halt, who goes there?' position. Leans in and checks out the interior of Sandra's sedan, ignores her attempts at being matey and says, 'Hold it there.' Goes back to the intercom. Buzzes, returns, and says where to park. Metal wall shifts sideways and we park next to a couple of jeeps. 'Maybe we're too early?'

'Relax.'

Another Action Man with a walkie-talkie appears and grunts to go in. Through a door at the back of the double garage into the kitchen.

There are *no* other guests, let alone a party, in sight. WE ARE TOO EARLY. 'Are we too early?'

'*No!* Hi, I'm Madonna.'

'And I'm slightly stupefied. Happy Valentine's.'

She is tiny and alabaster-white, bleached blonde with a smash of scarlet lipstick and altogether startling in the flesh. Much softer-looking than the image affixed in my head. And so petite. Sculpted into a Dolce e Gabbana black corset and knee-length black leggings with her well-documented cleavage quietly heaving like *Sleeping Beauty* at Disneyland. I am in a somewhat transfixed state for a few minutes, and am guided lamb-like to sit down in the high tech, steel and shiny wood-floored eating area. 'Wanna drink?' Sandra is 'Hi-honeeeey'-ing and hugging her, and I am wondering why the hell *we* are here alone on Valentine's. There *are* no other people coming. A large television is mounted way up a wall and bleating MTV very loudly, below which there is a steel frame with cross-wires over which is draped every glossy magazine like a sort of media clothes-line. Three have her face on their covers. 'This is Tony' – who wanders in through the garden doors in low-slung jeans, Calvin Klein shorts exposed, shirtless with a waistcoat, fag in mouth and bottle of beer in hand, like he is in a Levi's commercial. Which he may well have been.

'Wanna eat something?' Madonna opens the fridge, which is the size of a walk-in wardrobe, and offers up Chinese take-away from Chin-Chin on Sunset. 'It's all vegetarian.' Her voice is a slightly nasal high-pitched twang and comes at you FAST. Get to work with some chopsticks, while Sandra sits beside her and dangles an arm around her bare shoulders and cups her hand around the right mammary, making it ever so slightly difficult to concentrate on getting those beansprouts affixed betwixt sticks and into my mouth.

'I loved *Henry and June*.'

'Thank you.'

'Can you sing?'

'Why?'

'I'm gonna do *Evita*.'

'No, I can't, but thank you for asking.'

'My pleasure. Goddammit, you English are so polite!' This sounds half complimentary, half accusatory. 'Something *you* could learn, Tony!'

'What?'

'Manners!' and within seconds they are having a Burton–Taylor 'moment'. Which, as I have never met either of them before, is instantly embarrassing. Especially when they start yelling, challenging the MTV decibels. I 'eyewide' Sandra who shrugs a shoulder, like this is 'average'.

The dispute ends as abruptly as it started and Madonna returns to the subject of *Evita*. I ask what it was like working with Woody Allen on *Shadows and Fog*, to which she cryptically replies, 'Like the title. Script pages only the night before, he doesn't say much ... Mia was funny, 'specially about Sinatra and Ava Gardner.' But she's pissed off and starts slagging off the various singers on MTV. Which, considering her current chart domination, comes as a surprise. Sandra and I duet about our recent *Hawk* doings, to which Madonna headshakes from side to side saying that at least with the music business you have some control.

The intercom buzzes, and one of the hulks delivers a shoe-box-sized gift that just arrived. Madonna says her dustbins have to be guarded, else fanatics and nuts raid for *any* vestige of *anything*, to claim proximity. She opens the present and it's full of her favourite sweets – as well as a smaller wrapped parcel. Her 'I know what this is and who it's from' galvanizes Tony, and the air revs up for Round Two. The parcel contains a thimble-sized gold frog with diamond-encrusted back and emerald eyes, which instigates accusation and comparison – 'This is what I call a proper Valentine's gift. Not some cheap shit aluminum heart-shaped fuckin' balloon, dick-brain!' – referring to the helium-filled Happy Valentine tied with string to the back of a stool. I take this as a cue to wander out into the garden as they verbally Beatty each other over who 'gifted' adequately.

Tony joins me by the oblong pool, cracks open another beer and warns me not to go too far down the garden, ''cos there are alarm wires and lasers and security shit'. This top-of-the-hill position looks out over the sparkling sprawl of all Los Angeles below. The house resembles a clean-lined Palladian bungalow and is unexpectedly modest, with minimal furnishings and high profile Art. Legèr over the fireplace, Picasso above the immaculately neat desk, a Frieda Kahlo alone on a white wall.

'How do you cope with being Mr Madonna?'

'Fuckin' insane, man, insane.'

I think he earns a living as a model but don't ask. Go back inside, this time to the state-of-the-art gymnasium where S. and M. are yakking. I cannot work out why, having stared me so intently in the eyes earlier, Madonna is now talking over my shoulder while straddling a bench-press, until I turn and discover that the 'wall' behind me is floor-to-ceiling, end-to-end mirror and that she is staring at herself. Which is understandable, as she is a lot prettier than I am.

A friend of Tony's lopes in and says, 'Hi, Madonnaaaa,' like he was bored already, at which she queries Tony, 'Why are all your friends such losers, huh?' His friend seems immune to this insult and the two of them go off to get some beers.

'Let's get outta here,' and we follow our leader into a Cherokee Jeep, rev up, career down the winding roads to Sunset Boulevard and head for a club in Hollywood, our hostess at the wheel, causing adjacent drivers at the traffic-lights to pose in paralysis as they grapple with her real-life apparition. The music is too loud to talk through and I turn down the volume with a 'Do you mind?' and now it's my turn to get a little of that 'burn'. Madonna chews gum, and chews and chews, and *then* says, 'OK,' establishing – as if any of us were in any doubt – just *who* is in control here, which makes me feel like a wretched five-year-old having asked if I could set the house on fire.

The club is a converted theatre and we are here to see one of her back-up singers, Nikki, sing a set of songs she is releasing on her own. Midnight, and the place is packed to the gunwales already. Having just 'snitched' me in the jeep, she now arm-in-arms me through the doors into the foyer where managers, doormen, bouncers are all having that 'paralysis' thing to a man. Buzz, buzz, cram, cram in seconds and we are engulfed and siphoned through a side door. She is giggling now at all this and says, '*See?* as grown men, walking backwards down a narrow back-stage corridor, look as if they wish they could red-carpet-lay their very tongues for her to walk upon. This attention clearly feeds her capricious nature. Sandra and I are each side of her now, like tall attendants, having been assigned our roles, arms entwined. Tony and Greg smoke up the rear-guard. No one can fail to notice that something or SOMEONE is a-comin'.

We meet up with Nikki, who is akimbo with anxiety, dressed in a seventies bell-bottom cat-suit *à la* Carmen Miranda. And flapping. But pleased to have some mega-star support here. 'You gotta get better publicity pictures, GIRL!' quoth M., eliciting a puncture-faced mini-collapse of confidence in Nikki just as she is about to platform-shoe her way on stage. Which seems a bit much. Sandra rolls her eyes heavenwards.

We are then entreated by the grovelling clubsters to make use of the balcony in the theatre to see the act. About turn and we entourage our way up a narrow flight, through a door and on to the balc. Arms disentangled, duty completed, I move to the far corner to watch. To see. Madonna, like a Moth to her Fame, grips the balcony rail, leans forward and gives the 'house' her once-over. It's dark in here and the value of being sepulchrally pale and platinum blonde pays off. Everything else *is* dark around her, and by the count of twenty, the heaving, dancing mass below has become a swaying choreography of one. All gyrating, all looking up and only at her. Like a gospel gathering. It is pure Peron. As if timed, once the 'room' is hers, she turns her attention to the much-insulted Tony and 'eats' his face, kissing him like they were condemned.

It takes Nikki some pumped decibels to dislodge the focus from this 'impromptu' Romeo and Juliet scene. And I think, were I her, a quick call to the Capone School of Valentine's Day Messages Inc. would have been my response to this guest's arrival. The managers/club-owners are now squelching around the crammed balcony with offers of 'anything you want', wide-eyed and willing.

Had big M. wanted to, she could have snuck in here incognito but this is clearly *what* she wants. Right now anyhow.

Having arrived here as a group of five, we make for the car park surrounded by five hundred. People screaming. Moving. 'MADONNA? MADONNA?' I wonder what they would do were she to stop, sit down and say, 'OK, SO WHADDYA WANNA KNOW?'

She wheels us out of there FAST and says, 'SHUDDUP!' to Tony and Greg, who are discussing the car-theft scam they've heard about on Sunset Boulevard. All their kissing like an aberrant blip. We career back up the winding road to Mount Madonna and I am despatched into my own car with a sharpish 'G'night and thanks, see y'around.'

I meander down again, sedately, grateful to have had the opportunity to be plugged into this circuit and relieved not to have any more domestic jolts assaulting my synapses.

15th February
Flew home. Never got any of the parts. Never minded. Not *too* much.

1st May
'Columbia-Tristar Pictures request your presence at the press conference and première of *Hudson Hawk* in LA.' Fly Thursday 16th May.

17th May

Start of two-day press junket held in a big hotel ballroom full of round tables and assembled cast. We are given a pre-ball tactic-talk: 'WE ALL HAD F. U. N. RIGHT?!' 'RIGHT!!!'

Into the fray. In relays, each actor follows another in twenty-minute 'sessions' at each table to encounter assembled journalists who declare their hatred for this film and especially its Star. Hoo Boy. Lunch with Joel and Bruce will be the *real* test. Turns out the bad news has reached them before lunch and things swiftly frost up. Joel says, 'FUCK 'EM. Press have it in for us anyway. Gonna open massive next weekend.'

18th May

Like crates of flat Coca-Cola we are wheeled about for Round Two. Oy! Andie MacDowell and I are whisked off for a late-afternoon screening, being the only ones not to have seen the result. Empty screening room at Columbia Studios, each with our agents, each unable to look each other – or anyone else for that matter – in the eye at the end. Shell-shocked into the blazing evening sunshine. Agent Steve says, 'You and Sandra were—'

'PLEASE, STEVE. I BEG OF YOU. DON'T SAY A WORD. PLEASE.' And bow my head towards the car park, ABSOLUTELY SURE I will 'NEVER WORK IN THIS TOWN AGAIN'. The SHAME is entirely concentrated in my head, which seems to have heated up rather violently, leaving the rest of me limp and bloodless.

Crept round to Bruce Robinson's (he is here writing and directing *Jennifer Eight*) for some familiar 'face'. Having lost mine.

PREMIÈRE: same place, same time, same guests as last year's *Die Hard II* launch, except Robert Altman and Tim Robbins are seated directly behind us. 'What are *you* doing here?'

'I'm in it. How about you?'

'Oh, Tim and I are here doing a little research,' says he, *sotto voce*. 'What are you doing next month?'

'I'm going back to London.'

'Working?'

'No.'

'I may have something for you.'

This momentarily kick-starts my circulation until the reality of what this man is about to witness freezes thought.

There is a concerted cheer as the credits roll up front. But clearly the press and grapevine word has been out for too long already. A hundred minutes of ... of ... You choose, for a change.

I remember how this cinema ERUPTED at the end of *Die Hard II* and ENGULFED Bruce, while tonight you would swear some miraculous special-effects crew had been in to make a thousand people disappear. By the time the house lights are up, the stalls are all bare. Like that old Emperor's balls.

Hearse off to the 'party', held all too appropriately at a club called The Asylum, the cast like inmates. WAITING. For the guests who NEVER ARRIVE. Or precious few, anyway. The waiters finally outnumber the guests. I flee.

24th May

Memorial Day holiday weekend. Film opens on two thousand screens across the country and bombs in all of them. While Altman, true to his word, offers me a job to play a screenwriter in *The Player*. From the ridiculous to the sublime. At the very moment I think I will never 'work that cliché in this town again', I feel well and truly SAVED.

The *Hawk* reviews, if they can even be termed as such, are essentially poison pen letters, raging about budget, star salary and Hollywood excess, and the four-day box office result is 'dismal' at $7.5 million, in relation to expectations, budget, star salary, etc. ...

What began as a spoof 'Bond' caper movie, has ended up a capon. The film was awarded Turkey of the Decade by the Alternative Academy in the spring of 1991. SHOO BE DOO WAH WAH WAAAAAAAAAAAAAAAAAAAAAARGH!

The Player

20th June

Fly back into LA. *LA Story* is the in-flight flick. Three o'clock in the hotel and the bedside phone rings.

'Is that Richard? Hi, it's Bob. You get in all right? Listen I got some new ideas for the first scene. I'll send you the pages. I'm gonna hand you over to Signey about costume-fittings and stuff. If you're not too jet-lagged come over to Malibu for dinner. Katherine'd like to see you.'

21st June

Drive round to the production offices nearby and it's all as chaotic and apparently casual as a students' union. Open-plan. Phones, faxes, deliveries, 'hiya's and 'welcome aboard', 'Wanna eat something? Bob'll see you in a minute.' None of the power-suited officialdom of Executive Show Business. All of the ease and informality of a fringe theatre company. FEAR – of failing, big budgets, not sticking to 'the plan', bad weather, studio pressures, what's hot or what's not, seems resolutely absent. The 'Altman atmos.' is familial and so easy-going that you can't help wondering why every film can't be made under this ethos. Most of the staff are women, foremost among whom is Scottie Bushnell. I met her briefly in Paris two years ago, and she is as affectionate and 'how are ya?' friendly as you *don't* expect someone in her position to be.

Meet Stephen, the production designer, who is one of Bob's sons. Signey, production assistant, one of his daughters. Meet Bob, who 'uncles' an arm around me, like we have known each other all our lives, says, 'So what do you think? Wanna see some dailies?' and we flap through a makeshift curtain into the impromptu screening room. Plastic chairs in rows facing a white wall. Geraldine Peroni is the editor and obliges with running footage of scenes already shot. Stuff with Tim Robbins that looks like a documentary. Lights up, and while getting a drink from the cooler I experience that out-of-body levitation when he asks, 'So what do you think so far?' ALTMAN ASKING SWAZI? Which no doubt colours my 'Well, Bob, what can I say?' reply. He then relates this idea he has which is that, as the film is about Hollywood, he wants to populate all the scenes with real movie stars playing the 'background crowd' or extras. (Or Crowd Artists, if we are being PC.) 'There is the risk that some lurking Legend might overshadow the foreground action, but don't you think it's a good idea?'

Even though I know that this avuncular 'intimacy' is something he must have used to get people to do *anything* throughout a myriad movies, the very fact that he is even ASKING flatters. Involves. Includes. Dispels THE FEAR.

Dean Stockwell, who plays my 'producer-partner' in the film, arrives, slightly unhappy about having his golf routine interrupted for a costume-fitting. 'Do you play?' I know my negative has already lost me Brownie points. The two things he wants in the scene we have together, scheduled for this coming Monday, are a message bleeper and Geena Davies. He looks distinctly scowly about the gills when told that though he's got the bleeper the lady will be Andie MacDowell and that I will be playing his 'writing-directing partner'. Never heard of either of us and his off-handedness is the first note of unease of the morning. However, his scrapey 'front' is swiftly smoothed out and appeased by Scottie and Bob and he is on his way to eighteen holes before lunch. I am given extra dialogue *for Monday night*: the 'pitch' I have for the film within the film. Peter Gallagher moseys in, all friendly and 'welcome to town'. Bob likes to know *everything* and asks where and with whom I am having dinner. 'With Rachel Ward and Bryan Brown.'

'Are they both working?'

'I don't think so.'

'Ask them if they wanna be themselves in your scene on Monday night. Scottie? Who else do we have for the St James Club?'

'Malcolm McDowell.'

'Is he related to Andie?'

'No, different spelling.'

'Ask them. Just one night. Wear what they want. Equity minimum which they either get in cash or donate to the Actors' Benevolent Fund. If they do, call and I'll get Scottie to do the business.'

22nd June

Breakfast with Bruce Robinson, who is renting a vast villa owned by Gore Vidal on Outpost Drive. Some remove from their terraced house in Wimbledon. It's a Spanish stucco job, surrounded by palms and a series of terraced slopes that resemble a miniature Hanging Gardens of Babylon. Convertible in the drive, Norma Desmond *Sunset Boulevard* staircase within and a smile slapped across the chops of my mentor, who is attempting some 'heh heh heh' modesty about his luscious surrounds. None of which I can even pretend to be blasé about and I blurt out a 'FUCK ME!' for starters. He is exceptionally smiley this sunny morn, having had his film *Jennifer Eight* greenlit to the tune of a generous budget from Paramount Pictures. Tours me round the house, says he is giving up smoking Monday morning, and offers up a cabaret of the kinds of things writers do when pitching a film to the Men in Suits. Which is what my part requires me to do in two days' time. He suggests that, as I have to conjure up torrential rain in my opening gambit, I should try doing some 'ghhhurssshhhhh' sound effects.

'ARE YOU KIDDING?'

'No! ANYTHING. People will do ANYTHING to get their pitch across.'

He takes me through my whole speech, offering ideas and stories, which are cruel and funny, and which I console myself are all in the name of Research, that particularly prominent recent phenomenon that seems to have taken hold since Robert De Niro gained tonnage for *Raging Bull*. Every profile you read harps ON AND ON about RESEARCH, like actors were about to discover a cure for cancer. Bruce opines that my pitch will *only* be funny if it is delivered *dead seriously*, making me long to work with the old goat again. 'Why the hell don't you make another English comedy with ME in the LEAD, you fool? Why are you doing a thriller? That's not funny. Or political. Without me!'

'No money for flicks in England. What's Altman like, then?'

RED ALERT. Bruce is a very possessive 'landlord' and doesn't take too kindly to other directors being praised out of hand by upstart protégés like myself. So opt for 'Well, he gave me a part on the strength of *Withnail and I* so he can't be all bad.'

'Mmmmmmmmmm. Likes all that improvising shit, though, doesn't he?'

'Yes.'

'Hate it. If it's not on the page, it'll never make it on to the big screen.'

'I love it.'

'You would. You're a bloody actor. Think it's easy to just come up with good lines? I sweat blood over the dialogue and won't have some poxy ponce prancing about saying, "I think I'll just say this instead."'

'Yes, but, Bruce, your dialogue is brilliant, my old darling.'

'Every single word of *Withnail* was scripted.' (I KNOW, BRUCE! I WAS THERE!!) Cue for a ramble down his well-worn Memory Lane of mutual delights.

Wonder whether this kind of INSULT-DRIVEN relationship is characteristically English, or just typical of the ribald honesty that evolves from any true friendship?

Lunch with Steve Martin and Glenne Headly. He is still doing *Father of the Bride* duty, she 'resting' restlessly. We go to an exhibition of Bruce Weber photographs and leave depressed at our obvious physical imperfections compared to these heroic images of Michel-los-angelo perfected biceps.

Tea at the Four Seasons Hotel poolside with Kevin Kline and very pregnant Phoebe Cates, delineating which actors we have worked with are definitely certifiable or psychotic and reach a common consensus on a couple.

I have only been here forty-eight hours and can already hear names being dropped and diarized as I plunge Alice-like, down, down, down into Wonderland. Delicious. Ready to obey any instruction that declares 'DRINK ME' or 'EAT ME'.

23rd June

Lunch in Venice Beach with Steve, Glenne, Kevin and Phoebe, where nothing on the menu promises to add a millimetre to anyone's waistline – Lean, Mean Cuisine. Self-obsession is given a couple of spin-dries and someone points out that everyone round the table is currently in a movie playing somewhere in town. 'Lucky you to be doing an Altman.' Indeedy. LUCKY LUCKY LUCKY!

Go alone to a five p.m. showing of Julia Roberts in *Dying Young* at a Cineplex in Santa Monica. In the queue, I meet Suzanne Todd and Demi Moore (who is seven weeks shy of giving birth). I am curious. With *Ghost* a massive hit last summer, and having experienced the bodyguard and hoopla surrounding Bruce in Rome, I am taken aback to see her mingling with the general public. And ask why. To which she replies, 'Why not? No hassles unless you make a hassle. Plus I wanted to see the movie with a regular audience.' True enough, some folk notice her and people do a little whisper-and-point work, but otherwise no big deal, which confirms my conviction that a celebrity may pass through the GREAT UNWASHED unharmed, so long as he or she doesn't make a great song and dance about it. In everyday circumstances, of course, acknowledging that in the event of a publicized première, hysteria prevails and has to be controlled and cordoned off.

'How's Bruce?'

'Burnt. The *Hawk* press has been really tough.' There is nothing to say, really, and we sit together in the stalls.

24th June

First night-shoot on *The Player*. Five p.m. call. Location: St James Club on Sunset Boulevard. Originally owned by Mae West, but revamped and done up in deco style, it looks like a mini-skyscraper thirties radio, with curvy top and concrete sculpted palm trees up the sides. The film unit is using their biggest suite for makeup, wardrobe, equipment, *et al.* on the top floor, with a perfect view of the city stretched below. Dean Stockwell and Tim Robbins are already here and very friendly and relaxed, as is Bob, as is everyone. No sign of THE FEAR in these collective eyes. We sit down together, once dressed, on the balcony, and talk around the scene and about the scene, and anecdotes about various writer-producer pitches are related. Then we seem to fall into 'doing' the dialogue, offering ideas or variations. Bob says to keep him surprised and not over-rehearse. Dean is telling stories about Hollywood going right back to his days as a child-star playing in *The Boy with Green Hair*, the end of the studio system and how the town is now governed by fleets of accountants.

We are called downstairs to the poolside area, which, though real, looks like an especially built set. It's a narrow pool, built on a cantilevered balcony with a line of concrete palm trees along the edge. Blue lit. The cameraman is the French-Canadian Jean Lepine, with whom I jumble up my pidgin Franglais. The camera is mounted on a large metal arm, or jib, enabling it to swing round, up or down, and during the rehearsal you have no idea whether you are in close-up, wide angle or even out of the shot. The usual format of shooting a scene, with a 'Master' shot including the entire action, followed by the coverage of individual close-ups and over-the-shoulder shots, is dispensed with, so that everything is filmed much more quickly and fluidly and you have no notion of whether the camera is on you or not. Which means that instead of actors saving themselves for their close-ups, they remain completely involved and in character through-out the shooting of a scene. Bob encourages us to improvise and add whatever we think appropriate to the existing scripted scene, with the assurance that if what we do falls flat it's for him to decide and worry about and edit out, rather than for us to feel we have either succeeded or failed. His conversation is peppered with 'I don't know how it's gonna be and I don't want to. Surprise me.' Each of us is fitted with a radio microphone, hidden in shirt collar or pocket and linked to 'Altman Central' – Bob's headphones, meaning he can earwig everyone's conversation off-screen and on! He is EAGLE-EYED and HAWK-EARED. Does not miss a thing.

The first part of the scene involves some typically Hollywood 'schmoozetalk' from the writer-producer partners, played by myself and Dean, trying to grab the attention of Andie MacDowell, who appears as herself, supposedly having a drink in the club bar. The last time I had worked with Andie was in Budapest and her good manners have avoided any delve into the horrors of that epic. Or the resultant flick and première. Suffice to say, we are both mightily relieved to be 'outta there'.

Just before shooting I go for some obligatory bladder relief, stare at my reflection and have a mini-seizure about not looking 'in character'. Panic and maul my withered locks this way and that and suddenly see possibilities in a 'neo-Adolf' style. I take a deep breath and push through the swing doors, wondering whether someone will send me back with a 'Come off it'. Nobody does and, having done it, I feel different. Now, I know this is not the kind of in-depth Method-motivated decision expected of a serious artist, but sometimes these instant decisions are unavoidable. Point is, I've convinced myself that I now look every bit as pretentious as my character requires. Bob suggests I smoke thin cigarillos.

Malcolm McDowell is here to appear as himself in the club lobby and, having been so mesmerized by him in A Clockwork Orange, I find myself unable to say much more than 'pleased to meet you'. But I stare out of the corner of my eye every time he hovers, thrown back to 1972 and sneaking out to see a midnight screening while supposedly cramming for 'O' levels. The film was shown late, and at an exorbitant ticket price, as it was banned in neighbouring South Africa. It arrived in the Kingdom with huge fanfare and prohibition-type publicity and played for about two years, mainly for Afrikaner farmers and tourists, coming to view the 'forbidden fruits of Western Decadence'. Alex and his 'droogs', cavorting and marauding through a futurist thugland to the synthesized sounds of Beethoven made an indelible, terrifying impression upon this fifteen-year-old brain and, even though I know how films are made and a performance created, there remains something about a screen creation I find hard to separate from the actor who has embodied the role. With the result that no matter what else I have seen Malcolm McDowell in, his Alex is forever lurking. A bit like Anthony Perkins and Norman Bates. Indelible and inseparable. A kind of casting curse. Which, no doubt, inhibits any attempt on my part to ask, 'What are you up to, Malcolm?'

Most of the night is taken up with the car-arriving scene and initial meeting with Tim, Dean, Andie and me. The actual 'pitch' is given a stay of execution till tomorrow night. Tim asks if I will be in his scripted and directed first feature *Bob Roberts* this October, which is flattering and ironic as my character in the scene is hell-bent on selling his character a movie script.

25th June

Call Carrie Fisher, who's about to leave for Europe. She wants to know the lowdown on *Hudson Hawk*, and I pitch the epic in condensed anecdotes, like a dry-run for the speed required for the scene to be shot tonight.

Dailies shown at production offices at three o'clock. Everyone is invited, unlike the usual Fort Knox security, which 'protects' the actors from seeing their efforts. Gets laughs and the Adolf hairstyle does not seem as extreme as I feared it might be. Bob is pleased, says, 'Happy?', to which I 'ish'. Dean and Tim seem so naturalistic. When we get to shoot the scene that evening, there is no apparent break between when they are just talking and when the 'performance' begins. Can't see the join. Enviable.

My pitch involves selling Tim Robbins the condensed storyline of a movie 'in less than twenty-five words'. READY SET GO, and as I am playing someone in a high old state of anxiety *and* punctuating with quick drags on the cigarillo, my lungs are now apoplectic and hyper-ventilating. After a couple of takes my stomach caves in and three meals hurtle out of my mouth. Only I haven't managed to make it off the set and am forced to offload into a large potted palm at the entrance. 'OH, MY GAAAD' gasps in the near vicinity, as I begin a round of apologies for having 'heaved' so publicly and violently. 'You should have told us you can't smoke. We woulda got you some herbal cigarettes.' I mumble something about not being able to get herbal cigarillos. Feeling like a right wally, I lie down for a bit before going back for another go.

'This ever happen to you before?' asks Bob.

'Not quite. During the final rehearsal day for *Withnail*, but then I *was* leglessly drunk.'

'Cut the cigarillo, then.'

'I'll just have a go trying not to inhale it this time. Got a bit excited during the last few takes, that's all.'

'So it's not my direction, then?'

26th June

Three p.m. dailies. This is the first 'audience' and, albeit partisan, it is ruthlessly critical about what works and what doesn't. Grip the seat when my movie pitch gets underway, and wonder whether my nausea will somehow be 'visible'. People laugh and the relief is huge because when doing it the night before I had forgotten how funny the scene, as written, actually is.

Bob says to feel free to come and watch the big party scene scheduled for the evening. Mostly, when filming, free days are so valued that going to watch other people work is about the last thing you want to do. Except my time on this is a total of a week's work over a month, and the people are Jack Lemmon, playing the piano at a 'typical' Hollywood party by the pool, Sally Kellerman, Hotlips Houlihan from *M*A*S*H*, leg in plaster-cast humming to Mr Lemmon's tinklings, Rod Steiger, standing in a window figuring out how a window-waterfall is working, Jeff Goldblum descending a spiral staircase, director Sydney Pollack playing a power-broker, Harry

Belafonte in conversation with Robert Wagner and Jill St John, Marlee Maitlin speaking in sign language to Danny Thomas, in the midst of which Tim Robbins and Cynthia Stephenson are operating as REEL characters among the real thing. Everyone is radio-miked and a large track on the edge of the lit pool accommodates the camera crew on a moving 'dolly', the camera again on the mobile jib moving in and around the action. It takes time to co-ordinate everyone moving and talking and 'being themselves', with Bob as ringmaster, cajoler and joker. As midnight approaches he is full of 'I warned you guys it would be boring and none of you were gonna get paid anything much for showing up, I warned you!' to which Jack Lemmon rejoins. 'Will you just shut the [hits a chord] up!' Nobody minds. Nobody complains. Come one a.m., Bob announces, 'I'm sure I could keep you lovely folks out here all night and shoot the shit out of this scene, but I can't think of anything else to do, so I suggest we all just go home. Thanks very much. You were all wonderful. Brilliant performances of yourselves. G'night.' Gets a round of applause.

Sydney Pollack, the Oscar-winning director of *Out of Africa*, is asking, 'How does he do it? I took this part just so's I could figure out how he does it.'

27th June

Early morning earthquake. Six on the Richter scale. Sleep through it. Go to Columbia Studios to see a preview of *Prince of Tides*, not the final version, we are told, but 'Work in Progress'. The director herself slips in as the lights lower and sits at a console of controls surrounded by her team, including ex-husband Elliott Gould. The first-look audience goes doo-lally when BARBRA STREISAND comes up on the credits. Cheers at the end.

29th June

Eeny, meeny, miny, mo – to which party do I go? An agent from a rival agency is on the woo. The Altmans' for dinner in Malibu? A producer for dinner and the screening of Madonna's film, too? Susan Sarandon and Tim for a barbecue?

Tim and Susan have rented a big house in Brentwood Canyon to which they have invited all the actors in the Actors' Gang Theatre Company, which Tim co-founded and for which he still directs between films. He is the one in the movies. They are doing theatre in LA and the financial division is like that old title, *To Have and Have Not*. It's mostly men and rather like a sophomore social. Guitars, football, songs and very competitive water-polo in the pool. An antidote to 'Hollywood'. However, Susan embarks upon a theory that divides people up into men with predominantly feminine qualities, and women who are predominantly masculine, which neatly segues into actors and actresses, concluding somewhere late and bleary-eyed about Marlon Brando being very feminine and Meryl Streep being masculine, with various people falling into masculine-masculine or feminine-feminine categories, after which we divided up the world and everyone we knew with that kind of fervent intensity you have around three o'clock in the morning when everything seems *so* clear – and almost incomprehensible the following dawn. Like trying to retrace a dream. We are quite sure, though, that all the real 'greats' of either sex had a potent supply of the opposite gender in their souls.

'So how about you and Tim?'

'Oh, c'mon, he's very feminine and I'm masculine, which is why it works so well.'

Tim giants to the fridge and says, 'What "feminine" bullshit are you two on about?'

'YOU ARE,' choruses out of both of us. Which seems especially daft, looking at this six-foot four-inch man towering over the kitchen table.

'He IS!' cackles Susan.

'I'm going to bed.' He lopes, I leave and there are some bodies asleep on the sofas.

30th June

We are at a warehouse somewhere in Culver City, to shoot the finale of the film within the film that my character has written and directed. Having stipulated 'no stars, no pat Hollywood endings' he has inevitably capitulated to the Hollywood system. The set is a gas chamber, where the heroine is being executed.

Altman has hired Julia Roberts and Bruce Willis for a day to play these characters. Bruce is delivering a send-up of his *Die Hard* heroics, and Julia is giving her best victim Bambi-eyed acting. Added to which, Louise Fletcher's Oscar-win for Nurse Ratchet in *Cuckoo's Nest* is reprised as a gas chamber attendant. The reporters and onlookers include Susan Sarandon and Peter Falk.

Someone has computed that the collective salaries normally demanded by the stars who have agreed to do a day or two on this film would budget at around $110 million. Why do they do it for 'nothing'? For LOVE? For Bob, which is one and the same thing. All this for a man who has been working in Europe for the past few years. For a director who has fallen from grace in the eyes of Them. More than once have I heard the bleat of 'But WHY? That guy hasn't had a hit in years.'

1st July

Universal Studios for location lunch with Steve Martin and Diane Keaton. She is very funny yet 'unwritedownable'.

I have a meeting for *Dracula* with Francis Ford Coppola the following evening and ask Diane if she has any advice. She looks into the middle distance, as if her *Godfather* pasts were just hovering there, pauses, then says, 'Ohhhhh, Francis is just ... well, like Francis.' Again she smiles at some private recollection and looks up as if her enigmatic answer was perfectly clear, and, almost as an afterthought, says, 'You'll be fine ... fine.' And that's it. She leaves you sort of dangling mid-air, though you know her sentence has full-stopped. Like a private stream of thought that *might* just spill over into conversation, but then again most likely will not. With the result that you half drop your jaw expecting some more, and then she is 'gone'. Like a Woody Allen scene for real.

Steve Dontonville calls to give me the details for my meeting with Mr Coppola: 'Go down to Culver City, take a left on West Washington Boulevard, left again into Columbia Sony Studios and ask Security for directions to the Joan Crawford Building, where you will meet casting director Vicky Thomas. Five thirty. Prepare pages twenty-nine through thirty-one and page fifty. Good luck.' End of answerphone message. Second message: 'Give us a call when you're done to let us know how it went. OK? Bye.'

I pass the giant doors of various studios the size of aircraft hangars. *HOOK* SET CLOSED TO ALL VISITORS. DO NOT ENTER WITH-OUT AUTHORIZATION. This skull-and-crossbones message is painted red across door after vast door. Scenery-trucks are piled up with dying foliage outside, and chunks of fake tree-trunks render adults the size of Lost Boys. Which is about what I feel like on my way to finding and meeting Mr Coppola. Past the Judy Garland Building, and into Joan Crawford and there is Francis, all in black, with red braces and psychedelic tie, and 'well . . . like Francis'.

He does not sit, and pads back and forth talking and gesticulating as if kneading invisible pizza dough. Whereas I was told to prepare for a screen test, he has overshot that already and is telling me what a great role Dr Seward is, how many ideas he has, what the shooting dates will be and how he is currently hassling with the money men to make a deal possible. I sit wondering when he is going to ask me at least to read a scene for him but then the meeting is over, he is gone and I am out and vaguely dazed. Wander along in a WAS HE? DID HE? state of flux when a voice with short red hair yells, 'RICHARD!' from some distance. Knowing no one here I turn to look behind me to see which Richard is being hailed. 'RICHARD!! C'MERE.'

I obey and am greeted by the kilowatt smile of Tinkerbell, a.k.a. Julia Roberts, sporting pointy elfin ears, red boy's wig and leather shift leaf costume. 'What are *you* doing here?'

I tell her, and she asks 'Will you stay and play awhile? D'you wanna meet Steven?' Tink links arms, and leads me on to a soundstage, past the beefy eyes of uniformed Security, to meet Mr Spielberg. BLINK BLINK. Eyes adjust to the interior dark and an upstanding Legend. Manage a 'pleased to meet you', surf his pause till he replies, 'You're *Withnail*, right?'

A gigantic lantern, erected in front of a blank screen, is where Tinkerbell is perched, so big as to make Julia look very small. He explains that the background will be 'married' to a background via processing. Wearing regulation baseball cap, jeans and T-shirt, he is like someone's teenage brother. 'I've gotta meeting with your Prime Minister, John Major, later this year about funding the British film industry. Listen, would you mind trying to make Julia laugh in this little scene? Problem is, all her scenes are to no one as her stuff is all Blue-Screen processed.' YES, YES, MR SPIELBERG, HOWEVER MANY BAGS FULL, MR SPIELBERG. He talks so fast and so unassumingly that there is no time to fart and quaver, and Julia is hoisted up, and I launch into some Hudson Hawkery, as it's still 'freshly roasting'. She *does* laugh, although I wonder at the ethics of getting Tinkerbell to chortle at the shenanigans of Sandra Bernhard. Couple of takes and Mr Spiel is 'glad to meet you' and off on a caddy-cart to another set, apparently go-karting his way from one set-up and camera unit to another, such is the scale of the production and pressure on his time. Murray Close, the English stills photographer, whom I know from *Withnail*, is snapping *Hook* and says to come and see Bob Hoskins. Julia asks if I want to meet for dinner later. 'I'll call and leave the address.'

This is all getting a bit too Never-Never Land.

Bob is bearded up to play Pirate Smee and reassures me that 'Francis is brilliant, will cast you, you wait and see', and relates how he was cast in *The Cotton Club* on a Friday, flown to New York and started shooting the following Monday. When he speaks, his eyes widen while his voice gruffs, with a fluctuating expression of surprise. Like a grown-up child. 'C'mon, meet Dustin!'

Mr Hoffman is slumped in a chair on the deck of Captain Hook's ship, which is a huge, life-sized re-creation designed by John Napier and is crawling with Lost Boys, Pirates and technicians, afloat in a shallow tank of green 'sea'. No doubt he has met boatloads of folk today and I am reluctant to disturb his Hook-heels *off* time.

Bob 'Go on's and I mealy-mouth a 'Sorry to disturb you, but very pleased to meet you!'

He asks, 'Have you signed the visitor's book yet?'

The reputations of the director, stars and sets have attracted Head of State visitations.

Get back to the hotel and a message to meet Julia, Jason Patric and Co. at a nearby eaterie. Get there and find a message to go to another address. Third restaurant looks shut, and I'm ready to give up playing Snakes and Ladders when a car attendant asks who I'm looking for. *Sotto voce*. Nods to go inside. Julia apologizes and says they have literally been hounded out by the press and followed all over the place. 'Well, you shouldn't have dumped your bridgeroom at the eleventh hour,' is what plops out of my mouth, which makes her already wide one gape. This, out of Mr Patric's earshot. Being the only Limey in their 'bunch' might be the reason why Julia has taken to speaking in a cod Noël Coward accent, by way of including me in the conversation.

3rd July

Doldrummed. Stalled, waiting to hear about *Dracula*. *'If you're gonna shoot me, then shoot me, but don't dawdle about!'*

Queued for the six p.m. first day showing of *Terminator II*, counting on Arnie to blast away the pall. Place is HEAVING. Loud talk all through the previews and ads, dead silence for the Studio Logo. Decibel BOMBARDMENT greets the title. There's a 'Mexican wave' when ARNOLD SCHWARZENEGGER prints out and it's a two-hour Testosteround climaxing in gladiatorial applause and cheering. 'YO! YOH! YOH! MAN.' Tears from some who can barely believe that everything they hoped for and then some has been delivered. Head-shakings and mutterings that 'HE TRULY IS A G-O-D!' puts any of my purpling into perspective.

4th July

Independence Day. Altman party in Malibu. Dress code; red, white and blue. Buy US Flag stickers and plaster my clothes, hair and face with them, and trek up the coast looking like a stamped parcel for just about the best party I have ever been to. Why? Well, I will try . . . EASE. In every sense. Their condo is on the Pacific Ocean. I don't mean NEAR, but ON the beach. The living room is dominated by the sound and sight of the pounding surf immediately beyond the wall-to-wall windows. Katherine is the coolest, keenest hostess I know, makes everyone feel hugely welcome, every detailed arrangement seem effortless, unfussed.

She has been married to Bob for thirty years, and they kind of 'top 'n' tail' one another with an outward show of EASE. Like hand-hewn spoons. They are somewhere in their sixties chronologically, but are indeterminately ageless and inquisitive, yet without any vestige of that certain strain that develops like a virus – 'middle-aged trendism' – whereby desperadoes attempt to be-bop themselves into frillier fashions, tighter pants and nightshade red or black hairdyes, the haunted look of 'last call at the singles bar' furrowing up a pack of brows. Please, God, when my turn swifts up, do NOT let me fit a rug to my balding cranium or wrench some designer jeans around my saggy 'cheeks'. Remember this wisdom. EASE . . .

Most of the cast cruises in, and the unexpected coup is to have cast musicians in the film. Angela Hall, fresh from the Broadway run of *Black and Blue*, has brought her tap shoes and starts dancing and singing with the jazz trio. She's followed up by Annie Ross, who lays down some true smoked-Scottish salmon-pink blues. People are listening, eating, dancing, talking, Fourth of Julying. Then it's Lyle Lovett's set, of lyrical, haunted, Texan-dry ballads, accompanied by a cello and that drum that sounds as if someone is falling asleep while swishing something across the floor. He, in turn, gives way to Tim Robbins playing guitar and singing Tom Waits songs, then Gospel. Then there are fireworks over the Ocean, from Malibu Patriots. Food, candles, dancing, singing and I know no matter how I try to write this it will be a mere cornball to what it was like to be there. Apart

The Player • 219

from the absence of wife and baba, THIS is a night of perfect happiness. Unalloyed. PURE. Enough to make me cry, *knowing it now*, in the moment rather than reconstituted in memory.

11th July

Coppola's short-lived Zoetrope Studios in Hollywood are the location for the studio complex within the film. Bob has decided to open the movie with a record-breaking tracking shot that will introduce many of the characters and the daily activities of a studio. It's worked out with a model first, then set up on a huge crane in the parking lot. Everyone is choreographed to walk, drive in, enter, exit, pitch a movie, deliver the post, gossip, whatever, all apparently spontaneously. The whole sequence is rehearsed all morning until it coordinates smoothly, without breaks or cuts. The movie will start with a homage to the *movies*. Were this to be attempted by most other directors some steam would inevitably escape sideways somewhere. Not so with Bob. You get the impression that all of this paraphernalia is as familiar as a well-used Meccano set to him, and nothing is going to upset his enjoyment of the whole process. Even when he declares that he hasn't a clue what's going on.

I've only a couple more scenes to go. One involves a second script pitch in Tim Robbins' office via a telephone 'conference call', with me gesticulating to an inert phone cradle while Peter Gallagher listens in his car; the other is a scene in the screening room, in which I have totally sold out, capitulated to having stars and a happy ending, and end up *justifying myself.*

On my way back to the hotel I hear a radio DJ talking about having his mobile phone stolen, then calling his number, then having someone answer. Then his outraged disbelief that he was talking to the thief: 'I DON' BELIEVE THIS. YOU'RE THE GUY WHO STOLE MY PHONE?' To which the thief says, 'DEAD RIGHT, MAN, WHAT YOU GONNA DO 'BOUT IT?' Brilliant! Method-acting or hoax? Either way, Only in LA, I thought.

My room smells potently perfumed. Discover a huge bouquet of lilies and a note: 'Please come and visit the *Hook* set, love Julia.' How can I resist? Agent messages that say they 'hear' *Dracula* looks like a possibility. Hum a couple of choruses of *Pretty Woman* as I cha-cha round the room.

Have dinner with Robert Downey Jnr, who is so permanently 'wired' he makes me feel placid and turtle-calm. Watching and listening to him play five different synthesizers at once and flicking from one techno-gadget to another, I settle back feeling about seven years old to his turbo-charged FIVE.

12th July

Hooked and flattered my way down to Columbia Studios and into Ms Roberts's caravan. She is in her Tink gear, except for the pointy ears which await attachment on the makeup table. 'Check *this* stuff.' She is scrabbling through a pile of newspapers, cuttings and magazines spread around her. 'This business is insane.' Headlines, by-lines, short ones, tall ones – ALL declare variations on the same theme. That is—

JULIA ROBERTS FIRED.

REPLACED BY MICHELLE PFEIFFER BY FURIOUS SPIELBERG

THE PRICE OF FAME. ROBERTS COLLAPSES ON SET OF 'HOOK'.

ROBERTS ADMITTED TO RE-HAB CLINIC.

ROBERTS' CONDITION UNSTABLE.

CLOSE FRIENDS SAY . . .

She is laughing and shaking her head in disbelief. 'You tell me? *Have* I been fired? D'you see Michelle lurking around somewhere? You can tell me. I can take it. Haven't you noticed how drugged and incoherent I am right now? It must be true. It's written here on every page. Even got pictures of me with a bag over my head. I *must* be this drugged-out mad witch they say I am. Oh, this one says I'm having a nervous breakdown and suffering anorexia,' she says, chomping an apple. 'You're my witness that I have not been fired, drugged or hospitalized today.' She treats it like it's a game, but I can't help wondering at the price for this global attention and multiple-zero pay-packaged fame.

13th July

One of the producers of *The Player*, Nick Wechsler, and his associate, Keith Addis, are giving a party at a house above Sunset Boulevard. I follow directions up and round and round manicured houses, till a queue of parked cars and a VALET PARKING sign loom ahead. Flashing torches, and a smiling valet gives you a ticket, leaving you worry-free to wander along the candle-lit pathway into a party which has more stars orbiting than I ever saw *this* side of the silver screen. All yakking and drinking and snacking and schmoozing and I catch myself short and ask, 'Well, what did you *expect* them all to be doing, other than yakkin', drinkin', snackin' and schmoozin'?'

Among the waiters, agents and 'various' in a large living room with access to a terrace beyond, I bee-line for Bob and Katherine Altman to get my bearings. No sooner am I 'anchored' than a familiar but never-met-before face looms close and says, 'Hi,' with disarming familiarity. Split-second mental congestion – 'Are we related? Neighbours? Fellow passengers on the same train or bus route?'

'I'm Mimi Rogers, how d'you do?'

'I KNOW who you are. Pleased to meet *you*.' Exchange compliments and eat canapés.

'Can I join you guys?'

'Why, sure. You meet each other before?'

'No, but I know your work so I feel like I do,' says Rosanna Arquette.

This sort of conversation ebbs and flows for the rest of the evening. To my oblique left Gabriel Byrne and Ellen Barkin are talking to Barbra Streisand. BARBRA STREISAND!?! It is at this sighting that the room goes on a *Poseidon Adventure*. Upside down and inside out. I turn my head in what feels like slow motion and say, 'That's Barbra Streisand,' to which Rosanna says, 'Yeah, d'you know her?'

'That's Babs,' is all I can murmur.

'You *do* know her?'

'No, Rosanna, no, not *know* HER, but ... Jesus ... that's Barbra Streisand.' If you *are* a fan of hers, then no explanation will be needed for my apoplexy. If, perhaps, you feel otherwise (and I have been told she inspires the two extremes), then skip along down. Unless, of course, you are one of those sadists ready for a good cackle at how Swazi Boy made a good frothing of himself before her.

As with *any* obsession/fanaticism, there is some personal history attached to this one, which I feel duty-bound to share with you. It will inform the state I was in, being *this* close and panicking about *how* to get an audience. Reel back to an 'overseas trip' *circa* spring 1969 from Swaziland to Europe. Home Leave, as it was colonially called, although I was born a few thousand miles south of Piccadilly Circus. Aged twelve, in short pants and scropped hair, knees like knobbly knuckles, hairless and Hungry for Culture. Parents divorced and reshuffled. This was my first trip abroad with father and new stepmother, taking in capital cities of Europe before England. After Madrid, Rome, and days of Ruin and Cathedrals, we went to see *Funny Girl* in the cinema, mainly because it was in English with Italian sub-titles. None of us had ever seen anyone like her before. Having harboured an idea that I would one day become an actor, the effect of hearing this extraordinary person singing 'I'm the Greatest Star' was seismic. As if *she* somehow *knew* exactly what was going on in my head. I remember feeling a bit shivery, as if everyone must be able to 'see' my dream. That the Rags-to-Riches scenario was the clichéd plot-line of a hundred flicks didn't matter as I had never encountered it before. But more than anything else was this VOICE. I have never been a serial-faller-in-love and can count the number of times I've been THUNDERBOLTED. This was one. All great artists seem to share this common denominator: they make YOU feel that YOU are the only one being addressed. No matter that you are surrounded by evidence to the contrary and like-minded folk blathering about this brushstroke, that note, this phrasing, that concept, this vision, those comparisons. You just want to say, 'BELT UP. IT'S ME! – I'M THE ONE THAT GETS IT.' No matter that my parents came out and said, 'We have to buy her records.' WHAT DID THEY KNOW? I KNEW! I formed my own UNDERGROUND MOVEMENT right then and there. Membership – one. Mission – IMPOSSIBLE.

Having a secret is so fantastically sustaining and comforting, especially when teenage turbulence squalls up. My parents bought the records, but I was totally convinced that *only I* had the monopoly of true UNDERSTANDING. When I heard her belt through 'Gotta Move', I seriously thought this gal *must* be psychic. *How else could she possibly have sung this song without knowing that I was counting down the years ahead before I would fly this coop, become an actor, marry her, and hear her sing to our two children on a clear day?* I read in a magazine that having such fantasies was 'perfectly normal and just a passing phase'. It was an attempt to explain to worried parents *why* their kids had suddenly gone ballistic over some idol. How *could* they understand my depression when I read that, having divorced Elliott Gould to make way for me, she was now involved with Prime Minister Trudeau? Or any of the other pretenders to her affections down the next few years? When I heard she was having a relationship with Ryan O'Neal I felt as though I'd been stabbed. When news reached me that they had split up and that the pressures of fame were proving too much for her, my relief was so great that I almost believed that whoever Reuters was 'his' newspiece was the result of having to resort to printed press to reach me as she did not know my address. It prompted the only fan letter I have yet written and posted. (I of course kept a copy.)

Dear Barbra Streisand

I sincerely hope this reaches you personally. You don't know me yet, but I am writing to you to offer an idea you might like to consider. My name is Richard and I live in a small African Kingdom called Swaziland in south-east Africa. Since seeing *Funny Girl* we, my family that is, and I have been very big fans. I have followed your career avidly. We have all your records. I am fourteen years old. I read in the paper that you were feeling very tired and pressurized by your fame and failed romance with Mr Ryan O'Neal. I would like to offer you a two-week holiday, or longer, at our house, which is very beautiful with a pool and magnificent view of the Ezulweni Valley. Which the Swazi people call the Valley of Heaven. I think you will agree when you see it. Here you can rest. No one will trouble you and I assure you you will not be mobbed in the street as your films only show in our one cinema for three days, so not that many people will know who you are, so no chance of being mobbed. Please consider this respite seriously. You will always be welcome.

Yours very sincerely

And in anticipation of a hasty reply,
Richard.

P.S. I am studying Shakespeare's *Midsummer Night's Dream* and hope these lines will reassure you: *Theseus* – 'For never anything can be amiss when simpleness and duty tender it', or *Puck* – 'If we shadows have offended, think but this and all is mended. That you have but slumber'd here, while these visions did appear.' Yours, Richard

I typed her name and the 'care of Columbia Records' address on my father's typewriter to give it as much officialdom as I could muster, never, of course, breathing a word of this secret document to another living soul but posting it, resolved to deal with parental-accommodation details upon receiving her reply. An undeniable element of all this is *knowing* that the likelihood of ever *getting* a reply is small but it's a Message in a Bottle. Thrilling, fabulous and totally daft! As daft as drawing her profile through tracing paper and then practising, till doodling her nose while revising for exams, day-dreaming, whatever, was second nature. Getting the curve of her lips *just right* and imagining a smooch as long as any of the notes she was capable of holding, for things had begun to go hormonally haywire.

Every now and again my obsession would be aired, and inevitably ridiculed by the legion of Ali MacGraw admirers walloping around. Having sexual dreams and fantasies about 'Babs' sustained me through all the years I was told, '*Who do you think you are, thinking you will ever make it as an actor?*', which was heard concurrently with 'Nobody listens to that screecher anyway. Her nose is too big.' My reply to such remarks was to remain silent, filled from top to toe with psychotic plans to detonate such treasonous tongues.

Days, weeks, months, years I waited – there was no reply. Robinson Crusoe waited twenty, didn't he? And the 'phase' never passed.

The editor on *How To Get Ahead In Advertising* and *Withnail and I*, Alan Strachan, is similarly obsessed. I recall walking into the cutting room by chance one day and finding him working on a scene to the accompaniment of Babs. He confessed he had fallen in love, married, had kids and still felt honour-bound to tell his wife that his love was shared. Bruce came in at some point and offered some suitably withering damnation, but the secret pleasure of knowing that the editing of these two flicks, so close to my heart, was done to this 'other' soundtrack, was *deep*!

SWAZ MEETS STREISAND. This ticker-tape logo spools endlessly around my skull. It is flying around the room above everyone's heads as if attached to a light biplane advertising above a crowded beach: 'SWAZ MEETS STREISAND. TONIGHT. ONE PERFORMANCE ONLY!'

I have to admit that the now-crowded room is posing a problem. *How* to get introduced *without* making a total rumbaba of myself. I excuse myself as calmly as I can, locate the hostess of the evening, passing on my way Al Pacino, Whoopi Goldberg, Jeff Goldblum, Diane Lane, Christopher Lambert, Julia Roberts, Jason Patric, Sandra Bernhard, Isaac Mizrahi, Joel Silver, Annie Ross, Glenne Headly, Timothy Dalton, John Shea, Ken Wahl, Robert Downey Jnr, Annabella Sciorra and Winona Ryder, and splurge, 'I beg of you, *please* can you introduce me to Barbra Streisand? I've never met her and I know how private she is but the best man at my wedding was Alan Corduner who played in *Yentl*, my wife was the dialect coach on the movie and I saw a preview of *Tides* this week.' I dredge up *any* kind of résumé that might help. She says to wait, goes over, confabs, comes back and I sort of levitate my way towards her. Ellen Barkin moves off and I hear these words: 'Barbra, this is Richard E. Grant – Richard, Barbra Streisand.'

Petite, in a black hat and antique black lace dress with boots, she offers a hand and I 'platz'. What comes out of my mouth is a garbled, high speed, 'Alan Corduner from *Yentl*, Joan my wife, since I was twelve years old so pleased I can hardly believe this please forgive me but this is twenty years in the dreaming, oh my God,' which she rightly cuts short with 'Are you stoned?' Then a slightly slower less garbled apology and attempted explanation that 'No, I am allergic to alcohol,' fa-la-fa and to forgive the intrusion please and verbals.

Clearly used to the odd nutter breaking through her barrier, she says calmly, 'I know you from a movie.' I don't care a jot that she's probably lying, until she says, 'Tell me what you've been in.' I gabble the list and she said, '*Henry and June* – that's it, but you're English?' She then applies the calming tactics of a qualified asylum expert and asks me about the cinematographer, Philippe Rousselot, whose work she really admired. 'How's he do it?'

'Fast, brilliantly and with infinite love for people's faces.' She praises the extraordinary beauty of Uma Thurman and asks why I'm here. Once I'm relatively at ease, YEAH, LIKE WALKING A TIGHT-ROPE BETWEEN THE EMPIRE STATE AND THE CHRYSLER BUILDING, she says, 'So you saw *Prince of Tides*. Where? How come?' I tell her. But she wants the specific date and which showing. Then she grills me with questions about *everything*. During which time I have an overwhelming desire just to *kiss her* and wrap her round like that famous photo of the sailor in Times Square kissing a gal on the Day the War Ended. No doubt the dilation of my pupils has convinced her that I am either about to pass out or convulse. She keeps asking and wants *detail, detail, detail*. 'So you *hated* the music?' and I hear first-person-DIRECT come from my throat as opposed to the endless silent conversations 'we' have had over the years. '*No*, Barbra. I said I liked the music, but that I thought it was too loud in that breakthrough scene when Nick Nolte opens up in the office.'

'TOO LOUD?'

'I just think if it's swelling up that much, at that point, it seems like you're telegraphing what is already happening. Strong enough without that *extra*.' She nods and pauses and says, 'So what else didn't you like?'

I can feel the smile that has embalmed my face getting a second varnishing and say, 'Do you mind if I tell you something?'

'Go ahead.' Instead of respectfully sticking to the topic of *Tides*, I tell her about this letter I had written when I was fourteen, which makes her laugh, and then she says, 'I don't remember claiming to be exhausted then. Must just be the usual press stuff.' I know my time's 'up', because the very nature of any fantalk is a conversational cul-de-sac. How *do* you begin to reply to someone blathering worship-filled idolatries at you? It's embarrassing and, yes, flattering, but very soon a Dead End.

She proffers her tapered hand. I ask if I can kiss it, to which she laughs and says, 'OK,' after which she's saved any further frothings from me.

The remainder of the evening is a cocktail party haze. No one and nothing much else gets a look in. Save Winona Ryder, who moseys up with her younger brother, Uri, both of them teenagers, who together blow a duet of praise in my stupefied direction about *Withnail*, their compliments as remote from the encounter of the first kind I had just had *yet*, at the same time, they were doing *exactly* what I had just done to Babs. Then Winona gets very grown-up and serious about my being in *Dracula*. I tell her that I met Francis some time back and haven't heard a peep since. Although she looks like a 'child-woman', with perfect pale skin and jet hair, her self-possession is awesome. When she quells my doubting with, 'YOU ARE GONNA BE IN THIS MOVIE,' I believe her.

On my way out I cannot resist shooting a last glance at 'Babs' and I'm invaded by a strange emptiness – the cross that any fan has to bear – that while this 'idol' has such a significant place in my life and experience, I, of course, can have NONE in hers. I'm just another geeky gusher. Twenty-two minutes I had. Timed them. Replayed everything and can't quite believe she even told me about her eating habits in response to my asking how she managed to stay the same shape. Oi vey, Swaz. Some night.

14th July
Last shooting day. To complete this 'circle within a circle' go to a midnight showing of *A Clockwork Orange*, which I haven't seen since Swaziland twenty years ago. Since writing to Ms Streisand twenty years ago. Now having met Malcolm McDowell and Barbra Streisand in Hollywood, while playing in Robert Altman's *The Player*, I as good as feel ready to be boxed up and sent home.

Dracula

August 1991

Summer holiday in the South of France and my family is subjected to the usual overwrought chapter and verse of 'Life With an Actor'. That is, days of total euphoria swiftly stymied by dragoons of doubt soldiering about all over the place and ruining perfect weather and wonderful food. Doubt about whether Robbins' *Bob Roberts* and Coppola's *Dracula* or neither will COME THROUGH. A clear week interrupted by the real world of agents and possibility. Nothing ever clear cut but forever 'maybe'ing about like a bloody hive. In my head. I try to imagine myself in the reverse situation and conclude that were it Joan who was see-sawing about all this whatnot a double-barrelled shotgun might just be in order. This temporarily quells my jelly beans.

17th August

Tim Robbins calls me at 2 a.m. from New York and asks how things stand. I still don't know about *Dracula* but tell him so much time has elapsed now that it seems unlikely so I hope to be able to honour his offer for his film. He is apparently understanding about this.

19th August

Eight p.m. call from agent Steve Dontonville in LA. 'We have an offer on *Dracula*.' Now, with a decision taken, you might expect a deep sigh of relief – but nay, nay! The vertical thrill is such that I am flapping my feathers about and clucking in readiness for a good

'potting'. Having put up with all my snivellings, the delivery of the
'good news' presages separation from Joan, who thus resists running
around the olive trees like a *euphoric* beheaded hen. As I do. Call Tim
to tell him that the 'Godfather has made me an offer I cannnot
refuse'. Difficult.

2nd September

YOU ARE CORDIALLY INVITED TO A WEEK'S 'BONDING' AT THE COPPOLA
ESTATE IN NAPA VALLEY WITH THE CAST AND DIRECTOR. FRANCES WILL
BE COOKING DINNER FOR 8PM MONDAY 2ND SEPTEMBER.

Leaving my family after six weeks' holiday together is ghastly. My
three-year-old daughter is keening and crying and we are all undone
in a mess of goodbyes. Eighteen hours of domestic rearrange,
adrenalin and mayhem as I have to fly to London ahead of them,
open up the house, replace the light-bulbs that mysteriously pop after
their six weeks off, retrieve the goldfish from neighbours, water the
plants, pack and fly to San Francisco.

I intended sleeping on the flight but too anticipatory as per. There
is NO ESCAPE from *Hudson Hawk*, which is the in-flight film. On
the small screen, without sound, it plays out like a neutered cartoon.
Well, at least I'm not bound for Hungary, but am winging it to
Coppola's country retreat in the Napa Valley instead. It is the Labor
Day Holiday and the airport is jammed. Greg meets me with the
Zoetrope sign and we're off, driving for one and a half hours north
of 'Frisco. He's twenty-seven and friend of Roman Coppola, fledgeling
screenwriter, assistant editor, and son of Francis. He worked on
Godfather III and reminds me about the tragic death of Gino Coppola,
Roman's brother, killed in a boating accident six years ago.

The countryside shows the effects of a five-year drought, everything
dusty and carpet-brown. VAST open spaces, like Africa, with a full-
sized SKY; free of any cloud claustrophobics; 94 degrees, dry heat.
We cross a railway line into vineyards and pull up at a clapboard
thirties bungalow. This is where Carey Elwes, Bill Campbell and
myself – the three 'suitors' in the film – are barracked. 'Pick you guys

up later and take you up to the main house,' and Greg leaves. Bill *The Rocketeer* Campbell introduces himself like a dripping giant, having just jogged a couple of hundred miles. He is all gung-ho, square-jawed, built like a walking wall and incredibly friendly and open. He's very excited about this film – and who is in it. Carey Elwes, who has a moustache, gets off the phone and offers me a cigarette in a mid-Atlantic Malibu-Marlborough accent.

I unpack and familiarize. This house looks like the one in *The Wizard of Oz*, and the fly-screen doors and incredible heat remind me of my uncle's farm in the south of Swaziland.

'Let's walk up to the main house,' says Bill. The road stretches between vineyards to a narrow point in the far distance with a couple of mirages in between. 'Twilight – perfect time. Not too hot.' We trio out and, of course, the closer it seems, the further it is.

The house is a three-storey white clapboard Victorian *Giant*-style manse, with wrap-around veranda, enormous trees with benches around, manicured garden, pool, trampoline, and a panorama of vineyards and the Napa mountains in the dusky distance. Norman Rockwell and Edward Hopper 'scapes. Perfect.

Whether it's the time of day, heat, or jet-lag, there is an air of pre-supper somnambulance, with people dotted about like American Chekhov.

Gary Oldman is sitting on the wide verandah, ambles over and hugs me with a 'Hello, my darling,' in his distinctive 'little-boy-lost' mode, and declares he is feeling 'rat-arsed'. Having recently seen him in *State of Grace*, brilliantly portraying an unhinged state of mind with brutal physicality, it is a measure of his art that his slight frame can transform so extraordinarily in performance. There is little in his demeanour that gives any clue to this volcanic interior. The last time I saw him was in Paris while he was romancing Uma Thurman, but he shakes his head and says his eleven-month marriage to her 'is over' and says ponderingly, 'Maybe I'm gonna be one of those people who gets married a lotta times.' He tells me he is now living alone and looks sad.

Winona Ryder appears wearing a forties flower-print dress, sporting her minute eighteen-inch waist, and looking like Snow White. 'I told you you'd be in it. This is sooooo great!'

Keanu Reeves 'Hey, man!'s over and he and Winona are sibling-close. Discover we know Peter Capaldi in common (from *Dangerous Liaisons*).

Anthony Hopkins tracksuits up, having done a vineyard circuit, looks suntanned and fit, asks after Joan, with whom he has worked, and reminds me of the day and date we met some years ago. His memory outstrips that of Marilu Henner. I met him once and only briefly, but his recollection is photographic and unnerving. I have read that he loathed any kind of 'family-type set-up', which this week ahead is designed to be, and I'm not surprised to learn that he is in a separate guest house, alone. Again, his shy, diffident manner is in *total* contrast to the seismic-quakery of his performing self. Feel a bit frightened of him . . . Awed.

It seems odd to be hanging around a strange garden, meeting actors away from a rehearsal room, without any sign of the host, who is also director and producer. A working guest?

'Where can I find Francis?'

'I think he's cooking.'

Go through to the copper-potted kitchen that is bubbling and boiling and smelling spaghetti-sexy. Francis is in Hawaiian shirt and shorts, bare-footed and rolling gnocchi pasta on a floured table, with his wife Eleanor and an assistant and a trainee cook. 'Glad you're here. You wanna drink?' They're cooking for a large number, Francis claiming he wouldn't know how to cook for two! Maybe *this* is how he managed to make two perfect *Godfather*s, with their huge casts, before he was thirty-five?

Meet Sadie Frost, big eyes and 'so glad to get out of LA to Napa' but missing her baby son madly. Tom Waits lives in San Francisco so won't be staying over and is due in for rehearsals tomorrow.

Go for a swim in my undies as it's too far to go back to the bungalow. Francis plops in later and we get a somewhat strained, polite banter going and end up comparing notes about pool mainten-ance. Cross-cut with him telling me what a great role Dr Seward is, saying how much he loves anything scientific and medical. 'See you at dinner.' It's getting dark and I meet everyone on the veranda and Keanu has decided to call us by our second names – *Leonard* Oldman, *Phillip* Hopkins, *Laura* Ryder, *Simon* Elwes and himself, *Charles* Reeves – neutralizing the Fame factor and comically rendering us like the cast list of some old B movie *circa* 1947. First *good* laugh. Dinner at a table laid for twenty on the verandah, wine from the surrounding estate and Gary says it 'beats working for peanuts at the Royal Court'. Francis sits at the head dispensing gnocchi and stories as *padrone* of this *ad hoc 'famiglia'*.

3rd September

Nine a.m. sharp. The 'clan' gathers in a converted barn that is a mini-soundstage. Big 'square' of tables and chairs, copies of the Bram Stoker original in lieu of a plate setting. Video and sound equipment in the corner to record *everything*. Snack table. Props table. I am playing Dr Seward, sidekick to Dr van Helsing (played by Anthony Hopkins) and one of the three men obsessed with Lucy. Francis arrives, everyone takes their places and he begins: 'Actors are like bank accounts on the first day of rehearsals. I want to fill those accounts full of new experiences and relationships so that the final product will be rich.' He has a passion to rediscover what it is about Dracula, especially as there are already over two hundred films about him. WHY MAKE IT AGAIN?

'All this we hope to discover in the coming weeks.' He outlines his belief in rehearsals, for which the studio is unwilling to fork out, hence our being guests at his house for this extra week, where there is less pressure to 'produce stuff'. A little 'luxury time'. 'This is time to try out *anything* and *everything*. Books, references, films, costumes, props, *all* are at your disposal. We are gonna begin by reading through the original novel. That way *nobody* can bullshit that they *have* read it and actually haven't. Gonna attach microphones to each of you and record it all. It's written as individual journal entries by each character, so everyone gets a go.' I don't think any of us anticipated this back-to-school agenda and there is a splutter of laughs and 'What the f—?' Keanu kicks off and boldly attempts a Brit accent for Harker. The day drags interminably on with some folk sight-reading painfully badly compared to others. Tea-breaks are more like gasp stations. Biblical names explode into the air.

Lunch relief. But my frustration has to vent itself somehow and it hits upon the theatre versus film attitudes experienced in Blighty, the notion that unless you have held ol' Yorick's skull to the painted skies and creaked about on 'the boards' for at least seventy-five years, you dare not call yourself an actor. Heaven forbid you should claim anything committed to film might be equally good. TREASON! While disporting myself of this lofty notion, Anthony Hopkins lets out a barky laugh and says, 'I agree. I had begun to think I was the only one.' Instead of being bravo'd up by his support, I am overcome with embarrassment for he is a Colossus who has strutted his stuff both classically and on film, shaming my *kvetch* into a corner. But, still, he grips my hand for a good shake, and the previous reserve is replaced by a bit of 'molten lava'. That's what it feels like when those blue eyes 'get ya'!

Emboldened, I offer my theory that anyone who says they would *never* go to Hollywood, would never make a film, must know in their water that either they don't have a chance in hell or no one is ever going to ask them. 'I have yet to meet a soul who is not, deep down, a starfucker of sorts. But then I don't know Ken Loach. There have to be exceptions . . .' Tony ('please call me Tony') says to me, 'You're none too tightly wrapped, are you?' I laugh, and gleefully trade the list I have been compiling of these Americanisms.

'We should call ourselves the AA, Aliens Anonymous.' Venting some spleen in the Californian sunshine with Tony Hopkins during lunch-break is about the last thing I have anticipated, but it sends me back into the studio 'revved-up' at having found a compatriot.

Winona says she finds this reading 'crippling'. Gary is using every opportunity to try out his Hungarian-Transylvanian, which purrs along and he seems to me to 'be' the Drac already. He has opted for a sinuous, low-pitched 'voice of reason' that is already potent. All his private turmoil seems to have either dissipated *or* concentrated into what he is doing. Perhaps both.

Tom Waits. How can I not introduce him to these pages *without* falling into the cheesy showbizzy-sleaze-shpeak of a lone motel lounge act compère – hit the snare drum, smash a cymbal, bang a drum and wind up with 'LADIES - AND - GENNLEMEN - THE - IN - HOLE - THE - WALL - BAR - AND - SNAKEPIT - IS - SALOON - PROUD - 'N' - PRIVILEGED - TO - PRESENT - FOR - YOUR - ENTERTAINMENT - AND - YES! - GODDAMMIT!! - EDUCATION - TONITE - THE - ONE - AND - THE - ONLY - MR - LONELINESS - OF - A - LONG - DISTANCE - SONGWRITER - HIMSELF - IN - THE - FLESH - IN - THIS - HERE - LOUNGE - LADIES - 'N' - GENNLEMEN - LET'S - PUT - OUR - HANDS-TOGETHER-AND-GIVE-IT-UP-FOR-(gasping for breath)- MISTAH!!! TOM!!!!!!! WAITS!!!!!!!!!!' Everyone else is in smatterings of designer casuals. Mistah Waits arrives straight off an old record cover in a '64 open-topped Cadillac, with fins, with a funnel of dust trailing down the dirt road. The gravel voice gets out some howdy-doodys and his clothes and hair are crumple-sculpted to him. Doesn't seem to have a straight bone in his bearing and kills me off with his cool by growling out a compliment for *Withnail*. Out the side of his mouth. Like we might be being spied on by the bailiffs. Him, rolling tobacco and reefer. Winona and I are 'We've got all your recordings, Tom!!' To which he just heh-hehs.

4th September

We meet at nine a.m. to complete the readathon. It's faster today, but still turgid. At the end Francis drops this little 'bomb': 'Now you've read the novel, anything you feel is missing from the script, please come tomorrow with suggestions and additions.' Light-bulbs up the arses as faces previously dimmed are illuminated with 'possibility'. Egos get the Jane Fonda Workout. So 'there is method in his apparent madness' gets hummed and nodded around the table. Followed by news that we are all invited up to dinner in San Francisco and a rehearsed reading of the screenplay by a group of actors in a theatre restaurant called Monty's. Never known anything like this before. We cram into a couple of mini-buses and it's very like an episode of *Fame*.

The theatre restaurant is a sweat-shop of San Franciscan Bohemia, all here to get in on the first *first* of the next Coppola event. The actors reading the screenplay are part-costumed, candle-lit, accompanied by sound-effects and a narrator, with one of those ten-gallon-gonad type voices, reading all the scene descriptions between the dialogue. BOOM BOOM AND 'SO IT CAME TO PASS', etc., etc. By this slightly bizarre means, you discover *exactly* what your role is and how sizeable in the scheme of things. In my case, decidedly shrunken from the illusion fostered by the book-read where Dr Seward is forever giving some journal entry. Objective, subjective, and a kick up our collective to get back and trawl the source for extra scenes, while we have the opportunity. Night-lights burned some early hours in our bungalow. Honeymoon over.

5th September

Back in the barn. Read the rehearsal script, adding scenes and suggestions as we wish. These are typed and collated into a computer as they are offered, producing new pages almost instantly and gradually adding bulk to the existing script. Everyone is a little shagged from the night before, and tetchy. Conclude early, at four. Tony asks if I want to go for a drive and dinner away. We do and drive and drive and drive and end up in a small town called Calistoga. He does a cabaret of impersonations of almost every famous actor he has ever worked with, accompanied by stories. What really does it is hearing him do someone in their voice, but with his own commentary. An uncanny *déjà vu* whereby you hear the 'original' sending itself up.

6th September

A drama teacher from San Francisco arrives to help us improvise scenes, throw balls about, exchange hats, keep eye-contact and 'loosen up'. We embark on parlour games between the three suitors, Sadie and Winona. Francis is bubbling today and humpty-dumpties about, delighted with this 'play', which he guides towards doing the actual scenes, which are very short, hoping that the improvisation will enrich and inform the way we do these pieces. Anaheed, his Armenian Girl Friday and stalwart assistant of ten years, types every idea and suggestion that Francis comes out with. Then they are printed out and new versions of the same scene evolve over the course of the day. A pianist has been employed to play classical music of the period for our dancing, and some ballet dancers arrive to writhe around Keanu for a scene he has when beset by Drac's vamps. I throw myself into all this and enjoy it for what it is, *but* I know all too well that, come the actual Day, the role remains the same. But this equivocating is diverted by the late-afternoon horse-ride. Drama school was definitely *not* like this! Carey, Keanu, Bill and I go careering off on a wild trail up the mountainside, through forest and up to the top. Exhilarating. Boys bonding stuff! Home-made pizza and then to a corner bar and basement joint in the cluster of shops nearby. Ping-pong table downstairs, darts and customers in lumberjack gear. Tony is the only absentee. Everyone gets legless, and I might as well be, cavorting about and gyrating in a 'Last Call at the Single's Bar' frenzy to a succession of Aretha Franklin's greatest hits. Like an end-of-school exam-party thrash. Inhibition is so overthrown that I have no shame in singing a duet with Tom Waits, which, considering small animals and children have been known to run screaming when they hear me yodelling, might give you some approximation of the state of general inebriation. Hit the trampoline and pool for a cool-down session at three a.m. 'I'M YOUNG AGAIN!! I'M YOUNG AGAIN!' I holler, with each bounce on the trampoline.

7th September

Three hours' sleep, then the wake-up call to go hot-air ballooning with Carey and Bill. It's six a.m. and we're dressed in frock coats and top hats and Francis is overseeing all this in pyjamas and dressing gown. Why are we doing this? It's not a scene from the film but Francis has offered up this privilege as an experience the three suitors could have. For the sheer grace of it. The tranquillity of travelling in this style literally takes your breath away as the currents of air swoosh you up and along. Whether this will profoundly affect the way we act our parts does not enter the equation just now. All I do know is that this horsing, flying, dancing, feasting week has been unmissable. Time has been elasticated in this responsibility-free zone. Very like teen-agerdom without 'spots' or restrictions. Francis proves something of a dandy, immaculately turned out in a variety of linen suits, monogrammed shirts, silk ties and poster-paint braces. His *appetite* for everything informs his huge energy and, I suspect, rage. Says he loves to invent things, make things. Revels in the 'making' process of rehearsals.

We rehearse all day. Francis is totally at ease surrounded by a phalanx of assistants, technicians, choreographer, dancers, musicians – in fact the bigger the extended family, the better he seems to enjoy himself. He seems determined to throw every possibility and option up in the air and see where and how they land. At one point there are so many versions and variations of a single scene, that it feels like direction by committee. Quite often I feel I am invisibly loaded with flying custard pies. Everyone wants to make a suggestion and some of them are so tangential to the straight narrative drive of the story, that I begin to wonder whether this method of working isn't counter-productive and just confusing.

As a consequence of my 'Aretha-ing' around, Gary has decided to send me up with a new nickname, fluttering his lids every time he passes by in rehearsal and during lunch, intoning, 'Hello, OUT-RAGEOUS.'

Tony improvises on the grand piano during the lunch-break, and produces hugely romantic sweeps of Beethovian-Chopinesque music. 'There' but not; a self-declared loner. When he is sharing his company with you, it feels like a privilege.

Rehearse the Renfield Lunatic Asylum scenes with Tom Waits, who is exceptionally open and easy to work with. We compare notes on being parents. He says his two girls get 'outta hand – you know how it is, so I say, "That's it, Time Out time," which means they have to sit awhile in the same place and regather their forces before the festivities can continue.' But the way he inflects and words this, you half expect him to start singing the 'Ballad of Time Out', in those tradesmark vocals. I discover that the desk in the corner of the studio, alongside the props table crammed with artefacts and reference books, is the one used by Don Corleone in that for ever shuttered study where Brando dispensed his 'justice'. Outside the barn doors, to the left of the car park, stands the boat that took Martin Sheen up-river in *Apocalypse Now*. The documentary made by Elly during the shooting has been available for us to watch in the evenings. Francis looks back on this time as 'A madness ... that's what it kinda was, a madness.' There is a large portrait of Gino, their lost son, over the fireplace in one of the drawing rooms.

This director, who made *Tucker*, clearly loves cars and arrives in a new light green convertible on this, our penultimate day here. 'A present to myself,' he says. According to the *Apocalypse* documentary, he gambled *everything* to get it made, even risking this estate we are staying on as collateral. He is the only person I have ever met who would gamble *all* for a movie. There is about him the confidence that *somehow* it will all work out *no matter what.*

His life has encompassed such extremes of wealth, success, failure, personal tragedy, near bankruptcy, that were Verdi still alive, I would expect the opera *Coppola* to be a sure bet. The film is being billed as 'Bram Stoker's *Dracula*' but after this first week, none of us has any illusions as to whose version will 'Count'.

After our farewell dinner on the veranda, we troop back to the corner-bar'n'basement, and vaguely attempt to resuscitate the Night of Aretha, which you can never do. Beer chased down by shots of tequila is the preferred entertainment and lays most people out, with Gary literally blacking out. We heave him into the back of Tom's Cadillac and to bed.

8th September

Carey Elwes piggy-eyes in and says, 'Rise and shine, old chap.' The Damaged repair and convene for breakfast *chez* Coppola. Francis is perambulating about in shorts and T-shirt and is shoeless, watering the garden. Gary is convulsed and sobbing. I assume someone has died. No. Just feeling razzed with guilt about the night before. He is apologizing to everyone, most of whom are pretty hung over themselves. Someone eases him down with the assurance not to beat up on himself. All ends up headachey and laughing.

Play croquet in front of the house and Keanu, never having played before, cleans up. Busload of hangovers pile off to Oakland airport for the flight to LA. Sadie, having started off shy, is yakking ten to the dozen and she and Winona are clickety-click.

I sit beside Gary on the plane and he says, 'I'm really glad you're doing this movie. You're such a great actor. You deserve to be a success.' I cannot quite accept this compliment without the feeling of being patronized, but I puncture this paranoid pustule by accepting it at face-value and say, 'Thanks, the feeling's mutual.' He calls his assistant from a mobile as we come into land and says to come by later and 'scrape me off the floor'. The man is in an agony just now. Says 'a shrink can identify your grief but they can't fix your Life ... You know what I want, Outrageous? I want a Mustang convertible. I want to buy a house, and I want to be immortal!!' which sets us laughing all the way down the runway.

Stretch and half-stretch limos await us at LAX, and I suspect that now we are back in the real world, this back-o'-the-bus camaraderie will be dissipated. Somewhat daft seeing all these young faces disappearing into these over-stretched motors. One of them could easily take all of us. I am staying with Bruce Robinson for a week before he departs for Vancouver to start shooting *Jennifer Eight*, which stars Uma and Andy Garcia.

9th September

No rehearsals. See *Dead Again*, *The Commitments* and *Paris is Burning*. Call Bob Altman, who says he has nearly got the first edit of *The Player* down, but is nerve-racked. 'Separate parts work, but as a whole? That'll be the trick. S'pose you've forgotten about us now that you're in there with Coppola?'

10th September

Rehearsals in St Patrick's church hall on Hollywood Boulevard. We all la-di-dah in and we carry on with the stitch-and-start process, but the company sense we had in Napa has dissolved somewhat. Wigs, makeup and costume-fittings and measurings occupy the time when we are not needed for scenes. Stuart, who did all the hair-work on my talking boil for *How To Get Ahead In Advertising*, is on the team and creating various guises for Drac, who ages and transforms over four hundred years.

At the end of the day everyone scrams off in the different directions of their own lives.

11th September

My three-year-old Olivia's first day at playschool, on the other side of the planet. My penalty.

Tony distracts me with an improvised 'lecture' he creates as Dr van Helsing.

12th September

Olivia asks why she is going to playschool AGAIN? 'But I've already been!'

The pleasure of working with Waits. Like jazz riffing. No vanity. No ego on show. Just lets it go. He has hit upon a debauched old British Boiler-in-the-Club voice for his deranged character, who believes that by eating worms, spiders and insects he will somehow become worthy of the Master himself, Count Drac. He plays the piano and sings during the breaks and has 'boneless' fingers. Well, that's what they appear to be, able to bend right back on themselves, fag in maw and winkle-picker shoes tapping the pedals. His singing seems to come from different parts of his body – limbs suddenly shift and move as if releasing a corner of hidden notes, all melancholic and blue, sweet and bitter. Gets embarrassed if anyone gets gushy, but doesn't mind anyone listening.

13th September

Japan meets Italy as Eiko the costume designer does fittings for clothes that Vincenzo will make. Costumes are extreme, flamboyant, stylized High Gothic via *art nouveau*-Edwardiana. There's no way round sounding poncy when you're discussing clothes.

Discuss with Winona the press rumour that she is having an affair with Gary. She is distraught. I try to console her by saying that what with the high profile of this film, that Gary is separated from Uma, that they are cast to play lovers, it does not take Einstein to work out why someone *wants* this falsehood to circulate.

'Remember the date today, Noni?' (It's Friday the 13th.)

14th September

Crunch Time. The church hall in an usually misty Californian morn. We are trying to rehearse the finale of the film, which is all action set-pieces, fights, horse chases, none of which seems tangible in this bare-walled hall. Fatigue and frustration.

Gary is having problems with how to resolve this overall action with the climax and dénouement of his character. He and Francis are heading for confrontation. Sword-fighting rehearsal intervenes but merely ups the stakes. Gary is pursuing the how and wherefore of 'walking upside down on the roof, slithering down walls and transforming into a bat' in accusatory tone. Francis retorts, 'I, too, have strong ideas. Don't discount mine.' This is a battle that you feel should be conducted in private but it's not and my eyes are examining the floorboards, and I'm wondering if everyone else's are doing the same. It's very still in here, except for their voices.

Temporary calm when Francis suggests we sit down for an end-of-fortnight summing-up session. He opens the table for individual comment and grievance. Gary is first at it, saying the rehearsals are generalized and confusing, lacking specifics and detail. Francis colours, puts both hands on the table and chews out his sentences: 'I acknowledge my rehearsal methods are unorthodox, free-wheeling, open to offers. BUT! The final choices and edit of the film are mine and mine alone. I am not answerable to ANYONE else but myself. I have been doing this job for over twenty-five years!

'I *too* am insecure and vulnerable in this discovery process. I have to accommodate and tabulate *everybody*'s input. I feel like I have *never* been understood and beg you all to trust me. I know one, two, three, four – linear numbers – but I see them in another order from the way other people do, and for *this* people pay me a lotta dough to make movies.

'Next week we will have a more streamlined script, having incorporated and edited all the good stuff that has come outta rehearsals. We'll video-tape each scene in order, with Michael Ballhaus [cinematographer] using a camcorder, from which we will then make a video-sketch of the movie, as well as the storyboards that have been drawn of each scene. So, at the end of next week, when you have a three-week break before shooting starts proper, I can work with the writer and cinematographer to rewrite, tweak and adjust everything into shape. Ready for shooting. Enjoy your Sunday.'

Lurch out into the rest of the day, feeling gutted by the unease within. I recount the day's events to Bruce Robinson and he offers this advice: 'Always ask yourself, "What do *I* want?" For any artist this is paramount. Make sure you deliver a Richard E. Grant performance, whatever the "cost", detail or size of role. Be ruthless in this pursuit.' It is precisely the focus my flailing-about requires right now.

15th September

Andy Garcia and Uma Thurman are round for rehearsals with Bruce. I ask Andy about his experiences on *Godfather III* in preparation for the actual shooting of *Dracula*: 'Francis operates from a basis of CHAOS. Surrounds himself and whips up chaos to establish himself and his creative control. Francis demands of the actor *every* variation and possibility in every scene. Everything is kinda extreme. New dialogue, reversal of emotions, playing scenes with dialogue, then without dialogue, doing everything in looks and actions. Exhausting. Can drive you completely crazy.'

'Would you work with him again?'

'That is not even a question. I would go to the other end of the earth for Francis.'

This capsule review of what has been going on is reassuring and inspiring. Coppola is *not* making safe or predetermined choices. He wants, EXPECTS you to do things and offer up yourself to every possibility. Andy signs off with this coda: 'If you go for it, you will have a ball. But remember this. Martin Sheen got a heart attack on *Apocalypse*. You go as far as you wanna go.'

Drive round to Mount Olympus off Laurel Canyon to British director John Irvin's house, which he regularly rents out to visiting Anglais. It is presently housing Leigh Lawson and Twiggy, who took over from Rupert Everett. They are about to move into their own house and, as I need to rent one, I'm here to look-see. They are amazingly marshmallowy with each other and lovey-dovey, freeze-drying my cynicism with their warmth. House has two bedrooms, jungly garden and small pool. Perfect.

16th September

All change to video mode. This week the whole script will be video-taped to make what Francis calls a 'video-sketch' of the whole film. Michael Ballhaus, the German cinematographer who has worked with Scorsese, is introduced, and has all the charm and distinction of a courtly European. Incredibly polite, genial, and gentlemanly in the true sense. He is working with a hand-held home-video-sized Sony camera that is attached to an aluminium arm, secured by a belt around his waist – in fact it's a miniaturized Steadicam. Attached to this is a miniature screen to avoid any 'wobblyscope' effect of hand-held filming.

For the actors, it is time to commit. Your part is now as it will be. No more. And, once the final film is edited, probably, less. So what is MY contribution? Dr Seward is work-obsessed, in love with Lucy, but a man who is destined *never* to have his love requited. A seriously intense, somewhat humourless lonely old dolt.

Horrible realization that my part is sort of 'just your part'. The 'honeymoon' of rehearsal is truly over. I suspect I am not the only one with this syndrome today – everyone seems to be irritating *everyone.*

17th September

Most of the day free. *Sunday Times* paper carries article about psychoanalyst Alice Miller, whose new book claims *everything* is traceable to childhood. Dare I read this?

Meeting with director Gus Van Sant at the Château Marmont Hotel. He is casting *Even Cowgirls Get the Blues* and is flushed with the acclaim for *My Own Private Idaho,* which I saw and did not really understand. He says he is a great admirer of my work, in a very quiet voice, and asks if he can take a couple of Instamatic snaps as we talk. 'Sure, Gus.' Chat for half an hour and leave not knowing which way his wind will blow. These meetings are an oddity. Unless there is script to read aloud or prepare, you tend to sit around massaging each other's greatest hits, talking about any old 'inner tube', the tacit agreement being that he is there to suss you out, and I am there wanting the gig, but both of us just chewing the cud as if this was as per. Chances are I will never see the man again. Yet here we are acting like we have known each other some time.

18th September

James Hart, the screenwriter, is present and he clarifies the structure of scenes and remaining confusions about intentions. As he is an 'insider', who has not been around till now, his 'outsider' view is welcomed. Improvise with Tony Hopkins, trying to discover why these victims are losing all their blood without visible wounds, and his intensity and involvement is electrifying. This man's mental metabolism is set way above the average and he seems to generate HEAT. His immersion in his role is TOTAL. At the end of the session he grips me in a bear-hug and says, 'You're as mad as I am!'

Gary is festering about a newspaper article which headlines, 'WILD MAN OLDMAN ABANDONS UMA THURMAN AND SEEN

CHOOSING MUSIC IN TOWER RECORDS WITH WINONA RYDER.' Shaking his head, he says, 'I mean, you don't think they're looking at you but they *are* fucking looking at you. You know? I mean, you've gotta be careful.' His accent is imperceptibly metamorphosing into an American aspect.

Encounter the 'Silver Fish'. This is a customized silver bus that Francis invented for himself, which looks exactly like a giant space-age pill capsule on wheels. The interior is fitted with a sofa, four television screens, which he uses for editing, galley kitchen, jacuzzi, loo, THE LOT. Francis shows me round with all the enthusiasm of having just opened a new present. 'They all laughed at me in this town when I had this made, twelve years ago, but look here, I can do everything from this bus.'

Word was that on *The Cotton Club* and *One From the Heart* he directed via loudspeakers from the bus: he could see the actors on his screens but they were unable to see him. There is some 'sore-pointiness' surrounding this and he says he is going to be on the studio floor for this picture.

19th September

Very hot and airless. Very tired. Soupy. Rehearsal plod after the inspiration of the day before. Francis visibly taking deep breaths to remain calm and patient. Until Tony takes the floor. He is ceaselessly inventive, provocative and thrilling to watch. Capable and willing to try *anything* that Francis throws his way. Buoys me *up*!

Suzanne Todd and David Willis invite me to the première of *Rambling Rose*, which stars Laura Dern and her mother Diane Ladd, both of whom I meet as part of a crush of congratulators. Meet a twenty-four-year-old scriptwriter called J.J. who wrote *Regarding Henry*, has a three-picture deal, and talks *real* fast, as do his friends, all of whom seem young, ruthless and rich. Holly Hunter introduces herself with a welcome line in flattery and declares, 'I wanna do a movie with you.'

'Oh, Holleeeeee, what can I say? Me too!'

She is the height of a pixie and has don't-mess-with-me eyes. Having so admired her work in *Broadcast News* I need hardly tell you how plinked I feel.

While partaking of some Southern Fried specialities, in keeping with the film's Southern locale, David tells me that bro' Bruce (Willis) earned around $43 million last year which causes me to near choke on something fried, to the sounds of a Dixieland band giving it full throttle a few feet away.

Bruce Robinson opines that when, and if ever, I write my autobiography, it should be titled *I Feel Unusual*. I just hope to hell the Bastard lives long enough to write and direct me in something else. 'Nobody else *does* your dialogue like I do, Bruce! What the hell are you farting around with Method actors for in the first place?' gets him stoked up for a bit of argy-bargy.

21st September

As this is our last day of official rehearsals there is an end-of-term atmosphere. We have no sooner begun with the final scenes of the film – Dracula's confrontation with the rest of us, fight, chase and death – than Gary goes for the jugular. *Déjà vu* of exactly what happened at exactly the same point a week ago, only today there are documenting strangers. Gary is vehement again about the absence of specifics, and accuses Francis again of being 'generalized'. Francis leaves the room for a few minutes' breathing space. A hasty lunch-break is called, tables set up alongside the back doors of the church hall. No sooner have we sat down with a plateful than a screaming match ensues inside between Gary and Francis. The rest of us carry on eating. Only things are interrupted now by the sound of tables and chairs overturning, and yelling. Francis storms out of the opposite door and Gary comes through for lunch. Tony attempts to talk him down, but there is no stopping him. Tension all around and no one seems to know quite where to look or what do do. By three fifteen an assistant suggests we stick to the day's plan and have a final read-through of the finalized version of the rehearsal script. Which we do.

Without the director. He is clearly not coming back. All of which I find excruciatingly embarrassing. *Apocalypse NOW!*

Go to a party feeling very jaundiced. Usual gang of arse-creepers and hustlers and hucksters, agenting and schmagenting about. Partied out. There is only so much bullshit and power-peddling you can take in one day. Get out. Fly home to London on Sunday, 22nd.

Three-week hiatus in England.

14th October

Fly back. New house rental. New start. Sony Columbia Studios down in Culver City. The sound-stages formerly crammed with Never-Never Land sets are now Transylvania, London and the English countryside. Winona's character Mina's estate has been built in a vast studio, with painted cycloramas, exterior mansion, interior mansion, terrace and sunken topiary garden and lake. The latter has been created in what was once the pool used by Esther Williams for her forties water-ballet extravaganzas. Grand opera. Victorian furniture, gas-lamps, sweeping staircases, horses, carriages, servants, gravel, High Gothic costumery, music-relay through loudspeakers, a multitude of technicians, set dressers and scene painters, lighting, camera tracks, in fact a BIG STUDIO PICTURE as seen in old movie annuals, re-created and come to life. This is where *The Wizard of Oz* was shot, and for once in Los Angeles, you can glean a sense of the past. Everything is going to be shot on sound-stages, making this an unusual production since most films these days are shot on location. It feels incredibly exciting and I am thrilled to the knickers to be a part of it.

The overwhelming smell of the English-country-estate set is that of a greenhouse. Real plants, trees and moss are planted in movable tubs of loamy soil and are regularly watered and tended. I have never seen sets on this scale and neither, it seems, has anyone else. It makes the transition to the end of the last century much easier to imagine, being surrounded by the 'real' thing.

Francis has forsaken the formal suit and tie look and generally sports a loose Hawaiian-style shirt. He's wearing headphones and his hand rests atop the monitor on which he sees what the camera is seeing. The sheer size of the enterprise and the numbers of people involved dwarf any of the minutiae of the rehearsal room. It is absolutely overwhelming and at its centre strides Francis, apparently undaunted by any of it. No mention of what happened when we last met. This is a FRANCIS FORD COPPOLA production and everyone knows it.

17th October

First screening of *The Player* in Santa Monica, with a small invited audience followed by dinner with the Altmans for the post-movie do. I go with Susan Forristal and sit next to Joan Tewkesbury, who wrote *Nashville*. The film is *so* good I feel ready to bust with it. The voiced worry is that it might be too 'in' for its own good. This pattern of 'Well, I loved this movie, but will anyone outside the industry "get it"?' repeats itself over and over in the coming weeks as more test screenings are held and the word-of-mouth just gets stronger and stronger. An especially important turnaround for Bob, who says he hasn't heard this kind of buzz in LA for many a long year.

An agent is discovered crying in an underground car park, having just seen the flick, bemoaning her life being so mercilessly portrayed in the film. Rumours that sales of Range Rovers, which Tim Robbins sleazeballs round the movie, are going to go down among studio executives as a result of the film.

29th October

Winona Ryder is twenty years old today! A veteran! Francis clearly dotes on her just now and is very avuncular. There is nothing he will not try in a scene, exactly as Andy Garcia foretold. Music is played to get the right mood. He sometimes talks through a take, between the dialogue, to infuse what he wants, *willing* the thing to come to life. Also he is not averse to having people's kids and pets around during shooting, and *nothing* interferes with his ferocious concentration. The story-board, which has now been collated and made into a quasi-comic book, serves as a reference for scenes realized in rehearsals that may now seem disembodied by the shooting schedules in the same way that the video sketch can be relied upon to remind or stimulate. In particular this works for a scene where Anthony Hopkins suddenly swirls Winona Ryder into an impromptu waltz on the terrace, and then enigmatically sniffs the air. It came out of rehearsal weeks back, and today the impetus or way into the scene is lost. Francis gets the scene linked up from the Silver Fish parked outside the sound-stage and, within no time, the video-taped rehearsal is on his monitor for both Tony and Winona to see.

Despite all the pre-shooting preparations, the on-the-day reality is always different: the sets and costumes add such a different dimension that rehearsed patterns have to be forsaken and new ways of doing things discovered. Which avoids any sense of merely re-creating what has already been done. Tony is reticent for this very reason about rehearsing *anything* for a film, and his point is proven as scenes change and evolve according to these new circumstances.

I cannot avoid the suspicion that the video version and rehearsals were more for the director's and writers' needs than of the actors'.

Crypt Call. Vast tomb set with stone vault and the problem of how to get Sadie Frost into her tomb, with her elaborate dress, fangs, and the baby she is 'feeding on'. Francis jokes that maybe the only elegant way to do the scene will be if the thing is shot in reverse. Lo and withhold your breath, but the dress is wired up, candles 'rigged' to ignite or extinguish when she passes, and the technical logistics of all this totally baffles my size-two brain. Michael Ballhaus is intrigued by these technical problems and does not seem in the slightest overwhelmed.

The trickiest part turns out to be the babies. Two-year-old twins are dressed in diaphanous shifts and alternate for each take, according to the strict rules laid out for working children. Social worker and mother present. Much goo and coo between Sadie and the tots. However, come the actual shooting and the insertion of her fangs, the children get hysterical. A mattress is laid down in front of the tomb out of camera-shot and the mother lies in wait for the poor tot to be 'dropped' by Sadie as vampire, when she 'sees' van Helsing and the rest of us hiding in the shadows. The process takes a whole day, and when one of the poor little things finally manages to get through it, there is a round of applause. *Never* will I *ever* allow my child to go through this malarkey.

7th November

Set designer has created a realistic, dank, falling-down interior and it has been peopled by the weirdest humans Los Angeles has to offer. Eiko has designed metal cages to fit around the asylum keepers' heads, and the keepers have been cast to look like Viking Thors. The inmates are hosed down with water jets. The cells are padded and metal-clangy. A very intense young man, who is a bug-trainer, is on hand with boxes of slugs, bugs and creepy-crawlies for Tom Waits to work with. He produces a creature that wiggles around very effectively but when touched freezes as if dead. This enables Tom to choose one, pick it up, pop it into his mouth and pretend to chew without having to eat the thing. All of which he handles with aplomb. By the end of the day people are fairly *au fait* and *blasé* even about testing an insect or two upon their tongues. That old adage about people looking like their pets is unfortunately realized in this instance. The bug proprietor looks just like a compilation of his clients.

Another day requiring beast-work is altogether extraordinary. As a result of those two confrontations between director and star, a solution to the 'difficulties' has been found, which is to have Gary in a half-man half-bat suit, ready to attack the posse, which includes Messrs Hopkins, Elwes, Reeves, Campbell and Grant. A hairy all-in-one body suit has transformed Gary beyond all recognition, and his rage at us doubles the horror. By this I mean that the makeup effects are grotesque in their own right but such is the intensity of the performer within that you really do believe he *is* this monstrous incarnation. Gary NEVER goes half measure on anything.

There is never any marking out of a scene. Five hundred per cent all systems firing Batmobile. During the shooting, Francis blindfolds the posse and has Gary whisper insults into our ears just to get us wound up even further. Wind-machines, music, screaming, shouting, controlled chaos. Plus rats. And a rat-trainer, whose biggest assignment has been on *Indiana Jones*.

My abiding image of Francis is of him standing amid mayhem, always at the epicentre of his own storm. Like a child that has magicked up every toy in sight to perform a frenzied puppet show. Exactly what would overwhelm most other mortals, *fires* Francis. As far as anyone thinks they are already 'reaching', Francis has a way of out-distancing even that. Whether or not *Dracula* is a masterpiece-in-the-making seems irrelevant. The process is all. All-embracing and grand scale in these fittingly grand old MGM studios. On visitor's day, between camera set-ups, he often has a couple of kids on each knee, singing them Broadway songs – a benevolent real-life Stromboli, the larger-than-life puppeteer in *Pinocchio*. Like that cartoon despot, he is also capable of rage and wrath, but even when this is occasioned, it always seems to be in the service of the film.

14th November
Tony Richardson dies at sixty-three of Aids. Natasha holds a wake party in his house that is celebratory and brave, with all his friends carrying on as if he might have just slipped out into the garden. There is a large photo-portrait of him on a table. Music and squawking birds. She is, as ever, the perfect organizer and seems to get through all this by consoling other people who capitulate along the way – not that there are that many, for his friends knew what was coming and to survive being his friend, sentimentality was not on the agenda.

2nd December
Family to stay for three weeks. Life is complete. And I am undone when they leave. Imelda Staunton, who is godmother to Olivia, comes to stay for a week as she is here to promote a BBC film given cinema release in the States, and to meet studio executives and agents, all of which she says is pointless. 'Who the hell in Hollywood is going to

employ a five-foot-tall Irish potato-face like me in a movie?' She takes me round to meet Kenneth Branagh and Emma Thompson at Rita Rudner's house. Get nervous and talk too much.

6th December

Not working, and do a day's worth of photo-shoot with Ed Harris and Cindy Crawford for *Vogue* magazine, wearing designer dress-suits, bare-footed and playing croquet in a lookalike *High Society* garden in Pasadena. Much mockery from my 'height-impaired' friend Imelda for spending the day hitting balls about with Cindy, who is around six foot. Or seems to be.

7th December

Week free, and I accompany Glenne Headly to the Kennedy Arts awards in Washington, DC for a weekend of American high society for real. Dinner in the State Department ballroom, which is the grandest hobnobbing I have ever encountered. Anthony Hopkins is the only famous person in here whom I know to speak to, and he grins at me and says, 'They really do know how to do all this kind of thing. It's like a movie. Totally unreal.' The tables all have name-cards and enough glass, crockery and cutlery to sink the Armada all over again. The other guests at our round table for eight include a senator, George Baker, Martin Scorsese and, to my immediate left, Lauren Bacall. She has seen a screening of *The Player*, which serves as an introduction, and she runs through the actors she knows in London to see who we have in common. The combination of her deep voice and direct manner is initially unnerving, but she is so down-to-earth that my tongue is fast untied. I knew in advance of this dinner that Scorsese was casting *The Age of Innocence*, as Winona had told me she was in it and said I should get my agent to make appropriate noises, even though the main part was already cast with Daniel Day-Lewis. The film is set to go in March next year, a month after *Dracula* wraps. I resolve not to mention it in these surroundings and asked him instead why *New York New York* and *King of Comedy* were deemed failures in the States, while acclaimed in Europe. He speaks fast normally, but when embarking upon answering this question, he 'bullets' off. Scorsese's film knowledge is legendary, but I am totally floored to discover that he has seen everything I have ever been in, including *Hudson Hawk*. At this point he mentions that I am on his casting list of possibles for *The Age of Innocence*. CAN HE SEE MY FACE STRAINING NOT TO CRACK A BIG FAT BEAMER IN HIS DIRECTION – I reckon that this opulent banqueting hall – dinner-jacketed and bejewelled up to the throttling nines, chit-chatting with Lauren Bacall and nodding appropriately at the ancient senator opposite – is the best impromptu audition for playing a society type that anyone could have planned. Being currently employed by his friend Mr Coppola took any edge off the usual desperation that hovers around my wanting something too much!

9th December

Fly to New York. Three days of entertainment with Steve Martin and Victoria Tennant. Lunches, dinners, museums, shopping, walking and gossip. Back to LA but the new sets are not completed and schedule alters. Meaning the Xmas flight to London is delayed till the nineteenth. I miss Olivia's first Nativity play.

Complete everything bar the horse-chasing finale, which will shoot in January.

23rd December

A veritable hat-trick: Altman, Coppola – and now Scorsese has come through with an offer of a part in *The Age of Innocence*! However, this excitement and jump-up-and-down is put into strict perspective when I realize that my role is about eighteen lines of dialogue. In other words, a glorified bit part. But for Scorsese, baby! The opportunity is something I am not willing to miss out on and I gladly say, '*Aye.*'

6th January 1992

Return flight to LA cancelled due to fog at Heathrow and I am rerouted via San Francisco later in the day. *Dracula* – THE FINAL PUSH INTO TRANSYLVANIA. I mainly work with the second-unit camera crew, directed by Roman Coppola. This involves the gypsy caravan chase through the snow-covered landscape and mountain pass towards the Count's castle. Biggest sound-stage is transformed into Eastern Europe with steep sloping 'mountains and crags', trees, snow, wind-machines, central driving area for the truck upon which the camera is mounted. A huge operation requiring a great deal of planning and patience. Stage fifteen, which measures the size of a football field, is the largest in LA. The oval shape allows for the longest stretches of 'mountain pass' to effect distance. Trees are moved in and out to create the sense that the journey is much longer than it actually is. Fake snow is blown down from the gallery, which gets the horses all chivvied up and raring to hurtle. Which they do, round and round the track, like *Ben Hur* in winter. Clothing is extremely uncomfortable and hot and the makeup department has to rally in and powder everyone down before the next relay begins. Carey and Bill are expert horsemen. I'm not. The horse clearly knows this and tries to unseat me every which way it can. During one thunderously fast chase around the track, with whooping and hollering and stuntmen hurling themselves off the gypsy cart, guns firing and camera-truck revving to keep up, my horse careers too close to a crag of 'rock', which is made of polystyrene and cement. My left knee collides at speed with this and I can feel my mouth 'oval' and gasp, but no sound comes out. Delayed. Out of shot, keel over and am rushed to the nearby hospital. The film company seems very worried that I am going to sue them, which thought never crosses my mind. I'll be on crutches and strong painkillers for a few days and I curse the wretched beast that did this. The irony is that my horse is called Pop-Rock. The *Boy's Own Adventure* novelty of this horse-chase palled for everyone as it seemed without end, dust and fake snow by turns clogging up your gills. It's the same phenomenon as experienced on *Hawk* – action sequences take quadruple the time to shoot, because they require so many set-ups, stunts and time, which have to be edited down into something fast. Billy Burton co-ordinates the sixteen stuntmen, thirty-five horses, the bunch of actors and Swaziland ponce with supreme patience and good humour.

31st January

Last day, and I go to say thanks and goodbye to Francis and Keanu who are on another sound-stage shooting a Vampire Valkyrie scene, where Keanu falls asleep in the Count's castle and finds that the floor is literally erupting with female vampires intent on getting a pint. As they still have a way to go to complete, there is no communal sense of it climaxing or curtain-calling to an end.

1st February

Fly home.

23rd November

Fast forward to Mann Chinese Theater on Hollywood Boulevard. *Dracula* première. About as BIG and BROUHAHA as it gets. Wojciech Kilar's pounding score fills the theatre and for the first forty minutes my jaw is dropped, trying to relate the experience of what we shot with what is up there on the screen. And I know now that Francis is a techno-wizard. It's almost like a homage to every type of cinematic development over the past century. At first viewing I can't be in any way objective but it does seem impossible to keep the pace and pitch of everything this high through to the end. It seems almost overwhelmed by its own elements, and forsakes a straightforward narrative line to its cost. But there is no doubting that you are watching a movie, as opposed to something in the theatre or on TV and for sheer boldness and chutzpah it is exhilarating. Get outside feeling shell-shocked and am given a mansized handshake of congratulations by Liam Neeson. The party afterwards is a blurred mass of people and candles and questions about whether the public would turn out in sufficient numbers to justify the budget and hype.

30th November

Steve Martin faxes me this ironic note in *LA Story* style.

Dear Richard

    I have never known anyone who has been in a movie that did over thirty million on the opening weekend ($32 million in three days), but believe me, this fax has nothing to do with the opening at all. I was just thinking that, well, I don't really know you that well and would like to get to know you better ... spend a little time with you and your lovely wife, Joan, and maybe discuss one or two projects with you. When you're next in LA I would love to take you and your wife Joan to the LA County Museum where I can get special VIP services that will make your trip easier. Although I haven't seen *Dracula* yet, I just know that you're very special in it. I would love to sit with you and just listen to what's going on in your head ... It would be great if your wife, Joan, was there too. Hope to see you soon, and give my regards to your wife, Joan.

All my best, Steve Martin

(Which is best appreciated if you imagine it read in the obsequious voice of *any* agent who is hoping one day to represent you.)

The Age of Innocence

February 1992

I'm back in London for two weeks after my stint on *Dracula*, knowing I have to be away for another few months on *The Age of Innocence*. It's raining, I'm restless and Olivia has her pre-school half-term break. I suggest to Joan that I'd like to fly home to Swaziland for ten days. Her 'OK' is too casual for her to have taken me seriously. This is Wednesday evening. By Friday, I have booked myself and child on a flight for the coming Sunday. Joan cannot come as she is committed to too many projects to leave them at this short notice. At three forty-five I screech into the passport office in Westminster to get my daughter endorsed on to my passport before they close at four. Bureaucracy is not accommodating to impulse and whim and it requires a little prostrate pleading to get the required stamp. Which is about what Joan does on my head when I tell her. 'But you've only just got home and will be leaving again for the States any minute. I lose husband AND child?'

'It's only for ten days,' is my feeble reply. Near-divorce proceedings ensue.

WHY? *Why* this compulsion to go 'home'?

I cannot be too rational about this but it's partly to do with having left the southern hemisphere a decade ago and wanting to pigeon back and take stock. Plus a need to spend one-to-one time with Olivia, to alleviate the guilt and jealousy of being apart for so long. Joan's 'well, what about me?' is justifiable and I can hardly blame her for headshaking with disbelief at my intransigence. Wilfully flying in the face of her objections is something I have not blatantly done before but I am unwilling to turn around.

Going back is incredibly emotional in a way that I couldn't have anticipated. Flying into Swaziland, and finding I had been at school with the air stewardess, know other people on board, seeing this beautiful unspoilt landscape below the porthole combine to *undo* my tearducts. The smell of it, warmth, familiarity and sense of belonging, just has my old heart a-heaving. My life in the so-called First World is instantly put into some sought-after perspective. Without consciously seeking to 'go back in time', the pace of life here affords a sense of continuity and ease that is absent from my activities north of the equator. Marriage survives this blip.

Return 'home' to London with recharged batteries.

25th March
Two p.m. flight to New York.

Taxi driver on the way to terminal four relates a tale of woe about the 50 per cent redundancies in the driving business. 'If Labour get in, I'm gettin' out,' is his final edict, while I worry away in the back seat about the wisdom of committing to three months doing a part that shoots for fourteen days with eighteen lines of dialogue. If I don't do it, will I regret it? GET A GRIP, MAN. You're two minutes from check-in. Doubt knows no boundaries – despite the four hours enjoying First Class which concludes with steaming towels proffered in ice-tongs to mop down. The mental fandango cavorts relentlessly.

The alternative of being unemployed has about it the sobering chill of a Siberian draught. Maybe ... maybe this is better than two weeks of *West Side Story* at Westcliff-on-Sea. Were they even offering?

The connecting flight to Albany in upstate New York is in a plane like a tinned mosquito and I am violently sick into the paper bag while it shudders about in the bad weather. Another pensioner in a saloon car with my name on a placard embarks on a history of the local roadworks *en route* to the Desmond Americana Hotel on the outskirts of town. The interior is American-colonial with a population of conference folk wearing name-tags. Call Winona Ryder. She is going nuts having been here three days and not allowed to visit the location yet. Has word that *Dracula* is going to be HUUUUGE.

26th March

Costume-fitting in a disused bank. The costume assistant is male, moustachioed, sibilant, coiffed, witty and knowingly widens an eyeball when I sniff the new leather gloves provided.

Gabriella Pescucci, the Italian costume designer, is chain-smoking in slacks, cardigan, scarf, flat shoes and strong opinions.

Hair and makeup team are instantly familiar, caustic, campy and deadly serious about whether or not to have side-burns or just a haircut. 'Saw you in *Withnail* and *Henry and June*, right?'

'Right.'

'RIGHT.'

There is not a whiff of sycophancy blowing about in here. Your head is their *business* and here there can be no secrets for these total strangers will see you first thing in the morning, will have to disguise your every wart, scar and blemish and console away whatever pre-shoot anxieties you churn out.

My costume is either a black-tailcoat-and-tie ensemble or dandy summer-white suit. All of which feel tight. I pick up *per diem* dollars and detour to a shopping mall, which is a vast concrete bunker, to while away the cold afternoon seeing a movie. A pair of toothless old men sit arguing about the Tyson rape case on first-name terms with a 'Mike this and I know Mike wouldna done that' conviction. Unemployment in this town is very high and the place feels abandoned. The production is based here initially as many buildings are unchanged since the end of the nineteenth century.

Cab back to the Desmond Americana with a local psycho. I receive a message to join Miriam Margolyes for makeup and hair test approval with 'Marty'. Meet Geraldine Chaplin in the foyer, who is spindle-slim and complimentary about *The Player*. Films are an easy access card of introduction and it seems hard to credit that *Dr Zhivago* was made twenty-seven years back. (The image of the dead mother in the glass coffin haunted my childhood.) I am driven to the set and relieved to have something to do. The driver has a thick accent and critical faculty: 'I think you guys goddit made, huh? This actin' business. Looks sorta easy t'me! I guess ya jus' need a lucky break, right? A lucky "click" an' then you goddit made, RIGHT? I mean, looka Daniel [Day-Lewis], da man is a *prince*, RIGHT? Sat in da frun' seat o' da car jus' like you. Godda Oscar fer doin' dat cripple guy, RIGHT? Da *Foot*. Ain't dat un-be-leeevable, huh? Fus' time aroun' an' he gets de Oscar! Whadda Prince. Goddit made now, right? So what you been in? Nah, didn' see dat . . . don' see foreign films too much. Picked up dat Winona kid de udder day. Di'n look like no movie star t'me! If you askin' me, right?'

Arrive at an old building that has been done up to look like a photographer's studio of the late 1880s where the marriage pictures of Daniel and Winona are being shot.

Into the makeup trailer, through a barrage of rain and mud. Miriam Margolyes is installed in one chair and greets me with 'ARE YOU CIRCUMCISED, RICHARD?'

'But of course, Miriam, aren't you?'

The makeup and hair team exchange looks and say, 'You two know each other from before, then?'

To which Miriam laughs and says, 'Oh, no. We've met *once* before, very briefly, but he's the *most* wonderful actor, you know. I am *so* thrilled to be working with him.' She is totally alarming and disarming at once. Spherical, pop-eyed and determinedly garrulous. 'I *adore* most people and only want to hear the *good* news about anyone. "Be polite to all" is my motto.'

Haircut and side-burns affixed and off to meet Marty, who is dressed up in costume to play a cameo in his own film; the photographer. INTENSE – VERY FRIENDLY, VERY WELCOMING, VERY SHORT AND VERY VERY FAST-SPEAKING. Like Shhoooooooaaaaaaaaah! Maybe it's the setting, the period trappings, whatever, everyone is noticeably *gracious* and ever so slightly *formal* for a movie-set. Winona glides over in her wedding dress and whispers, 'Can you believe this? Martin Scorsese?' Daniel Day-Lewis introduces himself and is also *graciously, formally friendly*. He seems much taller as he's so slim, with cut-glass cheekbones that render my face an oblong jelly.

This costumed and girdled set-up seems the furthest remove from Scorsese's *Mean Streets*, *Taxi Driver* and *Raging Bull*, and I wonder whether the real Marty is somewhere in hiding or in the custody of Rupert Pupkin and Sandra Bernhard?

Michael Ballhaus at the camera helm, along with Winona, plus the period trappings give a slight sense of *déjà vu* as we so recently worked together on *Dracula*.

Unlike the Coppola set, the volume level of everyone seems set really low, adding to the sense of 'Polite Industria'.

Needing hair and makeup approval from the director himself seems excessive, but it was requested, executed and approved. Detail. Detail. Detail. He will overlook NOTHING. Go back to the hotel and have dinner with Miriam. (Forgot to mention that she is playing Winona's grandmother, Mrs Mingott, the beached society whale and matchmaker of the story.) She shares *everything*. Speaks to fellow diners as if she knows them, exchanges opinions on the food, belches, farts and slurps her soup with stereophonic gusto. The world is her friend, and even if everyone does not yet know it, they very soon will! Surrounding forks momentarily hover when she asks, '*Is* Madonna a lesbian?'

27th March

Letter of welcome and compliments from Daniel written on parchment-type paper that is unexpected and cheering. I've neither had nor heard of an actor doing this before. Tim Monich, the dialect coach, is here to get the English actors sounding like New York society-types and is due to give me a coaching session for all of my eighteen lines. I'm not exactly on RED ALERT, and he delays our session. Day free. Join Winona and her half-sister Sinyatta for lunch.

Her filming schedule is back-to-back and means long separations from Johnny Depp, who is filming in another part of the States. On days off like this, the separation hurts. Which is what her next 'revelation' does to me. She tells me that Daniel heard in London that the three words I hated most in the English language were 'DANIEL DAY-LEWIS'. I sit down to take this load on board. WHO? WHO HAS PUT ABOUT THIS POISON? Get a bit psychotic here in her suite. 'But this doesn't even begin to make sense. I would not be here today if it weren't for the fact that I got *Withnail* because Dan turned it down, when he chose to do *Unbearable Lightness of Being*. I OWE THE MAN MY CAREER INADVERTENTLY. JUST DOES NOT MAKE SENSE.' Getting up a REAL froth by now, and we call him in his trailer on the set. He just laughs at my acute discomfort and denial. 'Who told you this?' I ask. He says he can't remember, but it did make him wonder what I might be like on this film if I was so infiltrated with HATE. 'On the contrary, in the light of your making *Withnail* available to other contenders, I have *eulogized* your double-barrelled name and have publicity material to prove it! I'd like to garrotte the little *fucker* who put that about right here and now!' – which makes him chuckle. 'Daniel! Do *not* torture me for this. When it comes to opining about people, I am up there with the best of the snipers but your name ain't ever been on my hit-list. Thank you for your letter, by the way, *especially* in the light of this little landmine.'

Winona suggests we go and see *Ruby* as an ex-girlfriend of Johnny Depp's is in it, as is Danny Aiello, after which Sinyatta, who is a masseuse, gives me a back massage while extolling theories about hypnotherapy, rebirthing and discovering your 'inner child'.

Dinner with three other English thesps. The reason for us imports playing locals is that Marty says it is easier for English actors to play this kind of Class and Society strata than it is to find American actors who would have to *act it*. 'No big deal for English actors to get up in period costume like it is for Americans used to doing contemporary stories.' The characters in Wharton's novel are mostly Anglophiles anyway. Plus, English actors are *that* much cheaper to hire than their American equivalents. This cynical assertion is quipped between Alec McCowen, Jonathan Pryce, Stuart Wilson and myself. All of us are here on the same minimal movie wage – *for Marty*! We have been told that the three stars have taken substantial wage-cuts, to justify the rest of us being on the Equity scale minimum, but the argument doesn't quite hold when we hear that the budget is around thirty million bucks. Alec raises his glass and with twinkly aplomb toasts us all for 'Doing It For Marty'. He says that the pleasure of having a *proper* dry martini is worth the air-haulage from England alone! I meet Daniel in the lobby. He is drenched, having just done a five-mile run.

I re-read the novel and decide that there is only so much you can do for a part like this, short of giving yourself a mental hernia, and reach the unavoidable conclusion that we are all 'over-qualified' to be doing these 'niblets' but chorus *'It's Marty!'* – and the salary joke has become a running gag. Stuart has just completed on *Lethal Weapon III* playing the bad guy. Jonathan has stories about fanatical fans during his Broadway run in *Miss Saigon* and Alec's double-entendres blast away all my preconceptions – this is the actor who did a one-man show performing the gospel according to St Matthew, but there's not too much piety *here*, thank God!

28th March

On stand-by for 'accent and etiquette' coaching. Meaning I hang around, which we all do till noon when we're given 'clearance'. Jonathan hires a car and we brave a snowstorm *en route* to finding somewhere to have lunch in Stockbridge near the Massachusetts state line. We compare and contrast the politics of *Showbiz*ness: Jonathan says he was approached about doing *Withnail* years and years ago, but they couldn't get it financed. Lucky for me they didn't.

They are noticeably beyond the gormless gush-and-gosh stage in which I still slosh about, and are much more hard-edged about the profession. Comparative lists of Loathed Actors are compiled while we notice a shortfall of those whom all three of us Love. Surprising how much consensus there is, and that the very person you would expect to be adored, as they are by the public and press, is the *very* one despised all round for being such a, such a . . . you fill in whatever comes to mind. Preferably from your schooldays, which is where this kind of personage usually reigns supreme for a while.

30th March

I would like to report that I have been worked to the bone by Maestro Marty, *but* schedule change meant that my first day was delayed and that I have the rest of the week free to skedaddle to New York City. Which I do, by train, accompanied by Alec McCowen, down the Hudson River to Penn Station in Manhattan. Alec has stories, many, many, many stories, all of which make the time swift by. He was in *The Importance of Being Earnest* with Fay Compton playing Lady Bracknell. She had problems remembering her lines and announced with great conviction that '*Yes!* Thirty-five *is* a very attractive name!' He was born and brought up in Tunbridge Wells where his father was an entrepreneur who owned a pram shop. In Trade, he was socially unacceptable to the Conservative snoots, until the day his mother's father became a Socialist member of parliament, after which they were inundated with callers and invitations. 'AAAAAAAH, England!' He is all smiles and forgiveness for this transparent behaviour and apparently finds it more bemusing than infuriating. 'What was it like working with Olivier and Vivien Leigh?' (which he did in 1952). 'Vivien was quite, quite beautiful, but had HUGE, COARSE HANDS!'

I check in at the Wyndham Hotel on 58th Street, which is where the production is putting us up when the unit moves into the city. It's just behind the Plaza Hotel on the corner of Central Park. I'm told, 'You'll like it there. Much favoured by English actors and the permanent home of Jessica Tandy and Hume Cronyn.' I'm curious – maybe it's the chintz factor? Or the ancient elevator that has metal grille doors and a red-uniformed old geezer operating within? Or the absence of any high-tech fittings and appliances and multiple-lined phones? The guests are not a day under five hundred and if anything is guaranteed to slow us down to the sedate pace of Ye Olde New Yorke Societeeee, *this* is the perfect place of abode.

Oscar ceremony live on TV. Go to Natasha Richardson and Robert Fox's apartment to watch, scream and bet. Anthony Hopkins wins, making it an Irons–Day-Lewis–Hopkins 'Brit-trick'. Win a hundred bucks for getting almost every category correct and am chastised for being an Industry Hog. Wonder how many *new* friends will have barnacled themselves to Tony this night on the West Coast. Feel euphoric on his behalf.

See Sarah Jessica Parker in *Substance of Fire* at the Lincoln Center. Terrible disparity between the theatre and film financials and the vagaries of each medium. Here is Ron Rifkin, incredibly potent in the leading role yet has never done movies despite his talent and having a brother who is head of the Triad actors' agency.

See Elizabeth McGovern and Bill Campbell in *Hamlet* at the Roundabout Theater and am transfixed by certain members of the supporting cast who, whenever witnessing the Dane's Agonistes, bend their hosed legs as if in constipated deference to the Prince's *Angst*.

I play Larry Lefferts, a lounge lizard of the Upper Order, who spends his time philandering, gossiping and trolling about. Edith Wharton describes him as 'on the whole, the foremost authority on Form in New York. He had probably devoted more time than anyone else to the study of this intricate and fascinating question, but study alone could not account for his complete and easy competence. One had only to look at him, from the slant of his bald forehead and the curve of his beautiful fair moustache to the long patent-leather feet at the other end of his lean and elegant person, to feel that the knowledge of Form must be congenital in anyone who knew how to wear such good clothes so carelessly and carry such height with so much lounging grace.'

Now the effect on me of reading this assessment is twofold. First I assume I *am* this very creature, apart from the blond moustache, and how astute of Mr Scorsese to have cast me to play him. Each sentence is read as a personal 'insight' and by the end of the paragraph I damn well *believe I am* this lounging lizard. Acting is 'simply transference' so long as you BELIEVE. Not the BLIND variety of belief but the WILLING and KNOWING kind. But second, there is the insidious undertow of DOUBT. In casting me according to the 'type' of Wharton's outline, *does* Marty know something about me that I don't?

Has he rumbled the fact that I am a deeply superficial personage? For Chrissakes, you're playing a bit part! It was probably your 'bald forehead' that fitted the bill. Will you just shuddup already, huh?

4th April

Ten-day wait finally rewarded with the call to 'work'. YOU ARE A TALKING EXTRA, BOY. YOU KNEW THE DEAL BEFORE YOU GOT HERE. RIGHT? RIGHT! Seven-thirty p.m. pick-up and off into Troy. Into a trailer and am greeted by a huge bunch of red roses and welcome note from Marty. More blooms than I have lines to speak!

I meet Dan, just back from his regular five-mile run around a school track. Miriam is in the makeup trailer pulling off her old-age prosthetic and being complimented by the team for having broken down all formal barriers with the crew. Hair-trim and tong. Thence to Makeup for the paintwork. Michelle Pfeiffer is in the adjacent chair, with her hair in a stocking and face covered in pale base. Like fine bone china awaiting the glaze. I'd been told that she is sensitive and shy – and had been warned to approach her with care but, come the face-to-face, my nerves have hit the question super-highway and I am *off*. Her 'You ask a lot of questions' unleashes a torrent of self-recrimination: 'EASE UP! THIS MUST BE THE THOUSANDTH TIME YOU'VE HEARD THIS,' but my interrogation seems not to have caused offence as she goes on to tell me about the trials of playing Catwoman in *Batman II*: going temporarily deaf wearing that tight mask, and having to get used to the clinging rubber suit that has to be smeared with silicone to make it shine and register in the dark.

Michelle is NOT to be TWISTED, SHAKEN or ROCK AND ROLLED at first encounter. However, she is wide-eyed when Miriam comes in and says how intimidated she was when first meeting her. Michelle's faraway eyes are caught in the headlights of a 'WHAT, ME?' look. It makes her laugh. Makes her say, 'What is it with you English? I thought *you* were supposed to be shy and retiring and us Americans all up-front?' Slow-forward to twelve thirty a.m. Freezing. Outdoor scene involving Michelle and Daniel arranging a clandestine meeting that is 'seen' by Lefferts. Horse and carriage, *Anna Karenina* style fur for Ms Pfeiffer and snow-covered streets and gas-lamps. As the story is made up of minute 'betrayals', of which this is one, *nothing* is deemed casual or arbitrary. DETAIL, DETAIL, DETAIL. Mr Scorsese is no longer Marty in this situation. The work is, as Miriam said, very quiet, very concentrated, serious, intense. It's unusual to maintain the monastic mood among a hundred technicians. The usual way allows for normal noise and talk between camera and lighting set-ups and adjustments. Not so here. Pass Daniel and he invites no greeting or exchange between takes. Is this his Method in action? Assume so. Four hours pass with repeated walk-bys from me rehearsing my surprised 'What are *you two* doing here?' look.

Four forty-five a.m. The carriage action and dialogue is completed with camera and lights turning around to film my contribution. Half-hour wait. Into Makeup for touch-ups. Dan comes in, all smiles, and we chat about people we know in common – Pip Torrens and Tony Hopkins. He has totally transformed from the remote, steely suspicion maintained earlier as Newland Archer. This comes as a surprise. He is like a soul released. The unspoken rule I assume, is that when in character, Lefferts is his enemy and when working he will not speak to me. Marty comes in, has a cold, apologizes for the delay, jokes and hopes we can 'get the shot before dawn breaks'. Despite the hour, and the cold, he is obviously happy to be making this film. Makes me think, even from our few encounters, that for him *film is elemental*. His 'fifth' beyond Earth, Air, Fire and Water.

My walk-by and eyebrow-raise is straightforward. Two takes and we are done. But the daft relief and pleasure of actually having pleased this man and doing something floods my old tired veins with glee!

Back to the hotel and Miriam is having early-morning tea with Siân Phillips, who has just arrived. Alec is already awake and it's slightly like a Mad Hatter's tea party at this six a.m. hour. I collapse like the Dormouse into the teapot of my bed.

5th April

Two p.m. train down to New York. Check in at the Paramount Hotel. Call the Altmans and arrange to meet for dinner at their fourteenth-floor apartment off Central Park's West Side with those views you've seen from a thousand movies. Except that this is the genuine thing in 3D: the Park, Broadway, dusk, drinks and jazz in this Uptown Eyrie. Bob, the benevolent Bird of Prey, taloning up the talent. Everything is ordered and modern without any slave-marks to fashion. The living space is divided up by glass panels that stretch from floor to very high ceiling and are imprinted with grainy photo-blow-ups of faces – these salvaged from the 1967 Montreal Expo. Cynthia Stevenson, Annie Ross and a self-confessed Russian melancholic are already here and laughing. Because the news is all good news and is piled up on the coffee table. The reviews of *The Player* are in the realm of the ecstatic. Bob is low-flying and saying, 'I think this means we're gonna get to do *Pret à Porter* in Paris next year. I've never seen reviews like this before. The press are kinda haemorrhaging, trying to out-praise each other. But whether this translates into numbers, and what the New York response will be, is a crapshoot. The screening in LA on Friday was a bonanza success.' Despite the note of caution, Bob and Katherine are 'sorta levitating'. The confidence that exudes is almost visible, and since I last saw them, it's as if they've been lightly 'varnished'. All shiny and new! Even when they kindly enquire about my family and exchange chicken-pox experiences, everything feels elevated. UP! UP!! UP!!! And out we go for dinner, to a French Provençal restaurant that is a series of intimate living rooms. Round table of witticism and songs. Bob sings a funny ballad called 'The Rabbit's Rhapsody', the Russian offers some folk love songs that make him laugh and cry at the same time, like people are meant to do in Chekhov plays but rarely manage to. Annie Ross sings some blues and then the food arrives. Bob is spinning the possible stories and characters for *Pret à Porter* and assures me that 'when and if' – 'You'll be there.' To say that the pudding just slides down to heaven about does it. I never went to dinner with folk who broke out into song before. It's strange to think that the Altmans *could* at a stretch be my grandparents! Their spirits are like some magic life-affirming genie.

6th April

Extraordinary day of great highs, low, troughs and assorted human meteorology. Go to Greenwich Village to have breakfast with Matthew Modine. He is incredibly proud of his three-storey house, designed to the last square inch, which is like an uncluttered, calm sanctuary in the middle of this city. Stickler-Shaker-style funiture. A dream realized for a boy whose dad operated a drive-in cinema in Utah. I remember reading that Alan Parker rifled the planet to find the right boy-man to play Birdy and finally chanced upon Matthew. Despite all his sophistication, he reminds me so much of some of the kids I grew up with in Swaziland, who knew every kind of plant, animal and other things, that I feel as if I have known him a very long time.

He takes me to a diner owned by a friend of his, with a warning that the man might be very rude but is a great opinion-monger and original cook, which is how Matthew earned a living way back, as a short-order cook, and where and how he met his wife. Ken is straight out of *M.A.D.* magazine's 'Slob Chef' section. Chairs and banquettes are torn and restitched, seating sixteen. Shelves are crammed with foodstuffs, pantry-style, and the proprietor's wife is an abrasive dyed-blonde who dares you not to enter but warms up some if you do. With Matthew, anyway. The daily special is four-letter verbal abuse from Ken, the menu an eccentric challenge: sun-dried tomato broiled bread, garlic baguette, pork and fried strawberries and mountain-goat stew. A health-hazard challenge to any Californian-cuisinery. EAT AND BE DAMNED.

Up the road to a printer, and Matthew picks up an order of posters he has designed featuring a triptych of George Bush, a beggar's hand holding dimes, and a skull. *Why?* 'This is my response to Republican-ism. Gonna stick 'em up wherever I can. When I was thirteen years old someone blamed my generation for being apathetic and I never forgot that.' Next we go to the painting studio he shares with another painter-video director. To my untutored eye he has obvious talent. Dumps the posters for later. Walk uptown to Central Park. Expounds his theory on *what* makes a movie actor into a STAR. He argues that if your character can kill people and still keep the audience on your side, then you've made the transition – *murder* as a career move. 'Take Bruce Willis – unless he's shooting people nobody wants to know. Same goes for Arnie and Sly, Eddie Murphy and Tom Cruise.' To my 'Yes, but—' he retorts, 'It's been the formula since the first film about the Great Train Robbery. Gary Cooper finally cracked the Oscar when he killed people in *High Noon*. Gable, Grant, Bogart, Connery, Brando, Pacino, De Niro, Newman, Redford, and now it's Anthony Hopkins for eating people in *Silence of the Lambs*, Jeremy Irons for injecting insulin into Glenn Close.' I think he is talking a load of nonsense at first and laugh at him, saying, 'This is exactly the sort of insane theorizing that actors get into when not working,' but Matthew is *serious* about this idea and there's no talking him out of it. He is convinced that if you can be sexually attractive, heroic *and* kill people, you move over into a kind of real secure stardom. 'Look at the career of Al Pacino. When he's doing a nice guy nobody wants to know. He may be a great actor doing that, but when he was in *The Godfather* trilogy he was untouchable. Mesmerizing. Because you *saw* him kill.'

'So how many people have you popped off, Matthew?'

'Clearly not enough! How about you?'

'I haven't killed anybody, except Julian Sands – and that doesn't really count.'

'Agreed! So we gotta get you a part where you kill people that the audience *want* you to kill, right?'

'Right.'

'If you can convince that it is justified and morally correct to kill then you become an icon and earn the admiration, respect and adulation of both sexes. Like Kevin Costner. Like Jack Nicholson, Harrison Ford, James Cagney, Spencer Tracy, Dustin Hoffman, Keanu Reeves and Alec Baldwin ...'

'What about the guys who are always killers, like George Raft?'

'Too ugly. Bottom line is if you kill you also have to be half-way good-looking and have people wanna fuck you.'

'Yes, but surely there's also the "cripple option". Retards, psychos, the blind, deaf, dumb and legless have always won through too.'

'Like?'

'*Children of a Lesser God*. Deaf, Best Actress. Two competing wheelchairs in *Born on the Fourth of July* and *My Left Foot* in the same year. Bette Davis going blind in *Dark Victory*, Jon Voight legless in *Coming Home*. Christopher Walken going awol in *The Deer Hunter*, Dustin Hoffman hobbling in *Midnight Cowboy . . .*'

'Jesus!'

'Him too! I suppose we better get to the nearest payphone, call our agents and demand they check out all scripts featuring a leading man who is crippled, kills, gets the girl and all the sympathy.'

His outward show of down-on-the-range ease thus unexpectedly reveals the same lurky demons that plague the thespian species: uncertainty, acute and intense insecurity and frustration.

Get back to the trendy ship-shape order of the Paramount and there is a message from Winona Ryder to come round to her apartment *en route* to *The Player* première. She is my 'date' for the evening. Message from the production office to say they may have to reshoot one of the shots in Michelle and Daniel's outdoor scene as the dawn light might be too obvious. Oi!

Walk to an apartment building beside the Ritz Carlton Hotel on Central Park South, and elevator up to the twenty-third floor. Winona's rented apartment belongs to Pavarotti and it's full of his huge paintings on orange walls, with truly operatic-sized views of Central Park beyond the grand piano. Winona, in a micro-tight black dress and hair curlers, introduces me to Brook – 'She was the girl in the pit in *Silence of the Lambs*.'

The première is only a couple of blocks away at the Ziegfeld Theater and we walk. There's a huge crowd of predatory-looking actors, producers, publicists, paparazzi, *Vogue*-ers, fans, hangers-on and professional first-nighters. I am speculating because I have no clue as to who anyone is, but this is my general impression. Winona says this is the theatre where she first clapped eyes on Johnny Depp three years ago. We crush up the escalators and check out other people checking out their reflections in the narrow strips of mirror, doing their mirror faces and lip pouts which dissolve again the moment they're *not* reflecting upon their wished-for beauty. I'm seated next to Jonathan Demme, who is still Oscar-hot from the record-breaking *Silence of the Lambs* batch. 'Will *The Player* play?'

And it does! Good laughs and solid outbreaks of applause, of the apparently genuine kind. Party at the Hard Rock Café that is as like being a smoked burger as it's humanly possible to get, such is the cram and squash. Lauren Hutton introduces herself and says the day they make a movie about the late designer Halston I will certainly get the 'call' as his exact lookalike. Maybe it's my polo-neck and black jacket.

Whoopi Goldberg growls out a compliment, Tim Burton says, 'We'll work together sometime,' Tim Robbins is lurching and holding on to Susan Sarandon, Marisa Berenson does not look a day older than when I first saw her in *Cabaret* twenty years ago, and compliments flush and flow all around. Buck Henry provides his customary acerbic view. Whoopi invites a bunch of us to her suite in the nearby St Regis Hotel, where Annie Ross gives an impromptu repertoire of songs. Peter Gallagher and his wife Paula appear later after his performance *Guys and Dolls*. Volume level is set at RAUCOUS and alcohol around INEBRIATE.

An industry and critical hit and I wish Joan were here to share this with. Walk back pondering the 'Geldof-query' 'IS THIS IT?', stop off into an all-night deli, buy a tub of Häagen-Dazs rum and raisin ice-cream, scoff the lot only to witness it reappear in the bathroom and disappear down the cone-shaped basin. To bed.

7th April

Waiting for 'dailies clearance call'. Meet Modine and see a basketball 'buddy' movie starring 'Wesley' and 'Woody'. This first-name star billing is a new one on me. Sorta says, 'Hey, guys, we're all buddies here. Come play. Come watch. Come pay!' which someone must have been, handsomely, for coming up with this publicity ploy. 'Snipes' and 'Harrelson' are in small print at the bottom of the poster. How would it be if *all* flicks were advertised thus? 'Come see CLARK and VIVIEN in *Gone with the Wind*. Rock and Doris, Fred and Ginger, Peter and Omar, Oliver and Alan, Richard and Vanessa, Elizabeth and Richard, Charlton and Sophia. Ooooh, Jesus, will you stop this already. Jodie and Anthony?

'Let's go up to the Russian Tea Room for Borscht and Caesar Salad?'

'Why not?' More autobiography that strips away his clean-cut screen persona. Many changes of school, fights, moving around, having to make new friends and 'how to succeed with the face of an innocent and heart of an anaconda'.

'Nobody makes it in New York City by accident. You gotta WANT IT pretty bad!' which even as he says it *still* sounds as if the words belong to a more recognizably ruthless-looking face than Matthew's.

I see *Howards End* and I know I am very far from home when the following line in the film gets no audience response whatsoever, but makes me laugh intermittently for a good half-hour. Pure Enid Blyton: 'Don't hog *all* the tea-cakes, Tibby!' Anthony Hopkins has audibly 'crossed over' – people in the lobby are saying just how extraordinary he is to have been Oscared for playing a cannibal and now playing this repressed Englishman in Edwardiana so consummately.

I fly home for a week, having done one day (night) of actual filming. John Major and his Gang of Conservatives has been voted in for another five Tory years.

I am playing with my much-missed three-year-old who, on being put to bed, orders me to 'GO TO SLEEP, YOU OLD BUGGER,' having no clue as to why I am trying desperately *not* to burst out laughing. The love felt is almost unbearable in its overwhelm. The desire to protect and nurture, unfathomable.

15th April

Reluctant return to New York. Straight from airport to Park Avenue location where they are filming scenes in the house of the Van der Luydens, who are played by Siân Phillips and Michael Gough. Costume-fitting, and meet my screen-wife, Tracy Ellis, who is a New Yorker and has an ironic, twisted humour about filming – 'Like being a mushroom left in the dark.'

Thence to the Wyndham Hotel and a chintz suite. Go round to the Sandcastle Production offices in the Delmonico Hotel to see Bob Altman. The film is doing great business in LA and NYC with reviews that read as if they have been written by your best friend or grandmother, a rifle-range of bullseyes. Scottie Bushnell schleps in and they discuss casting possibilities for *The Singing Detective* by Dennis Potter. 'Thinking of updating it to Chicago in the fifties. Maybe with Al or Nick or – excuse me a minute—' Sydney Pollack is on the line. And it's a scene from *The Player*.

It's precisely these series of 'maybes' that decide the fates in an actor's life. Names hanging on the line, flapping on a whim, who, who, who-ing in the wind. I sit here and quietly nurse the creeping paranoia that all my agents *must* have died or at least gone into a *coma*.

16th April

Note in the hotel. 'WILL NOTIFY BY 11 A.M.' Eleven a.m. call to 'GET HERE AS QUICK AS YOU CAN!' I do, stupidly forgetting that filming for the most part is all 'HURRY UP!!!!!! AND WAIT'. Which I do till seven thirty. Afternoon is taken up by a visit to Dan's trailer with Winona. For four hours. Opera music plays. We trade stories and exchange praise for one another's work. I am taken aback at stuff he has seen on television. He clearly reads all the publicity and is very clued up as to what other actors and directors are doing, which dispels the illusion I fostered of his being this reclusive, inaccessible enigma. We compare notes on childhood and displaced sense of identity. In my case, the White-African-Englishman push and pull, his the conflict of Anglo-Irish-Jewish blood and the contradiction of being a 'Posh' among the 'Proles' of South London. The acute embarrassment of being picked up from school by a chauffeur-driven Bentley sent round by his grandparents. Fighting for street credibility. For the role in *My Beautiful Laundrette*, which was released simultaneously with *Room With a View* (in the States) like the two disparate halves of his own background.

An opportunity for me to thank him properly for *not* doing *Withnail* about which he is disarming and generous. He details, with real fervour, the working process and eight months' preparation required to play *The Last of the Mohicans*. He had to stop jogging to gain twenty-eight pounds, and did Army Para training. He shows pictures of himself transformed into Mohican beefcake. It does not sound as though his dedication is torturous when he describes the process but is, rather, something he relishes. Confining himself to the wheelchair for *My Left Foot* for the duration of filming, which was so trumpeted by the press, is clearly the way he *has* to work to become his character. When he talks about preparing, all hullabaloo and mystification is replaced with a very practical approach.

'How'd you get rid of all the weight?'

'Ran it off. I like being thin. Like feeling hungry.'

I discover that he, too, was obsessed with the Glasgow Citizens' Theatre Company when starting out, as the pictures and reports of their productions in *Plays and Players* magazine were always so astonishing. Neither of us ever made it there. He asks about fatherhood and growing up in Africa and says he feels about Ireland the way I obviously do about Swaziland. A kind of longing that can never be requited. The best bits of childhood linger there. It's as companionable an afternoon as it's possible to hope for. He is witty and vulnerable by turns, without ever resorting to the kind of vitriolics that from time to time hurtle through my veins.

Our conversation is interrupted by his being called to the set. I go into the makeup trailer and Michelle surprises me with this greeting: 'HI, YOU SEX MACHINE!' and laughs at *my* gobsmacked face for a change. Turns out that an English makeup lady who worked with her on *The Russia House* sent her love via Michelle and said my nickname was Sex Machine. I have no recollection whatsoever of this person and reluctantly suggest that it must be some other Richard. Michelle is having none of this and is clearly determined to pay me back for asking so many direct questions when we first met, and calls me Sex Machine from then on. One of those things against which you protest but which you enjoy every time it's uttered. Well, who wouldn't, coming from the lips of Ms Pfeiffer?

Adding to this afternoon's welcome, Marty greets my arrival with effusive compliments about my Look. This being the glance filmed at four in the morning weeks ago in Troy! Which lasted all of a few seconds. His praise is an embarrassment of hyperbole. 'No, you have no idea. I got really excited because it's exactly these kinds of apparently arbitrary "looks" that define character and situation and are so telling, which is exactly what "happens" in this story while apparently "nothing" happens. Lives are betrayed and made by precisely these kinds of "looks" and "moments".' MARTY IS ON THE CASE. MARTY HAS THE SCENT. MARTY HAS THE PICTURES IN HIS HEAD and NOTHING is going to pass his highly tuned SCANNER!

The drawing-room interior is a detailed re-creation of Wharton-to-the-word and picture references in books. Exquisite. Sit with Siân Phillips, Alexis Smith and Michael Gough, looking as if they have just eased out of the society paintings adorning the walls. Siân has lost many New York friends to AIDS, but cheers up when retelling the ritual practised by an English actor who, before leaving his dressing room *en route* to the stage, would always look at himself in the mirror and say: 'YOU LITTLE TREASURE! PETAL FRESH AND PARTY PRETTY!' This refrain becomes the mantra for the night. Silently mouthed before each take, of which there are many, involving Michelle bustling from one suitor to another. Written down it sounds silly and soppy, but it has the wonderful effect of a childhood password and its repetition and absurdity keep us on the giggle. Till one a.m.! Marty is very considerate, always accorded the highest status by the crew, immaculately groomed and clearly enjoying this evening enormously. Looking at him I still cannot get round the notion of him filming the violence that so coruscates through *Good-fellas* and *Raging Bull*. He is so polite and contained that I wonder if he will ever turn into Rumpelstiltskin before we are done.

18th April

Rain. I walk down a deserted Fifth Avenue to Park Central Station, expecting to hear Gershwin float through the mist. Train out to somewhere upstate and am picked up at the other end by Tim Robbins and Susan Sarandon. She is about to 'pop' another babe. Bungalow amid acres of trees and tranquillity. It's laid back and casual and everything I'm not but to which I enjoy being in proximity! Kids and toys everywhere, and we pick up the cats from the vet. Visit a doll's-house shop. Yak yak. Get round to the research mania that is part and parcel of the Method. She says that Nick Nolte's preparation and study for *Lorenzo's Oil* was Olympian. We compare notes on children and what not to do and what to do. Susan is big on 'negotiation'. Is this why her two children are so self-possessed?

19th April

Walk into the lobby at Wyndham's and pass Peter O'Toole. Double-take, as Siân Phillips is his ex-wife and I wonder if they know they're in the same hotel? This EXACTLY replicates the scene I have in *The Age of Innocence*, seeing Daniel and Michelle. Going up in the elevator I wonder whether my expression in real life is anything like the acted equivalent? When you're alone these kinds of thoughts easily occupy space and time, which they wouldn't have room for at home.

20th April

Six a.m. call. Coming in and out of this film so spasmodically offers a chance to monitor changes, and the obvious one is the smooth-running rhythm of the whole operation in contrast to the relatively disjointed start. It is disciplined by the restricted hours allowed to shoot in the drawing room location, which *has* to be cleared by a certain hour.

'So what did *you* do this weekend?' makes it feel like school, except that this is Michelle Pfeiffer and she has spent the time in Miami! The subject of working in Eastern Europe comes up and Michelle is as one with me about Moscow as I am about Budapest. *Never* again. Daniel says he didn't eat and exercised too much. Tracy Ellis, who as my much put-upon wife has even less dialogue than I have, finds my running commentary about all and sundry mildly hysterical, which of course fuels my tongue to further whip and lash. Michelle compliments *The Player*, but Siân Phillips says she fell asleep TWICE! And Alexis Smith describes what it was like working in Hollywood during McCarthy's witch-hunt, while under contract at Warner Brothers. Michael Gough resembles a bewhiskered sea captain from an illustrated *Boy's Own Annual circa* 1899, and dispenses stories and anecdotes with such charm that even when he is damning someone it is gilded with compassion. Siân on my O'Toole sighting: 'Thank God we never collided. You see he is a Leo and I'm a Taurean and both too headstrong. But how funny we should both be at Wyndham's at the same time.'

12th May

Dinner party scene will be shot over two days. This involves all the protagonists except for Madame Olenska (Michelle) who has departed for Europe, leaving Newland (Daniel) behind to marry someone he doesn't love. He sits at the head of the table as if at the Last Supper, surrounded by a guest list of Judases. The assistant director has asked us not to speak to Dan, other than in the actual scene, this being a dinner where everyone is seen to be his betrayer. Flower arrangements are copies to the petal from period paintings. Place settings and food are overseen by etiquette experts and a chef is re-creating the cuisine of another age. However, it's look-but-don't-touch time. The camera is fixed to an overhead crane, then on tracks, and all this stealth and smooth manoeuvring takes an age. In deference to Daniel and his character's turmoil we all natter quietly between camera set-ups, and need some cajoling from Mr Scorsese to rev up to tinkly chit-chat level when ACTION is called. Joanne Woodward is narrating and whole sequences and camera moves are choreographed and timed to the exact length of each passage. I often get the sense that the whole film is a private affair conducted in Marty's head, with the filming part a necessary activity, but nothing as rewarding for him as the editing process that follows.

At the end of two days' worth of dinner party acting, it is a relief not to have to drink any more ginger-ale and eat chopped banana – the substitute food, which is easier to chew and swallow and so avoids any close-up masticating mandible visuals! Ladies gasp with the relief of being set free from their corsetry.

Family here for two weeks. Zippy-dee-doo-dah up the Empire State, sail around Liberty, see the polar bears in Central Park and take out a second mortgage to pay the toy bill at F.A.O. Schwartz.

25th May

Family fly to London, me to Philadelphia. I'm here to shoot the opera-house scenes that open the film. Incredible re-creation of a foot-lit romantic opera set on stage and singers made-up in the over-painted style of the day. Endless playback of the duet to which two real singers mime. The stalls are filled half-way with real people in evening dress, but moving further back and in the circle, dress circle and upper circle are life-sized cardboard photo cut-outs that look like real people from a distance. Means they can collect these extras at the end of the day and shove them in a box. They don't require payment, feeding, direction or breaks to go to the bathroom.

A huge camera crane is set up in the stalls to swoop and glide from box to stage to auditorium, to introduce the characters at the opening of the film. Alec McCowen and I are positioned in a box opposite an upper-level box containing Michelle, Winona and Geraldine Chaplin, whom we keep under surveillance through opera glasses. Very like Staedler and Waldorf in *The Muppets*, grumping away.

The same opera is revisited a year later in the story, when Newland is in a real state of upheaval over his love entanglements. To facilitate the shooting of this scene, a box has been re-created in a tiny studio somewhere. For reasons that I cannot decipher Marty is tense and Daniel completely cut off, like his character. Whether an assistant mishears or misunderstands him, something goes up the Swanee and mid camera set-up Mr Scorsese goes ballistic. 'WHAT DO YOU THINK THIS IS? A FUCKING COCKTAIL PARTY OR SOMETHING? I NEED THINGS TO BE QUIET IN HERE!' He talks pretty speedily normally, and this sentence is punched out faster than Jake La Motta's finest. The normal crew-talk during the lighting readjust and camera checks on this film is conducted *sotto voce*. After this fusillade, it is eerily soundless. Eyes to the floor, Alec and I are fixed to our chairs in the box, knowing that this bullet-speed tirade is not *actually* about people talking, although it stops the blood in your veins, such is the shock of its raw ferocity. We indulge ourselves in a little light laughter when we're released. No mistaking now that Marty is a *Raging Bull* from *Mean Streets*.

5th June

Farewell lunch with Miriam Margolyes at Wolf's Deli round the corner from Wyndham's. She plunges herself at a piled plate of pastrami sandwich the size of a country-house door-stop. Then she finishes off my soup and, as we leave the restaurant, breaks wind very violently, which about finishes off the cashier. She throws her arms around me and says, 'We MUST work together again some time SOON! Hasn't the film just been pure HEAVEN?' Miriam is fantastically EMPHATIC about everything. ENTHUSIASTIC, GENEROUS and never anything less than OVERWHELMING. I wonder who will be the next stranger of whom she asks, 'Are *you* circumcised?'

6th June

Walk downtown to Isaac Mizrahi's apartment for Sandra Bernhard's thirty-seventh birthday dinner. On my way there I pass a blind, emaciated man begging on the street corner. He's wearing striped pyjama bottoms and has a piece of cardboard, propped on his concave middle, on which is scrawled: 'I HAVE AIDS. NO SUPPORT. ABANDONED. PLEASE HELP ME?' I was so shocked; just stood in a nearby doorway, stared and cried.

Uptown after dinner, to the Park Avenue apartment of Mrs

Parkinson-Peabody, a society hostess and philanthropist who is giving a welcoming party to the National Theatre Company tour of *Richard III*. An uncanny modern-day equivalent of Wharton's world. Or so it seems to me. The hostess's age is, no doubt, as indeterminate as her wealth. Her hair is steely and coiffed to the exactitude of a sixties helmet hair-dryer. She's indestructibly charming and greets me as though we have known one another for years, without being too tactile about it, and guides me through a gavotte of '*Do meet*' and '*Do have*' *en route* to a table laden with crab cakes and champagne. The walls are *trompe-l'oeil* panels of Tuscan vistas. Someone is playing a Broadway medley on the grand piano. Everywhere people are schmoozing and oozing their charms. Sir Ian McKellen, Richard Eyre, Rosalind Knight, Val Kilmer, Irene Worth, Bob Crowley, Bob Ackerman, Charlotte Cornwell, Edna O'Brien and the Pet Shop Boys. Among the English imports are various American patrons of the arts, and all of us are la-di-dah-ing about as if to the manner born. Charlotte Cornwell cracks through the *crème-brûlée* crust of charm by relating details of the company flight from Gatwick. The name alone introduces a howly note into the genteel proceedings. Irene Worth gushes a compliment my way about *The Player* and then declares loudly that one of America's foremost dramatists 'couldn't write a play if he tried!' which causes a momentary swivel of heads in her direction and makes me laugh out loud at the sheer velocity with which this opinion is launched from so 'left of field'! Richard Eyre, the normally reserved head of the National Theatre, embraces me with a bear-hug, causing me to blurt out, 'ARE YOU DRUNK, RICHARD?'

'NO. I'M IN AMERICA!'

This loosening up is catching and everyone is unusually friendly. Edna O'Brien is fanning herself and saying how exhausted she is from her sixteen-city book promotion tour, in a quiet lilty voice that draws you close and envelops you. She is everything you might hope a romantic novelist to look and sound like: flame hair and translucent skin and that voice, which spins the commonplace into whispery poetry. As if haunted by the Ghost of Glamour.

8th June

To the old studios in Brooklyn, where an entire ballroom has been re-created, and filled with rehearsing dancers and Strauss playback. It's like stepping into a Sargent painting. Marty is super-charged at the possibilities of shooting this sequence and is quoting from various versions he has seen of *The Great Waltz*. His knowledge of movies is encyclopaedic. No attempt is made to keep the noise down today and there's a carnival atmosphere. The camera is on a crane, which will sinew its way in and out of the dancers and introduce the various society characters, over which there will be narration. It takes hours and the extras complain about getting hot and sweaty in all their period finery, dancing under the lights on this humid June day in New York. Marty seems to enjoy the technical challenge of movie-making as much as he does dealing with actors and I never once see him look exhausted despite the long hours. When he talks about his private life it sounds as if he is married to the movies. It is his first and foremost passion and his appetite is that of a polygamist.

11th June

Library scene with Alec and Dan, cigars and whiskey. Final day for Alec and me. Dan is, as per, in 'private mode', having no social contact, maintaining his distance from me as Lefferts. Although I have found this disconcerting, it pays dividends in creating a real-life unease which matches that in this fiction. I wonder whether he will maintain it till I am gone, but as the final 'CUT' is called, Dan grips my hand, shakes it hard, then hugs me and says how good it was to have worked together, which, considering how little I have had to do, is slightly daft, but the relief of his instant and *total* transformation is wonderful. Marty leads a round of applause and thanks Alec and me for being here and for 'doing such small roles so perfectly', all of which is welcome embarrassment.

Dinner with Alec, and we exchange phone numbers and wonder whether we will ever clap eyes upon one another again in London, the vagaries of this profession being what they are. I have been in America on and off for a year now, and know that no matter the size of the parts I have played, the opportunity of working DO-RE-MI with Altman, Coppola and Scorsese will never be repeated in my future career. A unique privilege. A record for my own Book of Guinness.

12th June
Six p.m. flight to London. Six thirty a.m. arrival. An odd 'cocktail' of 'Yippee-aye-yay' and '*What next?*'

Pret à Porter

Autumn 1993

The relief and excitement when I get the call from Robert Altman cannot be overstated. 'Are you goona do the movie or what? What do you think? Well, you know the deal, there's no money, Paris for two months, models, multiple stories, no real lead roles, WHAT DO YOU SAY?'

'I'm jumping on the sofas, Bob. Jumping on the beds.'

Unusually, the script includes the cast list up-front: Ute Lemper, Lily Tomlin, Julia Roberts, Tim Robbins, Sally Kellerman, Lauren Bacall, Sophia Loren, Lyle Lovett, Anouk Aimée, Marcello Mastroianni, Forest Whittaker, Rupert Everett, Tracey Ullman, Stephen Rea, Linda Hunt and Richard E. Grant. Directed by Robert Altman. Copyright and confidential. Who is playing what and how often? Flick fast through and count up number of times Cort Romney, my designer character (a male version of Vivienne Westwood), appears.

A flurry of faxes from Catherine Letterrier, the costume designer, and finally, in late February 1994, we meet at Vivienne Westwood's workshop in Battersea. A dozen chain-smokers and the apparent chaos of a fringe-theatre wardrobe *circa* 1979 complete with Ms Westwood in platforms, fake fur, exhaustion and peroxide hair. 'Can't make out the script ... seems crazy.' Her Paris show is three weeks away and she leaves us with her team to squirrel out clothes.

Tracey Ullman is trying on stuff and says that so far most of the designers she has come across are antsy about how they will be portrayed or betrayed. She is now attached to an Artful Dodger top hat and leaves with it on. A very tired Austrian man with bad teeth takes up my case, and fittings commence. Pink three-piece suit and floor-length grey coat. I request a pair of those trademark platforms that Naomi Campbell fell off last year. 'Are you serious?' Half an hour later, a pair of twelve-inch-high black boots arrives, miraculously in my size, and the strapping begins. The boots are crotch-high with zips.

5th March 1994

Fly to Paris for *Pret à Porter*, and as my guts take to the sky, there is sink, plunge and panic. Who will believe me as a male incarnation of Ms Westwood? This happens to me on every job and, yes, it's another pit-stop, but always attended by the fear that someone is going to take it all away or yell, 'Fake!' just when you least expect it.

A driver is at Charles de Gaulle to meet me and the family, who are coming for the weekend. We motor past the Arc de Triomphe, skid right on Avenue George V to the lavish apartment hotel Carré d'Or. Large apartment with everything you could wish for and Olivia wants to play hide-and-seek behind the sofas. There is a new shooting script, breakdown of the scenes and revised cast list. I scramble through to see if I am still in it and deep-breathe at the prospect of playing a designer convincingly.

To the production office down the road, off the Champs-Elysées, and what a thrill to be paid to be here. The office is a bilingual smoke-filled warren of people experiencing pre-first-shoot anxiety. Sally Kellerman is five inches taller than me, trying on a pair of Japanese-style Westwood mules in the wardrobe room, and it takes all my self-control not to yell out, 'Howdy, Hotlips Houlahan!' Not a moment to reveal that I saw her in *M*A*S*H* when I was thirteen years old. She plays Sissy Wanamaker, editor of *Harper's Bazaar*.

6th March

After a clear-skied trip up the Eiffel, we throng to the glass pyramid in the middle of the Louvre, where we are to attend a fashion show. Thousands of people dressed in Liquorice Allsorts. We are escorted to the backstage loading zone. The TV monitor on the white ramp is intermittently watched by Ms Westwood, who is transfixed and intent and, apart from her visibly fluttering diaphragm, seems calm. Dressed in pearls, caramel beige sweater and matching trousers, she could be housewife-ubiquitous. But her shoes are twelve-inch tartan platforms and I don't think she is wearing a bra. Joan assures me that no one of her age could have la-las as well appointed as those without a good undercup. We are surrounded by flamingo-legged models, lengthened forever by the various boots and shoes with the cartoon-high heels, in various states of undress and re-dress. They are all here: Naomi Campbell, Kate Moss, Linda Evangelista, Christy Turlington and Tatiana Patitz. They all seem to be dragging on fags and slurping champagne from plastic cups while being trussed into miles of tulle, tight-fitting bodices, corsets, bustles, hats, jackets, coats and leggings. It is curiously calm despite the catwalk call for a new outfit every minute. Being in the midst of all this is undeniably thrilling. I had met Mlles Campbell and Moss at the British Fashion Awards and they say, 'Howdy,' as if we knew each other, which helps ease my unease at being a tall visible fly on their wall.

I am shuffled round to another vast hall where the makeshift movie Makeup and Wardrobe are set up to meet the cast and crew. Bob Altman guides me round and does the intros with all the charm and ease of a Chinese Mandarin.

Back to the second Westwood show, this time to the front row, and I'm placed with Azzedine Alaïa, Claudia Cardinale and Diane von Fürstenberg. This is a reality wobble, like *Vanity Fair* for real. Diane, whom I have seen photographed in a book about baths, leans over and thinks she knows me but cannot quite place from where, then reveals that her daughter played a gypsy in *Dracula* in a tiny scene with the 'Keenoo' actor.

Each model, isolated, lit and slinking down the runway, has a hypnotic effect quite separate from the hands-on fix, zip and pit-stop profusion witnessed earlier. They really do seem to have been 'made', for surely no human ever had legs that long, a face that cheek-boned or salary that high for walking without talking in someone else's clothes? The weirder clothes elicit the most positive response and while it is all obviously highly original and flamboyant, I cannot fathom just where or when such gear could be worn. This is clearly beside the point, but the point of it all is *what*? I turn to the programme for enlightenment: 'On liberty: the word libertine was used to discredit the best thinkers three centuries ago. We claim to have progressed. But orthodoxy still challenges the heresy (heresy is Greek for choice). Liberty depends on encouraging minority views and the 'bien' must not be allowed to abolish the 'mieux'. As for fashion, couture must exist alongside mass production, just as socialites who nourish heretical coteries and salons will not stagnate but flourish.' There you have it.

Go back to my hotel on the Métro among the legging-and anorak reality of Paris street life.

7th March

Joan and Olivia are on the first flight to London and the goodbye is always hard, even though I know it's not for long; her little face and the 'I love you, Daddy' always undoes me.

Breakfast with Sandra Bernhard in some grand hotel, and the time-warped relief that neither of us is in Budapest in the 'smell hotel' in the middle of the sludgy Danube, weathering through *Hudson Hawk*. My problem for the day is to manoeuvre my enthusiasm for the Altman film around her blatant outrage that she is not in the movie. 'YOU MEAN TO SAY OUTTA ALL THE FUCKIN' FOLK THEY HAD TO CHOOSE FROM AND HOW MUCH I KNOW ABOUT THE FASHION SCENE THEY COULDNA' FOUND ME A PART? WHAT IS THIS SHIT? THIS HOLLYWOOD BULLSHIT PISSES ME OFF. WHAT DO YOU HAVE TO DO FOR THESE PEOPLE? OH, YEAH, LINDA HUNT IS PLAYING THE EDITOR OF AMERICAN *ELLE* MAGAZINE? MY ASS! MORE LIKE *MIDGET MONTHLY*.' At which point she catches herself at it and we both cackle into the croissants.

I have a front-row ticket for the Cerruti show and access backstage to meet the man. This freebie is part of 'research'. Mr Cerruti is calm and genial amid the last-minute pre-dress. The fashion show begins with multiple screens, pounding soundtrack and images of movie stars dressed in Cerruti from various films. A white slice of light as a screen parts, from which flows an endless succession of the beautiful in more damned clothes. They look like clothes mortals *do* wear. Mortals with money, that is.

The cast and crew are in a backstage holding area prior to the Issey Miyake show, and a few rows of seats are reserved for the real fashion cognoscenti and celebrities. The real-life equivalents are strategically placed at the head of the runway, including Suzy Menkes – the doyenne of fashion writers, we are told. Wherever she turns, it seems as if she has just got herself decked up in the appropriate clothes by the designer on show. She resembles a VW car bonnet with beady headlamp eyeballs, scanning all in her survey, and has declared in the *International Herald Tribune,* seat of her lettered powers, that Altman is not the man to make this movie. She would have preferred Fellini. Alas, he is dead.

Actors wrap fairly pronto and a bunch of us go to the Val d'Isère off the Champs-Elysées. It's open till two a.m. and is laid-back and *sans* pretence. Tracey Ullman and I get blathering about the Royal Family, taxes, fire and Fergie – to the bemusement of Sally Kellerman, who has adopted twins and discovered a new vitamin regime. Stephen Rea sidelongs with deadpan epithet. The sense of a company free of the usual paraphernalia of caravans, chairs-with-names-on and your-billing-bigger-than-my-billing bollocks is evident. This may sound like a case of 'So-what's-the-big-deal?' but I have so often felt that movies operate along the lines of a medieval court, with despots, divas and duckbrains.

8th March

At noon I am picked up by a driver who speaks too fast for my limited Franglais and drives equally so. I garble out some *histoire-tristesse* about my father's premature death from lung cancer to explain why I will not survive this combustion chamber of Gauloise fog. We swerve into the underground car park of the Carousel du

Louvre and I am met by an assistant and marched off to the makeshift dressing and makeup area. Suitcases are opened to reveal a mirror, light-bulbs and full monty of creams, lotions and mascaras. Lunch is piled high in individual boxes, containing terrine, pâté, salmon, salad, roll and half-bottle of red wine. Much mutter and complaint from the French crew at this culinary compromise!

Rupert Everett, first seen in *Another Country*, used to be as skinny as me and I am amazed at his physical transformation, his arms now thicker than my thighs and neck as wide as his jaw.

'Gym every day.'

'WHY?'

'Sex.'

'*Touché.*'

In a corner sits Marcello Mastroianni in a dressing gown reading the Roman news, somewhat less streamlined than *8½*, and how curious that the ambassador of *La Dolce Vita*, along with Sophia Loren, should now be the elder statesman quietly enjoying a fag.

I am sent off with a video crew to film walking through a crowd of waiting fashion servants in the Louvre foyer. Get stared at and photographed, then ushered to a front-row seat for Chantal Thomas's lingerie collection. What follows is forty minutes of turbo-charged teenage underwear fantasia. Cher slips into the vacant seat beside me as the lights dim. She is dressed top to toe in leather designed by Chrome Hearts. She looks like Cher, and I cannot detect a line to suggest she's older than late thirties.

Monsieur Pierre, chief talent scout from the Elite modelling agency, asks if I will have dinner with Naomi Campbell, Kate Moss, Johnny Depp and Christy Turlington at Natasha's restaurant, followed by a party for Naomi at Le Palais club. In the name of research I agree. At the restaurant the supermodels push their food around their plates and I wonder whether they ever eat anything. Naomi assures me she eats like a horse. About four jumbo packs of Marlboros are inhaled in between details of who is with who and who is in town and what happened at this show. They tell me that the 'girls' are incredibly supportive of one another and not bitchy at all, and it would take armour plating not to be charmed by their sheer form; so fresh, so young, so tall and so thin. I never saw money anywhere and when it was time to go, all had been taken care of. As I hardly knew them I was embarrassed by their generosity but was told not to be. Johnny Depp, whom I first met when he was with Winona Ryder and who still bears her name tattooed on his shoulder, is apparently possessed of Kate Moss. They look like brother and sister, blowing smoke into each other's faces between kisses.

To Le Palais club for Naomi's party. Naomi pays me the compliment that I can dance, having clearly anticipated the Prince Charles School of Rhythm and Blues, and I bleat forth some inanity of having grown up in Africa. At some point, lung seizure begins to feel an imminent reality, so I body-squash towards the loo and meet Donovan *en route*. As in Son of Donovan, purveyor of sweet seventies folksiness. How old must I be, here in this seventies time-warp, to meet this adult popstar with an eyeload of smudged mascara? It transpires he is a *Withnail* fan. Fast forward to when I am toothless and bald and still meeting the trendies who adopt and hold dear that vision of London life!

I lurch out into the freezing air, past the crush of eagers desperate to get inside, past the chunks of bodyguard. 'NAOMI, LINDA, KATE,' choruses up like a desperate plea as we scramble into the cars and I can go home to savour the fast lane of a Paris night.

9th March

Still in the name of research, I am ticketed into more shows, the first being Valentino, and I am seated with Jackie Collins and Rupert Everett. Jackie laughs a lot, a sort of baritone gurgle that seems to underscore her every observation. She offers her mantra on publicity and chat-show technique: always convert every question with a cross-reference to a character or situation in your book, play, film, advert, rep season in Scunthorpe, etc. Her irony organ is very well developed.

Valentino struts down the runway, surrounded by the applauding models, and seems the most comfortable yet in this starring role of the designers; sleek, suntanned and coiffed.

The open invitation to watch the dailies every night is the closest equivalent to the binding process of rehearsal. Ensemble-playing abolishes the usual hierarchy of director, stars and spear carriers. The director is undeniably omnipotent in terms of the final version, but you feel that the actors and crew are the unfinished film's first audience and their response to whether a scene works or not is going to be that much more critical in this safe-house and will affect the editing. Plus you get to go out for dinner afterwards! Not that this is all rosy-glossy hold hands and sigh AAAH! In every company there are inevitably going to be one or two prize arseholes and this one is no exception. The competitive quotient is high and the egos yoyo-ing. Which perfectly mirrors the tightly wrapped fashion world we are imitating. We are given verbal invites, in honour of Cher, to a club called L'Arc. Naomi, Kate and Johnny are due and we drop the right names at the door and are reluctantly let inside. Word filters through that there is a roped-off area deeper within to which we might be privileged and we crush thither past buffet tables laden with almost bleeding beef. We foolishly get a leg over the rope, but are stopped mid-straddle by bodyguards, who rattle off in Franglais, and it's like being a teenager unable to get into an eighteen-certificate film. None of us is particularly keen to be here in the first place and now it's 'exclusive pour les stars' – two Gs in BUGGER-OFF time.

10th March

Tracey Ullman is a self-confessed fashion-*obsessif* and we go to the Chanel show together. Naomi and Kate are cavorting about and berating the press for prying into their every waking moment. Time to meet Karl (Kaiser Supremo of the fashion world) Lagerfeld who, we have been warned, has decided against appearing in the film and has barred any filming at his show. It is therefore with some trepidation that we seek an audience with the potentate, who is short, bulgy and sweating like a pack-horse despite the constant fan at his face. The half-shaded sunglasses do not disguise the obvious founda-tion of makeup and lip-liner, and he speaks at Scorsese speed. The podgy handshake is damp. Tracey is flattering and bemoans his prestigious absence from the film, to which he replies, 'You are professional actors. This is your passion and what you do. I am a designer not an actor, and therefore cannot try to do zis kind of playing.'

André Leon Talley yells into view. He is the giant artistic director of American *Vogue*, a Savile-Row-suited dandy with a booming Southern voice and the only black man encountered in this strange cosmos. His laughter is of the shriek school and when it charges forth his eyes whiten and widen, nostrils steam and expand and a train-entering-station shunt signals his delight. 'Lunch at the Ritz with Naomi *et al.* after the show, darling!' he commands.

This seems to be the show most eagerly awaited so far. Mr Lagerfeld, far from turning his back on the *Pret à Porter* filming, has offered his own twist: each seat sports a fake film can with the Chanel double-C signature, plus a free bottle of No. 5. The backdrop is exactly that, a film-set backdrop flanked by cardboard cut-out cameras, Klieg lights and sound-boom, and I wonder whether this homage was always intended as a one-upmanship ploy, or whether the King truly was to have been in the movie.

André guides Tracey and me backstage; he is like a bulldozer at six foot seven, and major attitude to match when faced with the surly security. André is in a state of near-euphoria and the words, 'Genius! Genius! Genius!' flute forth. We are guided like heat-seeking missiles to where Karl is sweating in the afterglow of his latest triumph.

Word filters through that Suzy Menkes has fainted somewhere, to which André retorts that she does this all the time. Ms Menkes recovers, manoeuvres her frail self into a corner with King Karl and secures a first-hand interview with him about his latest ideas, while being offered sips of Coca-Cola and being fanned by Karl's very own fan.

Then to the Ritz: Naomi is wearing eyeball-swivelling lingerie that could be comfortably packaged in a matchbox, inducing near-fatal thrombotics from the old prostates in pinstripes. Johnny Depp, in trademark just-outta-bed denim look, is stopped by the maître d'.

There is a tie-and-jacket dress-code altercation and within seconds voices are rising; Naomi gets up and charms things down. Travel plans are the conversationals; Kate is off to the Caribbean for a shoot, Naomi to Dublin to see her fiancé, and all the eggs Florentine and Perrier and champagne is signed to a room number so that yet again I fail to pay for my share.

11th March

My first proper filming call is scheduled for early evening at a famed restaurant in the gardens near the Place de la Concorde. Jeweller Bulgari is the party host in conjunction with the film production. This is true Altmanism: real-life and reel-life, with a *bona fide* event interwoven with film actors playing characters attending the kind of party usually created in a film studio. The entrance is a red carpet and candle-lit extravaganza with the name BULGARI on a framework of mini-candles.

I do not expect to see Sophia Loren and Marcello Mastroianni chatting to one another in dressing gowns and hair curlers, but they are. And then it's a go-round of howdy-doody to Kim, Tracey, Rupert, Lauren, Lili Taylor, Ute, Lyle, Forest Whitaker and the rest. Bob Altman announces that the night will be long and declares that he hasn't a clue as to exactly what will or won't happen, but to all hang in there and that everyone who has dialogue will be covered by one or other camera.

It is with some trepidation that I get my Vivienne Westwood gear on: it's its first outing in the film. The eighteenth-century white makeup, beauty spot and kiss-curled hair help me feel 'hidden', before I strap into the crotch-high black boots with the twelve inch heels, dinner jacket, hat, pearl earrings and gold penis-shaped cufflinks. Plus floor-length velvet double-breasted coat. I take a very deep breath before sallying forth into the critical eyestorm of the other thesps. Lauren Bacall guffaws her disbelief while others offer approval, especially La Loren, which is no small encouragement at this point. Helmut Newton, the legendary German lensman and leather *obsessif*, is here to cover the night, and is much taken with the sheer endless length of my boots. Once costumed and bouffed, we are trooped off in small groups to be mixed into the party.

Elsa Klensch, fashion editor of CNN news, sets up an interview with me 'in character', which induces palpitations – having yet to do anything in the movie, this is a one-to-one in depth about the fashion philosophy of Cort Romney, the designer I am playing. Having spent some time absorbing Westwood at first hand, I intone with as much sincerity as I can muster, just why and what and wherefore it all leads and means. Having this unexpected interview, which I am told will play on the TV in the back of scenes, has been a sort of birth, and gives sufficient confidence to go among the real folk and enjoy and see what reaction is on offer. There are so many people and scenes to be covered that by the end of the evening my sum-total of on-camera work is merely Hello Dollying down a crowded staircase.

I meet up with Vivienne Westwood, who wholly approves the character before her, and I feel that her approbation at this point is as important as Mr Altman's. Wrap. Scramble out and off to Le Bain Douche club, where the finale of the season is being celebrated. Or so we are told. There are crowds outside – bouncers, poseurs, drunks, bikers, wannabes, models. We are told to drop supermodel passwords to get past the human crush and squelch through a barrier of garlic fume and armpit, to get into the smogged interior that divides into upstairs bar and downstairs dancefloor. Simon Le Bon and Mick Hucknall are there. Rupert declares that this crowd is too 'boringly hetero-bourgeois' and kilts off into the night. Dancing is attempted in the lower depths, but such is the human glutch that I half hope those aeroplane oxygen hoses and cups might be released from the dark above like when the cabin loses pressure. Four a.m. and to bed.

12th March
Having felt like a case of Pepsi-Cola bottle tops exploding with self-confidence all week, nothing has quite prepared me for the phone call that comes at seven twenty this evening.

Catherine Letterrier, the costume designer, requests a fitting next week. "Ave you spoken wiz Bob?'

'No, why?' Red lights and alarms in my head.

''E is very un'appy wiz the rushes. Cannot use them and says you look a karakature and we 'ave to drop the 'at, makeup, earring, boots, walking stick,' and my head is now pounding red hot with embarrassment and shame. I cavorted forth thus clad at the Bulgari party all Friday night so the sense of humiliation is public and acute.

Why was nothing said before or at the time? Every recalled moment of that night is now replayed like some ghastly misprojected film in my head, as I look for clues ignored or misread. Oh, fuck. I instantly and petulantly want to leave and stomp off. There is the undeniable nag in my head that I have let Altman down and that he cannot bring himself to tell me straight. IT'S ONLY A MOVIE. Yes, but I cannot escape the gut-dread that this bodes ill.

13th March

A write-off, which my poor family has to bear the brunt of. Trudging through EuroDisney in rain, queues and cold all day cannot dispel this unease.

This yoyo feeling of self-worth and then having it taken away is frightening and crippling and just becomes endless self-loathing and doubt. Very unattractive. Negative. Boring. Sore.

14th March

Joan and Olivia are off home to London with relief to escape my paranoia. Everyone is invited to the dailies every evening. The response to my efforts at the Bulgari party is good and I feel slightly exonerated, made palatable when Bob comes up after and quietly suggests 'a few refinements'. He's ever the diplomat and seer, and I feel foolish but incredibly relieved not to have been sent to Ice Station Zebra by this man I admire so much.

Julia Roberts has arrived and is clearly jumping to be reunited with husband Lyle, despite the almost daily assertions in the British press that she has flown the marital coop. She is followed wherever she goes by paparazzi and autograph hunters. It does not seem to matter how disguised or careful she is when leaving the hotel, or diverting her route, they turn up and click. A large group of us swarm off to the Val d'Isère restaurant. Laugh laugh. Yak yak. Lili Taylor suggests a movie and we slip into *Romeo is Bleeding* long enough to witness Lena Olin earning points for kicking her way out of a car windscreen with her hands tied behind her back. Out into the bright late-afternoon light of the Champs-Elysées hoping never to have to be in such pulp and ruminating about how such a bunch of talent could have thought this was worth spending time and bucks making. Though, having semi-survived *Hudson Hawk*, I know part of the uncomfortable answer to that one . . .

16th March

As Altman has offered the world press access to the movie on condition they appear as extras, no day of shooting has less than a hundred people wandering about. Also, because this is France and he is ALTMAN, *auteur* and elder sage of *le cinéma*, there is a whole subculture of attendant goings-on. Altman has two cameras going at once and presides over both video monitors, watching both screens and listening on headphones to the multi-miked actors. You are often caught off-guard, which contributes to the elliptical life-like quality of the movie. At seventy, there is no sense about him of someone jaded, or 'seen-it-and-done-it-all'. He is endlessly curious and eaves-dropping for something original.

The peripherals interest him as much as the centrals. This informs his approach to the screenplay, which, as with *The Player*, is essentially an outline structure with character relationships and some dialogue but which is by no means a finished product, leaving the actor free to inhabit a role and improvise accordingly. He replies to my question about how he directs actors: 'Tell them as little as possible and let them make their own judgements and take responsibility for them-selves,' which is at once liberating and problematic when it comes to working out just how far you can go, or how this 'freedom' is interpreted.

Inevitably some scenes fall flat as some actors are less comfortable with improvising than others, or the odd one takes this as a cue for hogging centre-stage. Which resulted one afternoon in a Vesuvian confrontation between thesps fighting a war of 'territory'. No names. The paranoia of the world we are supposed to be portraying and the internecine intrigue is mirrored in the cast. Enemy lines are drawn and codenames given.

A perfect example of the apparently 'loose' way in which he works is borne out in a scene I have with Forest Whitaker, who plays a rival designer in the film, and with whom I have to kiss in some 'romantic setting'. Forest and I know this scene is coming up and voice jokey trepidation whenever the topic arises. Come the day, I ask Forest if he has given it any thought, to which he replies, 'Hey, man, I've just been in a state of denial!' The script has a couple of suggested lines, no more. We turn up outside the Museum of Modern Art opposite the Eiffel Tower, early evening, with forty-foot-high carved merman and mermaid murals as a backdrop and fountained pool in the foreground.

Bob suggests that we are discussing our cuckolded partners' ignorance of our liaison and how devastated they would be to find out. He says, 'Come up with something, but whatever it is, be totally serious about it.' Yak with Forest, write some lines down and Bob listens to our efforts and suggests a couple of adjustments. Altman goes back to his video monitor and the scene is shot very quickly. By not making a song and dance about our snog and leaving it up to us to interpret it as we like, any tension dissipates and we offer up a variety of the old lipsuck that we mightn't have if someone had done a 'caring and sharing' director shtick on it. Because he is so apparently casual about doing a scene, it seems relaxed and somehow makes you feel as if you are just 'behaving and reacting' rather than hoicking yer girdle up to do ACTING.

21st March
Paris Opera House: a half-page scene that will take until midnight or beyond to complete. It involves a huge press corps and assembly of real designers and the film-fake ones – myself, Forest Whitaker and Anouk Aimée – in the first-floor foyer of this baroque extravaganza

of gilt and gold opulence. No one knows whether all or any of the designers will show up as there have been rumblings in the press of mutiny.

I have now discovered why I have been through the grinder about my costume and overall 'look'. The actress playing my wife is, unluckily for me, Altman's daughter-in-law, married to his son, the set designer. She decides for round two. Meaning that she has my outfit reappraised by all and sundry, and articles of 'excess' are bodily removed. This kind of intrusion is a new one on me and, as I do not want to throw a total wobbly, I affect as much nonchalance as I can muster, while fantasizing about guillotines and all manner of garrottings. Logic argues that this must be jealousy on her part, yet the manner in which she has complained about me has been so underhand that I can only fester and wait.

Just when it looks as if only the minor designers will show, there is a sudden influx of Cerruti, Gaultier, Westwood, Agnès B, Rykiel, *et al.* Vivienne Westwood is wearing her trademark twelve-inch tartan platforms, mini-sofa bustle and see-through body-hug sheath. I cannot help feeling like fake-fur among these real Big Cats, and pose about in the back row as best I can in broken Franglais.

The dialogue preceding the photo-call is abandoned in the foray and a free-for-all develops with a surge of people from cocktail bar to seats. Two cameras are running, and numerous thesps and 'real' people are miked up. This feels chaotic and uncoordinated and requires deep inhalation and *c'-est-la-vie*-ing. It's a style of working that requires every preconception and rule to be abandoned. During dailies or during the shoot one of Bob's utterances, 'Who do I have to fuck to get off this movie?' becomes well quoted. He freely confesses to being bewildered by the sheer size and scope of what erupts in front of and around him. If most other directors were to say so panic would ensue, with executive accountants and actors calling agents. With Bob, though, you cannot help feeling that we are all under the Big Top together and that demanding rules, results and regulations would kill it. Whatever 'it' might turn out to be.

Vivienne Westwood and I go off to the canteen for dinner and she fills me in 'on a couple of things I would like you to think about and possibly incorporate'! This results in two hours of a unique personal history and philosophy, covering everything from her relationship with Malcolm McLaren, how punk came to be, numerous quotations from Oscar Wilde, her sons, her theory of beauty, and her great passion to form a salon for artists and thinkers 'like they had then', all punctuated with constant cigs, all of which might have ballooned pretentiously, were they not couched in her resolutely northern 'solid' sounds, which make even the most bizarre and extreme thoughts seem quite reasonable to my ignorant ears. Most of all, her passion for clothes and everything to do with them is as relentless as a heartbeat: the cut, The Cut, *The Cut*. The Feel of the Fabric. I am brain-buzzed with everything she has related and wonder how much, if any, I can trasmute into my part, but know that, whatever, the opportunity to meet someone like her and everyone else extraordinary on this film is what makes this 'job' seem the most wonderful and privileged of professions to be in. Purpling at the edges, I know, but true.

The crew and cast are now on the first floor of a nearby hotel, preparing lobby scenes where various characters meet. Late-night snack in the bar with Sally, Tracey, Sam, Lyle, Julia, Lili and Linda Hunt and I ask for their personal philosophies of life, 'in a sentence'. To which Linda incisively replies: '*Learn to ask for help!*' As good as the work gets, it has to be said that the downside of this hothouse epic is the overload of egos, with too many people hanging around with too little to do and the inevitable fissures and frustrations beginning to show. A sort of thespic-fatigue is discernible, so that the initial sweet-talk of, 'I thought you were so great in . . .' gets replaced by, 'If I hear that anecdote or "my-therapist" kvetch again, blood will be spilt!' Home James.

25th March

Teri Garr is in town briefly for fittings before returning at the end of the shoot for her scenes with Danny Aiello, who is a cross-dresser in the story. A new face means new stories and we magnet our way into the Val d'Isère for her low-down on the legends. This film, more than any other I have worked on, seems to have legend link-up by the starload. Lauren Bacall chatting about Bogie and Niven and Marilyn and Orson and Rita and Kate brings all the film-lore in print to a personal recall that is riveting. Sophia Loren on Brando, Chaplin, Burton and Peck; Bob Altman remarking that Sophia looks in real-life as much like a movie-star as she does on screen, which leaves me quite often tongue-roped and throttling for something to say without film-buffing and puffing. Teri speaks fast and tinkly, and I feel like I am in *Tootsie*, and she tells us about her times working on four Elvis movies. 'His party-style: invite a bevy of belles around to his place, offer no chips, no dips, some booze, watch TV and indulge in some heavy petting in between', but keep 'little Elvis firmly zipped up' *circa* the early sixties.

Despite having worked with and having met so many actors, I still feel starstruck and take vicarious pleasure in hearing stories first hand, though recall Carrie Fisher's pronouncement that, 'You're no longer a tourist; you're one of the attractions.'

28th March

My character's fashion show is being filmed outside Paris in the Château Rothschild. The show is a hybrid: we have the real models who did Vivienne's show, most of her collection, half of her staff doing the styling and dressing, along with the actors and film crew, mixed in again with real media video crews from around the globe. There are distinct grumblings about being hauled in at the crack-of and not used for hours. Much yoyoing of French assistants with walkie-talkies and mobile phones cannot ease the language/communication barriers. Sophia Loren is not happy, primped and coiffed hours in advance of working. This is the drawback of working in this 'loose' style. All is forgotten when I finally get to cavort forth with the models, wearing the platforms. A wonderful sense of the fantasticals, prancing about as a male Westwood for the afternoon.

It worries me slightly what she will make of what I have come up with and whether the satirical slant will seem like a betrayal. But, then, this seems like small sardines compared to the mother-of-all-punk that she is. Her passion for clothing is so intense and charismatic that I endeavour to convey this in every way I can possibly muster, assuming that anything done with enough obsession is inherently comical.

The film re-creation exactly mirrors the real fashion show, with everyone trying to hustle and get their three squeaks in. The difference being that, rather than brown-nosing the designer, here we have rabid actors trying to get themselves into the scene and their improvised dialogue filmed. How intentional this is of Bob I don't ask, but the sense of hysteria replicates the *real* back-slapping and slagging I witnessed at the *real* fashion shows. So Art is imitating Life.

Inadvertently, the sitting-around frustrations are given dramatic vent, which perfectly feeds the scripted faint that Sophia Loren stages upon seeing Marcello Mastroianni for the first time in twenty years. What ensues is nothing short of a free-for-all with press and thesp neck-and-neck to get in on the action. One actor feels he is being usurped by another and gladiatorial-verbals break out. When the naming of real names erupts, there is no doubting and assistants rally to divide the unruly. With enemy lines drawn, future encounters between these two actors (who shall remain nameless) are suitably charged with enough undercurrent to fill the *Encyclopaedia Britannica* with subtext! Altman being Altman makes no attempt to interfere and instead choreographs a scene wherein these two actors are in a mirror confrontation of their real-life combust. Another director might have a sit-down and peace-pipe session. Herr Altman uses the stuff to inform a new scene.

The differences between American- and Euro-thesp are curious; I sometimes wonder whether there is something wrong with me as I exist without therapist, futurist, assistant, nutritionist, manager, lawyer and publicist, all of whom, it strikes me, are fleece-merchants. But what do I know? The trappings and paraphernalia of the biz seem ludicrous but, then, my agent will not take kindly to such belittling. How does Shirley Maclaine cope with all these – plus them folk in outer hemispheres?

27th April

As Cole Porter mused, 'I love Paris.' Who could disagree? The few scenes I am in could have been scheduled down to eight days or so, but this applies to all the actors, and despite the odd bouts of WHAT'S IT ALL ABOUT, BOB-EEEE! I cannot deny the unmissable pleasures and privileges granted by being in this film, in this city, in springtime.

Bob shakes his head and declares bewilderment at the sheer volume of material. 'I got something here, God knows if I know what it is, but I'm sure there's something. Just hope I live long enough to find out what it is!'

Nelson Mandela is the new President of South Africa!

8th December

Fast forward to the *Pret à Porter* première, New York.

Lenny Henry calls and says while in New York he has seen the trailer. And I am in it. Relief. Not entirely the usual paranoids *but*, this being an Altman with twenty-four characters and multiple storylines, casualties are not unknown. What follows is little short of a full military manoeuvre, with a cast of foot-soldiers shipped into New York for the press junket. First Class.

London. Rain and last-minute pack and dash and domestic snap, crackle and ear-pop as Joan and I Concorde through the sound barrier. We are assisted through Customs fast, slink into a barracuda-length of limo and purr through Manhattan to a vast suite on the top floor of the Waldorf Astoria Hotel on Park Avenue. Plus cash in hand *per diem.* Pocket money. LA-DI-BLOODY DAΛΛΛΛH!

Joan to the big shop, and I join up with assorted thesps and Robert Altman for Round One of the junket. It's ten a.m. New York time and I am *here* before I left *there* at ten thirty. Each actor is assigned to a suite complete with TV camera crew, for the next six hours plus lunch, to talk for five minutes max, to a marathon relay of TV interviewers from networks around the USA. Reaction to the movie, which I have not yet seen, varies from the arctic to the equatorial, and all the while your jaw begins to ache at the Charm Chat required.

Lunch is school reunion time and, post the initial air-kissing and howdy-doody, it's every thesp for themselves.

WHAT ARE YA GONNA WEAR FOR THE PREMIÈRE?

The Altmans invite us all for dinner at Elaine's and we *are* in a Woody Allen movie now. Our body time is four thirty a.m. and eyes are stewed oysters.

9th December

Round Two: USA print and press. This involves moving from suite to suite for twenty minutes of round-table talk to assorted journos for another seven hours. Queries range from the intense to the not-so-acute.

10th December

Pret à Porter is set for a Christmas Day release on a thousand screens. A dozen others open in this Xmas jamboree as it's the last pit-stop for Oscar consideration. Opinion about every other movie is hurled at the wall and this marketing campaign has its own cast of Divas and Despots. NO WORD OF DOUBT OR DISSENSION. WE ARE TALKING HIT HIT HIT. MEGA MEGA MEGA. DO YOU COPY?

11th December

Re-group at the Altmans' apartment and Rossy de Palma diverts us with tarot readings in an undeclared atmos. of pre-prem paranoia. Mine anyway.

12th December

Free day to sample the WALK/DON'T WALK, ALL OR NOTHIN' nature of NYC.

THE PREMIÈRE. Faxes and flowers, details of the entering order, where to, how to, what to do. Line of black limos clogs the street to take us two blocks to the Ziegfeld Theater. My nerves are shredding at speed in contrast with the stately slow of the car. Rupert Everett and Rossy de Palma have to change cars as theirs has engine failure half-way there. THERE – a red carpet, bodyguards, mounted police, human corridor of cameras and crews and fans and revolving air-raid lamps criss-crossing the sky-scrapered night sky. Tim Robbins and Susan Sarandon ahead, Patrick Stewart and Richard Harris behind. CLICK CLICK FLASH FLASH SHOUT SHOUT.

Shift and throng around the crowds, who are rubber-necking the foyer for more famous faces, and into the theatre. Immaculately turned-out couture off-set by gallon-sized tubs of popcorn and Diet Coke. Lauren Bacall and Jean-Paul Gaultier are sitting just behind, Sophia Loren to the right, and now Bob is being introduced and casually says to the massed two thousand, to 'Give in and go along for the ride.' Scenes are applauded and the whole thing goes by without my being able to tell what is really thought or felt. Amazing to witness the turnaround in fortune for this seventy-year-old cinema veteran introducing his latest film, which is anticipated with antagonism by the fashion press and Altmania by the rest of us.

Walkie-talkied and ushered out, we limo another two blocks to the Roseland dance hall and are guided none too willingly upstairs, through a curtain and down a catwalk crammed with press and paparazzi. Once off this shop-window display of embarrassment, find your table and crash. Food finished and gossip swopped, lights go up on the stage and Prince dwarfs forth at speed, like that Duracel toy on ever-drive. Hysteria gets a grip. Jet-lag or something locks my brain, and after some greatest hits we leave. My last image is of Suzy Menkes standing on a chair surveying all and swaying to the beat of her own divining.

13th December

Donahue Show taped at the Rockefeller NBC Studios, four p.m. Lauren Bacall, Tim Robbins, Tracey Ullman, Helena Christensen, myself and Bob Altman, with Jean-Paul Gaultier. We get in the holding lounge for the Talent, as we are referred to, after a plastering of regulation all-over orange-tan makeup. A wired, headphoned, biconversational assistant chimes in with news that Gaultier has been excluded: 'Language difficulties, not an actor. Might cause confusion.'

Lauren Bacall is ready to walk. 'This is a national embarassment and a sign of the conservatism that is rampant. This man is an artist and fashion itself. How rude. How dare you?'

Suits and assistants are now manoeuvring in and out and Mr Donahue himself eases in with bright-toothed bonhomie and, 'Hey, guys, whatever it takes to sell the tickets, right?'

Ms Bacall is *not* to be bulldozed. 'I think it's a disgrace.'

'You're not gonna do the show?'

'We will do the show.'

We are trooped before the audience, sat in a row, and clips and questions make up an hour-long trailer for the movie. Tracey goes off into a shopping riff about red holiday sweaters and shamelessly imitates the twanging vocals asking her the questions. In between the odd serious attempt to probe, folk wanna know Ms Bacall's beauty secrets.

'I have none,' is her reply. Market research indicates that this show reaches the kinda audience who wouldn't normally go for this kinda movie.

Helena Christensen is asked what kind of bra she is wearing, to which she retorts, 'Your kinda question is exactly what makes models sound dumb.'

Leave sub-zero New York and land five hours later in sunny LA. Check in at hotel, hire a car, and have lunch with Steve Martin. Time warp back to *LA Story*.

Première pick-up six thirty. Rupert and Rossy and I wait for Jennifer Saunders to arrive. Having taken meetings with every top honcho in town for *Ab Fab*, including Mr Spielberg, we are drop-jawed at her tales of Hollywood's Highest humbling themselves.

Limo'd round the block; press line-up for the photo opportunity and TV soundbites. Volume goes up for the arrival of Madonna. We go into the theatre where cast and execs are cordoned off behind rope. Then we are introduced by Bob to the assembled perfumed people, and are each required to stand as if witnessing ourselves for an ID. The lights go down and it's a little easier to watch without feeling the onset of cardiac arrest at seeing and hearing yourself blown up large and studied by a thousand strangers. Applause and then another limo to ferry us over to Nieman-Marcus department store, to party on the second floor among the racks of designer clothes. It's an older crowd and there's no chance that Prince would make it past the sextet of violinists playing Strauss as you ascend the escalators.

After a couple of compliments *all* praise sounds false, and my brain clicks into *absurd person singular* mode. In the disco area, non-mega models are jiving up to some combo playing Abba and Barry White tunes, in the midst of whom reigns a bleached blonde with Mansfield mammaries. Jennifer identifies her as the damsel who is in liaison with an octogenarian multi-billionaire profiled in *Vanity Fair*. Hidden steel girders *must* account for the engineering miracle that keeps her la-las up and in harm's way. A six-foot person of indeterminate vintage can barely open her mouth, such is the sideways pull of her facial landscaping. She is matched only by a no-necked human with bright orange toupee that clearly makes *him* feel great, but renders his face beneath like a desiccated, ruined mandarin orange.

Until Christmas Day, the reviews are examined, the numbers are counted and audience profile scanners decoded and deciphered, predictions confirmed or thwarted. It's a WAIT.

February 1995
The French poster for *Pret à Porter* features five headless nude women with the title covering what would normally be the black stripe across their 'naughty bits'. It is plastered on every bus-stand in Paris. However, the city of Lyon has banned this advertising as has Versailles. Perhaps it is the beheaded aspect that has prejudiced the burghers of Marie Antoinetteville to put a stop to its display?

A Brit journalist at the press junket was scoffing at this prudery but conceded it highly unlikely that this poster would ever dare bare itself before '*les yeux anglais*'. His American counterpart said it would be *impossible* Stateside, and would only stand a chance 'if they were five fully dressed females riddled with bullet holes'. Returning to the same Paris hotel where we filmed exactly a year ago, *sans* the media hullabaloo and Equity stampede of actors hustling to get *any* morsel of a role, all is resoundingly silent. Like an afternoon at Miss Havisham's, except the rodents gnawing at the critical feast are the European press. The remaining guests are Anouk Aimée, Altman and me. The critical furore, with the odd exception, seems characterized by the kind of familial affront accorded the behaviour of a hitherto favoured member of the film fraternity who has been baa-baa'd into the black sheep pen. HOW DARE HE? HOW COULD HE? With some critters even going so far as to damn *all* his previous films, including the ones they once liked, and denouncing his thirty-year marriage to the movies as null and void because he didn't come up with the anticipated anniversary gift.

Altman said he thought it would be a couple of moons before the film would be evaluated for what it *actually* is, rather than the media HULLABALOO of what it was *expected* to be. Whichever way, the sheer velocity of the vitriol is shell-shocking when it detonates. And you have to remind yourself forcibly of what it was like to be here a year ago, when every ego was raising its flag to be a-flapping and a-filming.

Full circle. Fly out. *Fin.*

Epilogue

Having been briefed to convert my private diary into a fleshed-out public screed, which seemed like an impossibly daunting task at the start of the year, I have now completed it.

From the handing over in June 1995 of the 'manuscript' to the final edit in December, I have been struck by the parallels with the film-making process: first, the big thrill is the day you are told, '*It's you we want*', either to act or to write. The project, cash and confidence-boosting carrier-bag is the same. It is followed by the acute anxiety that rears up bellowing, 'HOW IN HELL AM I EVER GOING TO DO THIS?' A day at a time. Page by page, scene by scene, slowly. Until you have completed either film or foolscap.

I was commissioned to write one hundred thousand words – can't count and delivered 187,000. Likewise, the average hundred-minute film regularly runs twice that length when 'roughcut' together for the first time. Then the 'hacking' commences, by a highly astute Human who edits the performance or prose into something people might want to watch or read.

By the time it is ready for delivery, another year has 'lived' by and now it's time to get out of the house and sell. Something that is already a thing of the past. I can't think of any other profession in which you are so acutely dealing in Time. Simultaneously creating something in the present, from what is written in the past to be released in the future and then judged in the present.

Writing this epilogue is as peculiar as writing your own epitaph before actually being boxed up and buried. I had hoped for some wisdom at the cramped end of my thirties, but feel my hand moving inexorably towards my forehead in a gesture of 'nay, nay'. What I do know is this. No matter how intense, important, life-alteringly-fabulous or fiasco-laden a 'flick' is, it finally just that – a 'flick', of the fast-forward button or fade out. This year's 'MUST SEE' is destined to shuffle itself on to the overstocked video shelf six months after its release.

I ponder the question that's always asked, 'Did you know at the time you were destined to be in a hit or a howler?' And apart from an unequivocal 'NO!', three answers spring forth. *Casablanca* was considered 'unreleaseable', the Dakota plane 'unflyable', and the *Titanic* 'unsinkable'.

The other most commonly asked question is double-barrelled shotgun – 'WHAT'S NEXT?' If you aren't working, it's tantamount to an accusation, and if you are, an affirmation, guaranteed only till the last day of your present contract. If acting is a Licence, I'd like my card to be fully comprehensive until such time as my motor gives out.

Adieu!

Post Script

You'll understand why my collective noun for my profession is 'a moan' of actors as it's what bonds us all together. At some stage, every one of us has been out of work, overlooked, by-passed, rejected, demoted, underpaid, overpaid, overpraised or annihilated, stitched up or applauded. There is something innately *weird* and hilarious about making a living this way, and just when you think you've got a handle on how it all works, then something side-winds you off kilter and it's back to the old game of Snakes and Ladders.

Steve Martin mused whilst strumming on his banjo one evening that, 'If you're *lucky*, your career can be summed up in five YouTube clips.' Reminding me of a piece of advice my father gave me when he was dying, that, 'If you have five true friends in your life, consider yourself a rich man.' For this Swaziboy, born on the 5th May 1957, it's proved to be a significant bunch of fives.

Carrie Fisher sagely quipped – 'Richard, you're no longer a tourist, you're one of the attractions.' For a boy who grew up star-struck in a one-horse town in the smallest country in the Southern Hemisphere, it *still* strikes me as surreal that I have led the life I have.

'How do you see your old age?' enquired Roddy McDowall over lunch in Los Angeles. I was forty to his seventy. He was a child star opposite Elizabeth Taylor in *Lassie Come Home*, then most famously played Cornelius in *The Planet of the Apes*. Steve had arranged for me to meet him as I was researching what 'old-timers' did on a daily basis, for my Hollywood novel *By Design*.

'Never given it much thought, Roddy.'

'Well, you have a choice – you can either take the route of 90 per cent of actors down the bitter and twisted highway and end up raging at the moon like Kirk Douglas, furious at the loss of your fame, your roles reduced to cameos and "walk-ons", until you're finally wheeled out at awards ceremonies just to prove you're still breathing.

'Or.

'Look around and take note of just how lucky, fortunate and *blessed* you've been to have survived show-business, and to have met, worked with and befriended people of exceptional talent, *and* to have had a first-class ticket to some of the most extraordinary places on the planet.

'When you're on the plane back to London tomorrow, go through your entire address book and it will be patently obvious who is on which side of the dividing line. The majority will be made up of the "Could have, should have, would have beens". Jealous, envious, angry and disappointed. It's a choice and something that will resonate with you the older you get.'

Roddy died less than a year later and his wisdom has guided my thinking ever since.

'Who wants to go clubbing on Saturday night?' I posed this question to a group of young actors in Prague at the start of shooting *The Scarlet Pimpernel* at the end of the last century. There was an *audible* snigger, prompting me to ask:

'You think I'm too old?'

'Well, you are the same age as my dad,' retorted a young buck.

I was forty-one and computed that if an eighty-two-year-old thespian had fluted forth the same question, I too would have assumed he was suggesting a quiet drink in a comfy corner of the Garrick Club. Conjuring up a conversation I had had with Sir John Gielgud when he was in his early nineties on the set of *Portrait of a Lady*.

'How old do you *feel*, Sir John?' (That's how we all addressed him.)

'Thirty-eight, dear boy, but my body has other ideas.'

'What's the most difficult thing to deal with?'

'That terrible (rolling his 'R's) moment when you dial the number of a friend, then realize all over again, that they've "gone". So my advice to you is to cultivate younger friends.'

When a gang of us decamped up to Cumbria to an hotel on the outskirts of Penrith in 1986 to begin filming *Withnail and I*, Paul McGann and I were the youngest members of the crew, and for the next decade, I had no sense whatsoever of any change, until Emilia Fox, Jamie Bamber and assorted keen fresh faces openly doubted my 'Dad dancing' credentials in the Czech Republic.

Gosford Park was a seminal experience in that it felt like a dream-team repertory company making a film on a shoe-string budget, with the entire arc and gamut of an actor's life up for examination on daily display – ranging from the ingénues and just-out-of-drama-school fledglings at one end, keen, curious and testing the diving board of 'will I, won't I make it?', to the young guns who had tasted success, to the thirtysomethings who had already been around the block and no big career surprises anticipated, then those 'character' faces who seem always to have been there, and finally, the Bafta- and Oscar-awarded, feted, signed sealed and delivered living legends at the top of their league. Damed and knighted, trading 'war stories' of past successes and dissecting infamous flops with deadly anecdotal relish.

Thirty-three years in London and it *still* seems surreal to have cooked supper for Meryl Streep, eaten dinner with the Prime Minister at Chequers, attended the wedding of Prince Charles to Camilla Parker-Bowles, chatted to Nelson Mandela, heard Streisand sing from a privileged seat in the middle of the front row, played Higgins for the Sydney Opera Company, guested on *Rab C. Nesbitt*, written and directed *Wah-Wah*, created the Jack perfume brand, been paid to jump on five-star beds and lick the plates clean in the world's most luxurious hotels, had a role written for me by Lena Dunham in *Girls,* played tennis with Sir James Dyson, hosted a Pavarotti concert, and *still* get employed on a regular basis as an actor.

My father died at fifty-two, so every one of the past six years I've outlived him, feels like a bonus.

As for 'Five true Friends' – I feel like a billionaire to count Steve Martin as one of them.

'Chin-Chin'!

Richard E. Grant

PICADOR CLASSIC

CHANGE YOUR MIND

PICADOR CLASSIC

On 6 October 1972, Picador published its first list of eight paperbacks. It was a list that demonstrated ambition as well as cultural breadth, and included great writing from Latin America (Jorge Luis Borges's *A Personal Anthology*), Europe (Hermann Hesse's *Rosshalde*), America (Richard Brautigan's *Trout Fishing in America*) and Britain (Angela Carter's *Heroes and Villains*). Within a few years, Picador had established itself as one of the pre-eminent publishers of contemporary fiction, non-fiction and poetry.

What defines Picador is the unique nature of each of its authors' voices. The Picador Classic series highlights some of those great voices and brings neglected classics back into print. New introductions – personal recommendations if you will – from writers and public figures illuminate these works, as well as putting them into a wider context. Many of the Picador Classic editions also include afterwords from their authors which provide insight into the background to their original publication, and how that author identifies with their work years on.

Printed on high quality paper stock and with thick cover boards, the Picador Classic series is also a celebration of the physical book.

Whether fiction, journalism, memoir or poetry, Picador Classic represents timeless quality and extraordinary writing from some of the world's greatest voices.

Discover the history of the Picador Classic series and
the stories behind the books themselves at
www.picador.com/classic